# TO LIVE AND DEFY IN LA

# TO LIVE AND DEFY IN LA

★ ★ ★ ★ ★

## HOW GANGSTA RAP CHANGED AMERICA

. . . . . . . . . . . . . . . .

## FELICIA ANGEJA VIATOR

HARVARD UNIVERSITY PRESS · Cambridge, Massachusetts, and London, England · 2020

First printing

Library of Congress Cataloging-in-Publication Data

Names: Viator, Felicia Angeja, 1978– author.
Title: To live and defy in LA : how gangsta rap changed America /
Felicia Angeja Viator.
Description: Cambridge, Massachusetts : Harvard University Press, 2020. |
Includes bibliographical references and index.
Identifiers: LCCN 2019040585 | ISBN 9780674976368 (cloth) |
ISBN 9780674245839 (epub) | ISBN 9780674245846 (mobi) |
ISBN 9780674245853 (pdf)
Subjects: LCSH: Gangsta rap (Music)—Social aspects—
United States. | Gangsta rap (Music)—California—Los Angeles—
History and criticism. | Inner cities—California—Los Angeles. |
Urban youth—California—Los Angeles.
Classification: LCC ML3918.R37 V53 2020 |
DDC 306.4/842490979494—dc23
LC record available at https://lccn.loc.gov/2019040585

FOR AMALIA AND OTIS

# CONTENTS

# PREFACE

The title of my book is a nod to William Friedkin's 1985 film *To Live and Die in L.A.* For me, it's a movie perfectly evocative of the eighties because it is a story about artifice. The plot centers on the pursuit of a counterfeiter who is both brilliant and ruthless. His forgeries are expertly crafted, fooling both those too naive to recognize the trick and those on the hunt to expose the truth. Even the film's heroes engage in their own kind of con, deceiving colleagues, loved ones, and themselves. Indeed, the entire cast of characters is a tapestry of pretenses. Bilge Ebiri at the *Village Voice* put it elegantly when he described *To Live and Die in L.A.* as "a movie all about facades. The posturing characters, the synthesized soundtrack, the heavily art-designed frames, the gyms and the strip clubs and the avant-garde dance performances that put bodies on full display—all serve to create a world of whisper-thin surfaces, beautiful and magnetic and unreal."[1]

The thing I find especially interesting about *To Live and Die in L.A.* is the way the filmmaker uses artistic realism so purposefully as a backdrop for this tale about illusions. The

car-chase sequences in the film are relentlessly raw, devoid of
the sorts of special effects and jump cuts that, in other action
films, allow viewers some distance from the tension. Friedkin
makes you feel every bump and swerve and near-miss. It's
nauseatingly realistic. What's more, to portray Los Angeles,
the director skips the obvious cinematic settings: there are no
iconic neighborhoods or skylines and no glorified city land-
marks. Only the empty, concrete channels of the LA River, beloved by locals and not tourists, make an appearance. Like
film noir directors of an earlier generation, Friedkin seems
intent on blunting fantasies of Los Angeles by exploiting
popular fears of urban underworlds. So perhaps it should
come as no surprise that the white director took his production crew to black neighborhoods in Inglewood, South Central, and the Nickerson Gardens projects in Watts.

Like the film that inspired my title, *To Live and Defy in LA*
is a book about the relationship between artifice and authenticity. Here, it is black youths, rather than white artists, who
use these creative devices to subvert mythologies about Los
Angeles. They deploy both—fusing make-believe with real
life—to captivate, provoke, and entertain.

*To Live and Defy in LA* is also, like Friedkin's movie, about
the eighties. Although I conclude with the 1992 LA riots and
the music that emerged from that moment, the arc of the
story is largely defined by the decade prior. This means I do
not explore the generation of artists who took on the mantle
of LA rap in the mid-1990s, including Snoop Dogg, Tha Dogg
Pound, DJ Quik, Suga Free, MC Eiht, Cypress Hill, and Tupac Shakur.[2] Nor do I examine the stylistic and ideological
diversification of LA hip-hop in the 1990s following the me-
teoric rise of gangsta rap, an important development in the
genre's history exemplified by the growth of the Good Life

Cafe arts movement. The most impassioned music fan seeking an encyclopedic survey of Los Angeles hip-hop history
will not find that here. But my hope is that those expecting
boilerplate coverage will be pleased with the depth and discovery in these pages focused on the genre's origins.

I also, purposefully, avoided drawing this story forward to
the present. While it is tempting to wax poetic about a genre
I still love, arguments I pitch about current rap will inevitably
sound dated to even casual observers of music trends. For
many years I have been a devoted fan, a DJ, and a pop culture
scholar, and the thing about rap that has always seduced me
is the rate at which it transforms, innovating and adapting at
breakneck speed. I have attempted here, by carving out this
brief-yet-critical moment in the timeline, to detail some of
that dynamism with respect for the fact that this music is always in flux.

At the same time, it has also become quite clear to me that
as rap innovates some changes resonate longer and loom
larger than others. *To Live and Defy in LA* is grounded in my
contention that many of the themes popularly associated with
rap music since the early 1990s—its uncompromising black-
ness, its militancy with respect to the police and other institutions of white supremacy, and its reconciliation of commercial
success with rebellion—are rooted in Los Angeles gangsta rap.

# TO LIVE AND DEFY IN LA

INTRODUCTION · They Don't
Even Know

■ **In the late 1980s,** Los Angeles record producer Dootsie
Williams concluded that black youths were oblivious to the
racial oppression all around them. He complained to friend
and musician Johnny Otis that the new generation could not
see the problem, much less its nuances. Born and raised in
Jim Crow Alabama, and coming of age in the mixed community of Watts at a time when the Ku Klux Klan was enjoying a
resurgence in Southern California, Williams knew bigotry.[1]
He told Otis that he had always been painfully aware of the
ways racism shaped his life. It was once "so blatant," he said.
"But today it is so smooth and sneaky that our younger generation of Blacks is lulled into a sense of false fantasy. Hell, they
don't even know they're being discriminated against."[2]

Dootsie Williams had been part of an early wave of Los
Angeles migrants drawn by the promise of an urban utopia.
Though some would still mock it as the "Hell-Hole of the
West," LA by the 1910s had all the trappings of a California

1

Eden: a lush Mediterranean landscape, a thriving entertainment industry, plentiful jobs, and an abundance of cheap, single-family bungalows.[3] Around the turn of the century, Southern California boosters had begun to transform Los Angeles into a commodity to be carved up, advertised, and sold, not only to land developers and railroad tycoons, but to ordinary people (Fig. I.1). Los Angeles County in 1880 held just over thirty-three thousand people, a hamlet compared to the city of San Francisco with its roughly quarter of a million residents. But by the end of the 1920s, the county's population had exploded, topping two million, making Los Angeles America's most rapidly growing region and the premier migrant destination in the West.[4]

White Americans and foreign immigrants made up the vast majority of LA's transplanted population throughout the late nineteenth and early twentieth centuries. But the county was also the final destination for thousands of African Americans. Dootsie Williams's family was among those who left the Jim Crow South to go west rather than follow well-worn migratory routes to the north. W. E. B. Du Bois, prominent black activist and editor of the NAACP's journal, *The Crisis*, beguiled some with his poetic observations of "wonderful" Los Angeles, where the air was "scented with orange blossoms and the beautiful homes lay low crouching on the earth as though they loved its scents and flowers." There, Du Bois noted with enthusiasm, the black community was a "hopeful group—with some wealth, large industrial opportunity and a buoyant spirit."[5]

This was quite the tribute from a world traveler, a founding member of the NAACP, and the foremost African-American scholar of the "Negro" experience. Du Bois was an expert on the many cultural and institutional barriers in both southern society and northern life to black civil rights, black

Fig I.I Early twentieth-century postcard of what is now MacArthur Park, just west of South Central Los Angeles. Image originally printed by Edward H. Mitchell, courtesy of the Studio for Southern California History.

access to higher education, black economic autonomy, and black political power. Plus, he became a leading voice of protest against white violence, which reinforced the subjugation of his people "from Pennsylvania to Oregon and from Massachusetts to Mississippi." For Du Bois, Los Angeles was a black promised land by comparison.[6] Jefferson Lewis Edmonds, editor of the Los Angeles *Liberator*, agreed that African Americans who came to the West "in search of better things" were "not disappointed." The *Liberator* touted the "splendid conditions found in California" and opportunities for success available to all, regardless of color.[7]

Patterns of early black settlement in southern Los Angeles County, however, exposed racial boundaries in the Golden State. Du Bois conceded that "the color line is there and sharply drawn."[8] African Americans who migrated to South

Central Los Angeles and the unincorporated community of Watts in the early twentieth century bore witness to this. These newcomers were drawn by cheap land, access to downtown industry, proximity to transit hubs, and the relative diversity of the region south of downtown. Until the 1920s, the sliver of Los Angeles west of Central Avenue and east of Flower Street, along with the small suburb of Watts, where Dootsie Williams's family settled, was ethnically, racially, and socioeconomically mixed—a patchwork of wealthy, middle-class, poor, Mexican, Japanese, Native American, Italian, Jewish, and black residents. Outside of South Los Angeles, however, the region looked much different. Restrictive housing covenants and other forms of resistance to neighborhood integration kept most of LA's west side, including Culver City and Inglewood, in addition to LA's south side, including Southgate, Lynwood, and Compton, nearly exclusively white. In 1930, the US Census counted fewer than a dozen black residents living in all of the above-listed places combined.[9]

Dootsie Williams reached adulthood in the 1920s, at a time when LA's black communities began crystalizing, bound by housing discrimination and occupational limits but also by desires to be near other black Angelenos, black-run businesses, black churches, and black mutual-aid societies. New waves of African-American migrants came with their resources and their expectations, stretching the invisible boundaries of black Los Angeles by replacing the ethnic whites, Asians, and Latinos who moved further east and south.

By the 1930s, as African-American residents increasingly dominated the south-central corridor, the concentration of black talent reinforced economic, social, religious, and political networks. Buoyed by an activist black press and black nationalist slogans like "Don't Spend Where You Can't Work,"

grocers, butchers, restaurateurs, barbers, hairdressers, seam-
stresses, junk dealers, childcare providers, legal professionals,
physicians, construction contractors, and realtors thrived.
Black-owned music venues like the Lincoln Theater and the
Savoy featured renowned African-American performers, including Billie Holiday, Count Basie, Ella Fitzgerald, and Louis
Armstrong, while the lavish Dunbar Hotel hosted celebrities
from the realms of music, literature, sports, and activism, including bandleader Duke Ellington, poet Langston Hughes,
boxing champ Joe Louis, and high-ranking members of the
NAACP. The Fifty-Fourth Street Drugstore, Brother's, Love-
joy's, Honey Murphy's, and other popular after-hours joints
further enriched the district's nightlife scene.[10] This subsec-
tion of Los Angeles had its own churches, mutual-aid programs, political organizations, elite social clubs, and three
newspapers. Add to all this a distinctly Southern Californian
brand of home ownership—manicured lawns, backyard pools,
and palm trees appear standard in early century photographs
of South Central neighborhoods (Fig. I.2)—and these tightly-
knit communities exemplified the triumph of black life in the
West. As Du Bois put it in 1913, LA's African-American people
represented "the new blood of California with its snap and
ambition."[11]

Throughout the first half of the twentieth century, African
Americans made up less than 4 percent of this unusually diverse urban population.[12] Los Angeles was a sprawling me-
tropolis that housed, within its broad mix of cultures and
ethnicities, a postage stamp–sized black enclave largely removed from white society. As African Americans in the neighborhoods in and around South Central thrived, its people
remained all but invisible to the rest of the city, creating the
illusion of racial harmony.[13]

Fig I.2 Cover of W. E. B. Du Bois's *The Crisis*, August 1913 issue, featuring the Los Angeles home of Mr. and Mrs. William Foster. With its sprawling veranda, manicured lawn, and newly planted palm tree, it illustrated the "beauty and enterprise" of black life in Los Angeles.

Image courtesy of The Modernist Journals Project, Brown and Tulsa Universities.

War and further migration complicated this. Even before the United States officially entered World War II in 1941, the Pacific Coast had become a vital defense industry center, with munitions plants, shipbuilding ports, airplane hangars, military bases, and infrastructure projects transforming Depression-era Southern California into a labor mecca. From 1940 to 1945, migrants in search of steady, high-wage, skilled work flooded the state, with manufacturing centers like Los Angeles and Long Beach attracting the bulk of newcomers. The vast majority were from the Midwest and the South, and, after the federal desegregation of the national defense industries in 1941, a disproportionate number were black.[14] In the two decades following US entry into World War II, the number of African Americans in California rose from 124,306 in 1940 to 883,861 in 1960. In Los Angeles, the black population increased more than fivefold, from 63,774 residents to over 330,000. California's wartime economic boom, followed by postwar opportunities in the aerospace, energy, consumer manufacturing, entertainment, and service industries, spurred one of the most significant African-American migrations in the nation's history.[15] Southern California appeared, once again, to be the ideal destination for those "in search of better things," or as black wartime migrant Horace Tapscott put it, a "land of golden opportunity."[16]

As LA's population mushroomed, racial tensions that had once been diffuse, due in part to isolation and sprawl, took on more prominence. More frequent interactions between African Americans and whites inside the county's places of work and leisure aggravated frictions related to employment, housing, policing, and education. Even as divisions hardened and tensions grew, however, economic and legal gains for black Angelenos seemed to soften the edges of bigotry. The

World War II defense industry boom yielded new, lucrative employment opportunities for African Americans in Southern California. And even after war drew to a close and the scaling back of defense industries disproportionately affected black workers, African Americans in the region continued to make advances.[17] Sustained access to government work and training programs, successful protests against racial barriers to the skilled professions, GI Bill entitlements, and labor unions helped protect black interests. Housing reformers, too, used a combination of political activism and legal action to fight racially restrictive practices, allowing for the community's expansion westward into once lily-white neighborhoods like Inglewood and Baldwin Hills, and southward into the blue-collar suburbs of Southgate and Lynwood. Black Angeleno activists and homebuyers also succeeded in integrating the coveted "ideal home city" of Compton, which, by the 1950s, would become for upwardly mobile black families a promised land within the promised land.[18]

Viewed in comparison to southern oppression, even explicit examples of racial bigotry in Los Angeles could not eclipse the economic, political, and social wins. For many black Angelenos, California endured as an Eden relative to the Jim Crow South, from which most African-American migrants arrived. While Martin Luther King, Jr.'s civil rights movement battled state-sponsored white supremacy in the former Confederacy, Los Angeles seduced as "the land of the free, where segregation wasn't too tough."[19] South Central community leader George Beavers, a native of Atlanta, Georgia, noted that year after year, Los Angeles beckoned refugees from all sorts of troubled circumstances. But for black southerners who had known the pain of racial apartheid, lynching, and political disenfranchisement, this California "heaven" proved especially alluring.[20] The ideal of Los Angeles as a black promised land would remain powerful through the early 1960s, not only inspiring westward migration but framing narratives about a people's dream achieved.

The 1965 uprising in Los Angeles threatened to undermine this faith in progress. The five-day rebellion (enduringly labeled the "Watts Riots" despite the fact that the riot area spanned much of South Central, and the precipitating arrest occurred at the intersection of 116th Street and Avalon Boulevard, west of Watts's southern border) left thirty-four people dead, over one thousand injured, some four thousand arrested, and an estimated $200 million in property burned, looted, and destroyed. Until the 1992 LA riots, it stood as the most destructive episode of urban unrest in American history. Occurring against a backdrop of national civil rights victories, California's healthy economy, and the prevailing sense that Los Angeles was the black promised land, the uprising stunned the country.[21]

LA's police chief, William Parker, responded as if utterly flummoxed. To reporters, Parker insisted that his city had seen no signs of conflict among races. It was "quiet" as far as that was concerned, he said. In the days following the riots, Parker appeared on NBC's *Meet the Press* and dismissed a pointed question from journalist Len O'Connor about "a racial problem" in his jurisdiction. "Los Angeles offers more for the Negro citizens than any other city in the world," he said, noting the irrelevance of federal civil rights legislation for his exceptionally progressive city. As if certifying the laudatory words of W. E. B. Du Bois from half a century before, Parker explained, "All of the gains in civil rights in the recent years have already existed in Los Angeles for a number of years."[22]

In the fall of 1965, the California Governor's Commission on the Los Angeles Riots published its report on root causes. In a number of ways, the report undermined Chief Parker's public pronouncements. It cited, among other things, black unemployment in the riot area nearly three times higher than the county average, and a history of tension between African Americans and the Los Angeles Police Department. But the report also claimed of Los Angeles, after sketching its portrait relative to the nation's other urban areas, that, for African Americans, "the opportunity to succeed is probably unequaled in any other major American city." The neighborhoods of Watts and South Central, it noted, were not "slums" but communities where detached, single-family homes, a third of them owned by their occupants, lined "wide and usually quite clean" streets. Plus, the region's black residents had full access to parks, playgrounds, movie theaters, shopping districts, public transportation, and voting booths. But the commission's report seemed in conflict with itself, providing a litany of riot "causes and answers" alongside other evidence that, for African Americans, "Los Angeles conditions are superior."[23] Conclusions seemed as elusive as when *Newsweek* printed its August 30, 1965 cover. The weekly featured a photograph (Fig. I.3) of armed troopers in military jeeps rolling through the ravaged and smoky riot curfew zone, atop the question: "Los Angeles: Why?"[24]

For Dootsie Williams, the 1965 uprising simply confirmed that *de jure* segregation—that is, racial privilege dictated by the letter of the law—was only the most conspicuous mechanism of a far broader, more complex, "smooth and sneaky" system of racial oppression in the United States. For Williams, the riots revealed that in black Los Angeles achievements

Fig I.3 On August 6, 1965, a military convoy rolls through a Watts business district destroyed by rioting and arson. In the wake of the 1965 Los Angeles riots, the national press struggled to make sense of the rebellion and its precipitating events. RBM Vintage Images / Alamy Stock Photo.

ultimately reinforced limitations; the realization of progress threw racial injustices into sharp relief.[25]

■    ■    ■

Over the course of decades, Dootsie Williams had cultivated a black entertainment empire in Los Angeles, developing a keen understanding of the recording industry and fashioning a fruitful career, first as a trumpeter, then a bandleader, then doing "A&R" (artists and repertoire development) for a recording label. By the early 1950s, in the midst of a thriving Los Angeles Central Avenue black arts scene, he had formed Blue Records. The label was eventually renamed Dootone and became nationally known for popular rhythm & blues releases and comedy records notable for their dirty—or "blue"—material. Williams earned a fortune from the successes of a local doo-wop group called the Penguins (of "Earth Angel" fame) and the era's bluest comedian, John "Redd Foxx" Sanford. The Dootone label produced a wide range of African-American performers, most of them talents plucked from within LA's most segregated and racially isolated communities. Williams took pride in promoting myriad forms of black expression, all of which resonated with his own experiences living in Los Angeles.[26]

Dootsie Williams imagined black Los Angeles as the polestar of black entertainment—with his own businesses at its core. He pictured film studios, television and radio stations, performance venues, and, of course, recording labels not only housed within the African-American communities of Los Angeles County but thriving because of those communities. With this goal in mind, and bothered by the absence of modern, black-owned event spaces in LA, he opened the Dooto Music Center, a $300,000 multiplex in Compton featuring spaces for the production of music, television, and movies along with an auditorium. In 1963, the *Los Angeles Sentinel,* a black-owned, black-run weekly, described the Dooto Music Center as "the most-needed cultural and recreational center in Southern California."[27]

It was a space that Dootsie Williams would all but abandon in the 1970s, unable to recover financially from losses related to the 1965 uprising, a devastating slump in record sales, and a series of robberies. By 1975, Williams and his wife had cut their losses and invested much of their remaining wealth in beachfront property in Mexico. As Williams told his old business partner Doc Young, he was letting the Compton venue go because "I want to do other things."[28]

The 1970s was a decade in which black Angelenos like Dootsie Williams labored to adapt to the new challenges of a post–civil rights cultural and political climate. Black Power and black nationalism, which had thrived in LA in the wake of the 1965 riots, had been all but smothered by federal counterintelligence programs and internal divisions. Yet, African-American activists, including some former militants, funneled their efforts into electoral politics, with the goal of electing more black and black-friendly leaders, amplifying the African-American voice in policymaking in the state, and ensuring that state and civic leaders would give more attention to the needs of their constituents. These men and women registered black Californians to vote and nurtured alliances with Latinos, Asians, white liberals, and working-class voting blocs—efforts that helped bring about the 1973 election of Tom Bradley, LA's first African-American mayor and the first black candidate to be elected mayor of a predominantly white American city. Such significant political milestones came as unemployment among the region's African-American residents rose well above the general population's average. The local black press rang the alarm about joblessness specifically among black youth, which seemed to be turning relatively benign neighborhood social cliques and lowrider car clubs into criminal street gangs.

By the 1980s, deindustrialization, urban flight, and California's tax revolt had devastated predominantly black communities like South Central, Inglewood, and Compton, exacerbating the problems of unemployment and poverty. An influx of new immigrants into Los Angeles during the decade meant that, for scarce jobs and resources, black residents faced heightened competition from neighboring minority groups, particularly Mexican and Korean residents, who were often similarly restricted by racial discrimination in housing and hiring. The introduction of rock, or "crack," cocaine to LA streets in the same period inflamed the overlapping problems of substance abuse and violent crime.

But the 1970s and 1980s were also the decades in which popular culture and entertainment, much of it manufactured in and disseminated from Los Angeles, elevated a new generation of African-American stars, including Michael Jackson, Bill Cosby, Oprah Winfrey, Prince, Whitney Houston, and the Los Angeles Lakers' Magic Johnson. Plus, within two decades of the 1965 uprising, the region became, yet again, a beacon of racial progress. Pristine enclaves like Windsor Hills, Baldwin Hills, and Ladera Heights housed LA's black yuppies, celebrities, wealthy entrepreneurs like Dootsie Williams, and a rapidly expanding African-American middle class. Buoyed by enduring, and deeply cherished, mythologies about Southern California as an Eden of equal opportunity, LA in the 1980s appeared to be a bellwether for the future of America.

And perhaps it was. But not necessarily in the post-racial way the American public imagined. Los Angeles had the same economic, social, cultural, and political dilemmas as similar American cities, but managed to gild over them to save its reputation. That is, it was a promised land only on its glittering surface. When Dootsie Williams complained to his friend Johnny Otis about black youth in the 1980s "lulled into a sense of false fantasy," he was expressing what were then widespread fears about a post-civil rights generation ill-equipped to respond to continued subjugation because it couldn't see past the golden veneer. In Compton, where Williams had built his music enterprise, he knew kids old enough, many of them, to have some memory of Black Power. From his vantage point, these children had grown up amidst a political and cultural backlash to the Sixties but failed to recognize the implications of that backlash. By the mid-1980s, after all, the Huxtables were the most beloved American family on television, and President Ronald Reagan trumpeted the arrival of an era in which skin color no longer mattered and "all men and women have equal opportunities to succeed." Dootsie Williams saw this younger generation uncritically absorbing the cultural messaging about a new "color-blind society." Black kids in LA, he believed, were falling for the proverbial okeydoke.

■   ■   ■

In the early 1980s, a young Compton DJ named Alonzo Williams revived the shuttered Dooto Music Center by turning its auditorium into a nightclub. With some support from the Center's old owner, Dooto's became a wellspring of young black talent—a community of local artists that would ultimately prove Dootsie Williams wrong. The club helped to nurture the careers of Los Angeles DJs, rappers, producers, and entrepreneurs, among them, artists who would become the most controversial, and influential, entertainers of the late twentieth century. Sometimes the music addressed racism directly, and sometimes it didn't, leaving fans and critics to guess how this young generation of black innovators chose to engage with institutional injustices. In fact, though broadly derided, the "gangsta" aesthetic that became synonymous with this West Coast music scene not only helped its participants dramatize their oppression, but ultimately became their best tool for provoking national dialogue about it.

*To Live and Defy in LA* begins by, first, tracing the peculiarities of Los Angeles in the early 1980s, in the age of Reagan, when romantic notions of LA hid the lived experiences of black youths coming of age there. Then, it tells the story of the music that exploded from behind that veil. This is a history of a West Coast phenomenon that was, in the tradition of the blues, a form of blunt self-expression, and thus a potent, if not immediately obvious, response to systems designed to silence and control black people.

Los Angeles gangsta rap, like the Los Angeles rebellions of 1965 and 1992, seared into the national imagination the most explicit and sensational details of LA's urban crisis, complicating long-held, time-tested myths of the City of Angels. The music was sensational in its content, provocative in its commercial success, and radical in the message its makers and fans delivered: that America incubated inequality at its own peril.

CHAPTER 1 · The Batterram

■ In 1985, "Greg Mack" Macmillan was the most influential figure in Los Angeles radio. This was in spite of the fact that he worked for KDAY, a local AM station with a signal so weak it "wavered in a high wind."[1] From its hilltop location above Echo Park, the sounds of KDAY managed to spill southward. In the best of conditions, the station could reach audiences throughout the southern flatlands of Los Angeles County, from downtown LA to Compton, and Greg Mack made it his mission as music director to cater specifically to the young people of these mostly black communities. His unusual choice was to reject both the adult contemporary programming that had previously defined KDAY and the urban contemporary format embraced by most of the nation's other black radio markets through the 1980s.[2] Bucking all trends, Mack abandoned KDAY's former reliance on mainstream jazz, Motown standards, and disco. Instead, he showcased a unique selection of bass-heavy music, including the up-tempo electro music called "freestyle," and rap, the sound he heard blaring from car cassette decks from MacArthur Park to Venice Beach. Mack had embraced rap in particular from the moment he arrived at the station in 1983, a time when most popular black radio jocks were dismissing it as mere novelty. His choice to take cues directly from the kids he aimed to serve proved savvy. In just two years' time, rap music had not only revitalized the struggling AM outlet but had thrust KDAY into the vanguard of black radio.[3]

To curate KDAY's programming, Mack looked to hip-hop trends emanating from New York, the genre's birthplace and its heartland through the mid-1980s. His success in the Los Angeles market, however, relied on more than his attention to trails blazed in the Northeast. He also drew on his experience hosting a Majic 102 show at KMJQ in Houston, Texas—another urban radio market embedded in a car culture like LA's, with an African-American listenership that, in the early 1980s, favored funk from the West over disco from the East. In Los Angeles, KDAY's young staffers, who served the station by day and danced to rap and freestyle at South Los Angeles parties by night, constituted Mack's direct line to the station's core audience. Plus, the young programmer kept his ears tuned to "all the booming systems" in his South Central neighborhood. Rather than chasing the older listeners his industry peers were delivering to their advertisers, Mack sought to corner the local urban radio market by catering to the tastes of black youths.[4]

It was with this in mind that in the summer of 1985 Greg Mack gave "Batterram," a song made by a local rapper, its radio debut. Although KDAY's program director, Jack Patterson, had encouraged his staff to showcase promising LA artists, Mack's choice was still an intrepid one.[5] No record label had produced "Batterram," nor was it pressed on vinyl, virtually the only format used for promotional music distribution at the time. A Compton kid named Todd Howard, billing himself as "Toddy Tee," had recorded the track in a crude home studio onto a cassette tape. And although the song borrowed the instrumental track of a New York rap hit—the *Billboard*-charting single "Rappin' Duke"—its rhymes were in the local vernacular, focused on a problem not many outside LA even knew about. Toddy Tee's dub was a cautionary tale about the newest weapon being deployed in the war on drugs: a six-ton armored vehicle outfitted with a fourteen-foot steel battering ram. The Los Angeles Police Department was using it to execute search warrants, and as the local rapper's chorus warned, *"You can't stop it, baby/The Batterram."*[6]

■   ■   ■

Los Angeles County's deployment of two V-100 military surplus vehicles marked a new phase in its approach to two related problems: gangs and rock cocaine. Rock, also known as "freebase" and later "crack"—first appeared on the streets of Los Angeles in 1983, the same year Greg Mack joined the staff at KDAY. Demand for the new street drug, a crystalized derivation of powder cocaine that provided users with a potent high for a minimal price, quickly eclipsed sales of all other narcotics. Local gang networks, already adept at dealing marijuana, PCP, powder cocaine, and other illegal substances, shifted to selling the new product, which was cheap to get, easy to manufacture, and unusually addictive.[7] A sudden boom in the market for rock provided lucrative opportunities for the region's black gangs, who profited handsomely by collaborating with drug traffickers and by building their own complex distribution networks. But as the area's drug-dealing outfits—now linked to LA's Crips and Bloods organizations—sought to expand sales and defend against competitors, they were compelled to fortify drug houses, arm themselves with military-grade guns, and engage in ever-more violent campaigns to control their markets.

The changes for Los Angeles were dramatic, even for those who had spent years investigating South LA's metastasizing street gang problem. By the end of 1983, shortly after rock cocaine's arrival, Los Angeles County officials testified before the United States Congress about an emerging crisis. To the Senate Subcommittee on Juvenile Justice, LA County District Attorney Robert Philibosian characterized South Los Angeles as a warzone where "the sound of gunfire is so commonplace that law-abiding citizens no longer exhibit enough curiosity to go as far as their windows to see what is happening." Los Angeles Police Department Deputy Chief James Bascue also offered testimony about the social impact of the horror, describing the citizens of his city as psychologically paralyzed. He told the subcommittee that rock cocaine had so exacerbated the gang wars and drug-related crimes of armed robbery, kidnapping, and murder that surrounding communities were permeated by violence and terror: "People can't go to the store. People can't enjoy parks."[8]

The stakes of crime control were especially high in early 1984, as Los Angeles city leaders prepared to host the Summer Olympics. Press reports of "gang-related" homicides in the spring intensified pressures on Los Angeles officials to address the youth violence (and the homelessness, urban decay, and dysfunctional public transportation system) plaguing the central section of the city where athletes, spectators, celebrities, political figures, and the international press would convene in July and August.[9] The coming of the Games heightened LAPD Chief Daryl Gates's fervent devotion to get-tough policing, especially as it related to juvenile gangs. From Gates's perspective, violent youths—particularly African-American boys—posed the greatest risk to his city because they were those most likely to be involved with gangs and to traffic in narcotics. Gates intended to sharpen the police department's attacks on black youths who investigators tagged as criminals.[10] At a time when Los Angeles was in the international spotlight, the chief vigorously defended his officers against charges of harassment, implicitly condoned racial profiling, and cited the "war" on gangs as justification for "novel" law enforcement measures that included extreme force.[11] In spite of his aggressive leadership, and no doubt for some because of it, Gates remained popular among Los Angeles residents who were increasingly worried about violent crime. The public, including many black Angelenos, judged his department favorably through the early 1980s, supplying the chief with the mandate he needed to stay the course. Indeed, after the 1984 Olympic Games had ended, Gates saw an even broader groundswell of support, including from his sometime nemesis Mayor Tom Bradley.[12]

Faced with the unpredictable problem of gang violence and the vexing reality that his city had become a key battleground in America's war on drugs, Mayor Bradley called a press conference in October 1984. Since the closing of the Summer Olympic Games, more than thirty people had been murdered in Los Angeles, most of them in the communities of South Central where, he informed reporters, gang members had become "drug assassins" who used military-grade weapons and distributed rock cocaine from "rock houses." The mayor made the grim pronouncement that Los Angeles was under siege. His constituents were newly threatened by the Crips and the Bloods, gangs long known to be violent but who now moonlighted as drug traffickers, compounding the city's growing crisis of addiction and blight. He called the problem "urban terrorism," evoking LA's feverish recent efforts to avert any act of foreign terrorism during the Olympics; this urban threat, the term implied, warranted the same fervor from regular citizens—"community leaders . . . the churches, the schools, the businesses . . . the parents"—to collaborate with police. Moreover, by rallying officials from across the city to come up with "an aggressive plan of action" to "purge our community of this violence," Mayor Bradley gave Los Angeles law enforcement officials like Chief Daryl Gates the authorization to explore innovative, and even radical, solutions to gang-related crime.[13] That is exactly what the LAPD did in 1985 when it introduced the battering ram.

As Bradley explained, police task forces had to contend with a new obstacle in their efforts to halt the spread of rock cocaine: rock houses. Sometimes masquerading as single-family homes, apartments, or small business storefronts, rock houses functioned as centers for the production, distribution, and consumption of rock. Thus, a warranted police raid on any one rock house could lead to the confiscation of drugs, drug paraphernalia, cash, and weapons, along with scores of arrests of both users and dealers. Having positively identified some three hundred of these structures across the residential landscape of South Los Angeles, operating near homes, schools, churches, community centers, and playgrounds, police had the clear data and the moral incentive to pick them off, one by one.[14]

The problem, however, was that drug dealers understood this and prepared for it. After a few failed attempts in 1983 and 1984 to execute search warrants at suspected rock houses, police investigators discovered at these locations sophisticated fortifications designed to prevent theft, shield those inside from drive-by shootings, and thwart police. Leaders of SWAT teams (so-called for their use of "special weapons and tactics") reported encountering steel doors, iron bars covering windows, and, most remarkably, metal cages flanked with electronically controlled doors, in which entering and exiting visitors could be detained if necessary. By design, these extras turned rock houses into fortresses that could withstand a police onslaught or at least frustrate tactical teams. As Gates recalled, his men would arrive "with a tow truck and a cable, lock onto the front door or a window" and yank off what they could to create an opening. This highly visible, time-consuming work, while it eventually delivered police access to the premises, destroyed the element of surprise that was essential to any successful drug raid: "By the time we [got inside], the sellers would have taken the drugs into a bathroom—which would have a steel door—and flush them down the toilet." Dope dealers and users could escape all charges if they managed to hide or destroy incriminating stock and supplies before cops gained entry. And usually they did. "Without the drugs as evidence," the chief lamented, "we couldn't make an arrest that would result in a conviction."[15] When this happened, Toddy Tee's "Batterram" tells us, the hustlers celebrated, *"jumpin' up and down 'cause it ain't no case."*[16]

The SWAT leaders advised Chief Gates that they needed a strategy for conducting more effective rock house busts. His solution came in the form of a couple of V-100 armored vehicles borrowed from the US Department of Energy. The US Army had first used the two tank-like personnel carriers in the Vietnam War and, later, for security at a nuclear facility. By the early 1980s, they were out of commission, which created an opportunity for Los Angeles. The LAPD first acquired the six-ton armored vehicles as part of its crisis readiness in case of terrorism during the 1984 Olympics. Once the Games had closed, the US Government expressed no interest in reclaiming the twenty-year-old V-100s, and so they sat in storage for several months until someone in the LAPD's gang and drug tactical units proposed using them in rock house raids. To that end, they suggested a few basic modifications: paint them a dark blue color to mask the military camouflage and to better represent the city agency; label them with the Los Angeles city seal and the words "L.A.P.D. Rescue Vehicle" (because, as Gates argued, rock house busts aimed to rescue communities from drug dealers); and, most importantly, outfit each of them with a steel battering ram.[17] The idea was simple: a fourteen-foot steel ram, with six tons of bulk behind it, would be a "precision" tool for forced entry. As Toddy Tee rapped, the LAPD was *"sick and tired of snatchin' down bars"* with cables and tow trucks.[18] Here was a new weapon that vested raid teams with the power to roll up to the front of a rock house and, in seconds, punch a hole in the building large enough to allow police to rush in, expeditiously locate drug evidence, and make arrests.[19]

Chief Gates approved the proposal, and when the first "battering ram" vehicle was complete, he organized test runs in demolition zones along the path of the planned Century Freeway. Seeing the ease with which the V-100 punctured dilapidated houses marked for removal, Gates predicted that his department would, at last, gain the upper hand in its battle with cocaine traffickers. The chief understood there would be public outcry, and he anticipated some legal challenges to a municipal police force's use of a mechanism of war to carry out search warrants—a first in history for any

American law enforcement agency. In his mind, the potential benefits outweighed the risks, and it was also possible that the LAPD would be lauded as a model for others on the front lines of the nation's war on drugs. So confident was Gates in the success of the battering ram, in fact, that he invited photographers and reporters from the Los Angeles press to witness its maiden run.[20]

On February 6, 1985, Gates stood in front of the refurbished "rescue vehicle" facing a crowd of media observers. The plan was for a SWAT team to put it on the streets of LA that evening, using it for the first time in the field, to execute a search warrant on a suspected rock house in Pacoima. The chief conveyed optimism about the mission and christened the first voyage of the battering ram by cracking a bottle of Thunderbird wine on its port side. Then, with Gates riding in the passenger seat, the massive vehicle growled down Louvre Street, press vans in tow. As it rolled over the front lawn of the target residence, a neighbor screamed at the police to stop. The ram charged forward nonetheless. As intended, it demolished a front wall within seconds of impact, affording the raid team immediate access to the home's living room (Fig. 1.1).[21]

Inside the Pacoima house, the SWAT team discovered not a bevy of drug dealers and users but, instead, resident Linda Johnson, her small son, Marquez, and another woman visiting with her two children, all of whom were eating ice cream when the ram smashed through the wall. The ordinary domestic scene stunned investigators, including the chief, and the fruitless hunt that followed dismayed those who expected to discover a fully functioning rock cocaine enterprise. Police found no weapons, no conspicuous stacks of cash, and only a trace amount of cocaine, less than a tenth of a gram, an

Fig I.I On February 6, 1985, the Los Angeles Police Department debuted its armored V-100 "Rescue Vehicle," fitted with a steel battering ram. Los Angeles Times Photographic Archives, Library Special Collections, UCLA Library.

amount so insignificant that the LA district attorney refused to consider filing charges. Linda Johnson and her husband (who returned moments after the raid) were arrested on site and their child was placed in protective custody. But without sufficient evidence of any wrongdoing, the couple was released and reunited with their boy the next day. Attorney Johnnie Cochran, who immediately filed a claim against the city on behalf of the Johnsons, publicly condemned the Los Angeles Police Department for "negligence, violation of civil rights, intentional infliction of emotional distress, assault, battery and damaging property." The children in particular, Cochran noted, suffered from trauma as a result of the battering ram. "They have trouble sleeping at night. They cannot get it out of their mind. They see a police car and they remember it."[22]

In response to the debacle in Pacoima, the San Fernando Valley chapter of the NAACP, a group of Pacoima ministers, and the ACLU sought to block further police use of the V-100 vehicle. Its deployment had proven to critics that the Los Angeles Police Department planned to conduct drug raids as if it operated in a war zone, without regard for the safety of bystanders, with little concern for those living in the surrounding neighborhoods, and with disdain for the civil rights of private citizens. "These weapons may be appropriate for a battlefield," an attorney for the ACLU told the *Los Angeles Times*, "but not to serve an arrest warrant." Reverend Jeffrey Joseph, Sr., a Pacoima minister and a witness to the maiden run of the ram, denounced the LAPD for using his community for target practice. "We don't need new weapons to be tried out on us," he seethed, reminding reporters that three small children under the age of ten had been inside the home, in the direct path of the vehicle's destruction.[23]

■   ■   ■

The protests in Los Angeles over the use of the battering ram echoed decades of challenges leveled by black Angelenos against the police. In the 1960s, after the black uprising in South Los Angeles that came to be known as the Watts Riots, state and federal leaders conducted hearings on racial discrimination in policing, and national civil rights leaders including Martin Luther King, Jr. and NAACP director Roy Wilkins called for greater scrutiny of police practices and of Police Chief William H. Parker's leadership. In that same decade, *Muhammad Speaks*—the firebrand weekly paper of the

Nation of Islam—provided a steady stream of evidence to black Angelenos of all creeds linking law enforcement to white supremacy. By the end of the decade, the Los Angeles chapter of the Black Panther Party was functioning as a police watch organization, as well as galvanizing hundreds of young black militants with its armed resistance programs.[24] These were a few of the reasons why, by the opening of the 1970s, LA had secured its position as the primary battleground for the national conflict between urban black communities and police. Although much Black Power activism ebbed in the early 1970s, especially in the wake of coordinated federal crackdowns on black radicalism, LA's African-American communities remained acutely aware of police authority and intent on checking it. The concerted challenges to law enforcement endured. In fact, the grassroots campaign to establish true checks on police power gained its greatest momentum much later in the late 1970s, when Daryl Gates, Chief Parker's dutiful protégé, became the city's newest, most notorious top cop.

In 1975, three South Los Angeles social justice advocates resurrected the idea of police watch groups touted in the late 1960s by the radicalized men and women of the Los Angeles Black Panthers. Anthony Thigpenn, Kwaku Duren, and Michael Zinzun had worked as community organizers in the early 1970s, speaking with victims of police abuse and providing assistance for those who sought to file complaints. Zinzun, who had spent two years as a member of the LA Panthers, was particularly troubled by the "epidemic" of police violence that had only worsened since the decline of Black Power. His concern was that as the war on crime replaced the war on poverty, African-American people nationwide, but especially in poverty-stricken places like South Los Angeles, would become increasingly vulnerable to modern policing methods designed not to protect but to attack.[25] In response to a flurry of violent police-involved incidents—among them, the killing of sixteen-year-old Barry Evans in a shootout with the LAPD, and the killing of Betty Scott, mother of four, by California Highway Patrol officers—Zinzun and his fellow activists sought to form an organization of like-minded people committed to curtailing what had become the LAPD's new "reign of terror."[26] "Unity is the only way," Zinzun told the *Los Angeles Sentinel*, "to stop police killings and instances of police abuse."[27]

Their organization, the Coalition Against Police Abuse (CAPA), was created with the express goal of gathering and publicizing information about abuses committed by officers of the law. As the group's original statement of purpose declared, the time had come "to let the authorities know that we will no longer tolerate the senseless harassment, injury and murder of community people by the police, and that we have resolved as our main purpose to organize and mobilize the masses . . . against police terrorism in our communities."[28] To these ends, CAPA sponsored public demonstrations, including picket lines meant to obstruct the daily operations at police precincts and the district attorney's offices. Its members distributed proposals for community action and offered workshops inside South LA community centers. One South Central "Organizing Against Police Brutality" event, held in December 1976 at Fremont High School, featured Black Panther royalty Ericka Huggins along with Larry Williams of the Greater Watts Justice Center, a legal-aid organization founded in the wake of the 1965 Los Angeles uprising. At what the *Sentinel* called CAPA's "cop abuse seminar," Huggins issued to the packed hall a directive about police misconduct. "Publicize any and everything that occurs in your community," she said, imploring her audience to remember "the Martin Luther Kings, Fred Hamptons, Malcolm Xs." California State University Northridge journalism student Dwayne Waheeb Williams endorsed Huggins's message, and reminded the room that many others—not only lauded movement leaders—had also fallen victim to violent oppression. In fact, when it came to law enforcement abuses, every member of the black community was at risk. With camera in hand, Williams testified about his own violent confrontations with the police and proposed photography as one form of resistance. One could take photos, tell the press, take a complaint directly to the police department, or seek support from organizations like CAPA, Williams said: "The only way to alleviate police abuse is to report it. Make it known, whether it is a small complaint or a large one."[29]

When veteran LAPD officer Daryl Gates began his tenure as chief in early 1978, his department and the county sheriff's were straining to withstand pressures applied by CAPA and its partners. Pickets, marches, and protest rallies stymied operations at police precincts and sheriff's patrol stations throughout South Los Angeles. Thanks to the combined work of CAPA, South Central's New Mount Pleasant Baptist Church, the *Los Angeles Sentinel*, the Greater Watts Justice Center, and the National Conference of Black Lawyers, the LAPD faced a major lawsuit for "falsifying police reports, battering citizens, unlawfully discharging weapons, committing unprosecuted crimes and destroying records."[30] City Councilman David Cunningham, meanwhile, with the support of African-American California State Assemblywoman Maxine Waters, had expanded a campaign to create a citizen panel to supervise police shooting investigations, rejecting the LAPD's and district attorney's long tradition of internal reviews with little or no oversight. Adding to the department's challenges, Gates was forced in his first months in office to respond to charges of illegal spying. Gates was personally named in a civil suit filed in Los Angeles Superior Court accusing LAPD leadership of planting undercover officers inside CAPA and other police watch groups.[31]

Gates had reason to be concerned. Beyond organized protest, CAPA had a core mission: to expose abuses of police power to the public. In the years before Gates took office, CAPA conducted research into the unique sovereignty of LA's chief of police. Unlike chiefs in other major urban centers, including New York, LA's top cop was an appointee of a police commission rather than the mayor—and thus, did not answer directly to City Hall. Nor was the position subject to term limits. This had been the case since the late 1930s, when the Los Angeles City Charter was amended to remove the direct link between the mayor's office and the office of the chief; the thinking had been that this move would shield the police department from political pressure and corruption.[32] By the 1940s, the chief of the LAPD was more than the highest-ranking police officer in the department. He was an unusually independent political player, free to make decisions about his force without concern for the mayor, the mayor's approval ratings, or municipal elections. That meant that through the long and tumultuous tenures of William Parker (1950–1966) and Edward Davis (1969–1978), some viewed the chief of the LAPD as a beacon of integrity and stability in the midst of political turmoil. For others, especially leaders in City Hall, these freewheeling chiefs reeked of arrogance, and the "mentality" of the office too often empowered them to defy the mayor and, by extension, the people of the city.[33]

By the first months of Chief Gates's administration, CAPA secured court orders to obtain LAPD documents, including evidence showing the department's concerted move toward militarization—the steps that would lead to the battering ram. The group also got its hands on training bulletins, which were as much a window into the culture of the department as a detailed description of police procedures. One bulletin, among the first that Gates approved, revealed that LAPD policies for justifiable homicide were quite flexible. First, it listed protocols for using "deadly force," acknowledging a precedent set by recent court cases making homicide defensible only in action against "violent felons." The bulletin went on, however, to provide police with useful loopholes. If acting in "self-defense," for instance, an officer had broad latitude to decide what constituted "an immediate threat" of death or serious injury. The license to use deadly force, it explained, was an entitlement granted to those whose job demanded rapid response. If presented with immediate life-threatening danger, "it is not in the public's interest, the Department's interest, nor the officer's interest for an officer to hesitate and become ambivalent." Similarly, the bulletin outlined standards for shooting "fleeing felons" versus "fleeing misdemeanants." In the case of a felon, the officer was permitted to fire if that person had committed a violent crime and his escape would "constitute a threat to the welfare and safety of the community." In a case of misdemeanor offense, it noted that deadly force was "*never* employed"; nevertheless, it could be warranted in self-defense. This was the kind of fuzzy clause CAPA saw as designed to provide cover for overzealous cops.[34]

Then, it happened. On January 3, 1979, two LAPD patrolmen confronted Eula Love outside of her South Central home as she yelled at two representatives from Southern California

Gas Company, waving a kitchen knife in her hand. Earlier that day, she had assaulted another man from the utility, hitting him with a shovel after he tried to collect her overdue payment. With her twelve- and fifteen-year-old daughters just inside, Love warned the officers to leave. Witnesses said she was poised on the walkway, thrusting a boning knife in the men's direction, reportedly angry at the utility's threat to shut off her gas unless she made a minimum payment of $22.[35] Yelling obscenities, the thirty-nine-year-old mother ignored the officers' demands to drop the knife, and the men fired their service weapons multiple times, killing her instantly. Hazel Blue, a neighbor on the scene, described it as "a nightmare."[36]

In the days following the shooting, Chief Gates set about explaining his officers' actions to the press, hoping to limit what was sure to become a public-relations mess for his department. He told reporters that when the two policemen emerged from their patrol car and approached Love's residence, they observed the woman "flailing her knife" with "froth coming out of her mouth." (The "froth" observation had actually been made by the gas company employee assaulted earlier.) He said the officers perceived a mortal danger when she made a move to throw her weapon. Gates stressed that Love died because "she decided to solve her problem with a knife. That's why it happened."[37] The chief relayed details from an internal investigation, including portions of testimony from Lloyd O'Callaghan and Edward Hopson, the officers involved. Presumably trying to head off charges of racism, Gates was careful to note that, although Love was black, so was patrolman Hopson. The official account from the police was, in sum, that two LAPD patrolmen acted in self-defense, and thus their use of deadly force was justified.[38]

Eyewitnesses complicated this narrative. Neighbor Hazel Blue saw one officer knock the weapon out of Love's hand before any shots came. (The officers said the same, but claimed she promptly snatched it back up.) It was when Love got back to her feet that she was "shot down cold blooded," Blue said. Sheila Love, Eula Love's teenage daughter, said that her mother was on her knees when the shots came, and testimony from one of the gas company employees present that afternoon seemed to corroborate that account. "She never got up," the serviceman told reporters. "She was down on her knees all the time." Love's youngest daughter testified that Love was unarmed and retreating backward when the cops began shooting.[39] When the Los Angeles district attorney interviewed witnesses, two said that Hopson "fooled" or "fumbled" with the knife after the shooting. Although one later recanted and the other was unable to articulate what he had seen, it hinted at an extremely serious allegation, that the police officer had tampered with evidence. A month later, the magazine *Jet* made a further claim: "A neighbor reported that one of the officers kicked the knife across the street."[40]

Through the fog of conflicting accounts, one fact remained clear: a woman was dead, shot eight times by uniformed police officers. Word of Love's death spread quickly throughout South Los Angeles, and so did rumors about a police conspiracy to cover up wrongdoing. Black locals, already suspicious of the LAPD, expressed anger, frustration, and a renewed sense of dread about the continuing disintegration of community-police relations. One South Central resident, Marion Singleton, told a *Los Angeles Times* reporter that he and his neighbors spent their days "talking about the shooting" and discussing their fears. More than anything else, he said, "people are afraid nothing will be done about it."[41] Other residents and community leaders, many of whom knew Love personally, crowded into city council meetings to express their outrage at the LAPD and demand compensation for the victim's orphaned daughters. Many spoke of their own confrontations with violent and verbally abusive police, and described officers riding into their communities with guns blazing.[42] The local chapter of the NAACP, the National Human Rights Coalition (NHRC), and CAPA joined forces with Love's South Central neighbors to petition Los Angeles City Hall for a grand jury investigation into the shooting.[43]

South Central church and civic leaders also clamored for action against Gates and his agency's policies, which more often than not supported discrimination against their constituents. For instance, Assemblywoman Maxine Waters, a vocal critic of police strip-searches and choke-hold tactics— maneuvers used most brazenly against African-American men—went to the press. She blasted the police, claiming they were routinely "trained to be tough with blacks, and because of that they come into our communities thinking that all blacks carry guns and knives." State Senator Diane Watson called for "checks and balances," noting that "for too long, the police have felt they were above the law [and] have never been made accountable for their actions."[44] The city's most prominent African-American ministers publicly proclaimed that the Eula Love case was "bigger than Love's death" alone. Reverend Milton M. Merriweather, an outspoken critic of Police Chief Gates, called for City Hall to see that justice was done, for not only Love but all black folks in Los Angeles. He predicted mass uprisings if Officers Hopson and O'Callaghan were not punished for their actions, and reiterated this warning during a pastors' march following Love's funeral.[45]

The *Los Angeles Herald-Examiner* helped sow anxiety about the growing power of the LAPD. Day after day, it printed front-page, above-the-fold features on the shooting and the investigations that followed. Under provocative headlines like "The $22.09 Gas Bill Tragedy," the paper focused on the most macabre details, particularly the haste with which the police officers drew their weapons, the number of shots fired, and where the bullets entered Love's body. *Herald-Examiner* editors also railed against Chief Gates, his deadly-force policies, and his police-protecting processes, voicing serious doubts that any internal investigations into police misconduct could be fair. So scathing were the paper's criticisms that the chief issued a veiled threat to its editors. "Maybe you can get away with this kind of journalism in New York," he warned in a press conference, "but you can't in Los Angeles."[46]

Unfortunately for Gates, that kind of journalism circulated widely. Police brutality in Los Angeles was national news by March, when *Esquire* ran a feature on Love's death. The popular magazine posed provocative questions about whether the Los Angeles Police Department, the most powerful law enforcement agency in the country, protected and served black citizens with the same care and civility it did whites. The *Los Angeles Times*, which had not yet devoted much ink to a story that its rival the *Herald-Examiner* was reporting avidly, jumped in after this, reminding readers that the awful shooting of Eula Love was in no way the first incident in which Los Angeles police had used excessive violence against a black or brown suspect. It profiled several other recent cases of abuse under investigation by the LA District Attorney, including the case of James Richardson, an unarmed nineteen-year-old shot and killed by a patrolman who mistook the black teen for a robbery suspect, a shooting that occurred just two weeks after Love's death. Shortly thereafter, as the newspaper reported, three plainclothes LAPD officers fired at Cornelius Tatum, an African-American gas station employee, when they misidentified him as a burglar. It was Tatum's first day on the job at the Vermont Avenue business, and because he was aware that it was on one of South Central's most dangerous blocks, he was armed with a shotgun. Witnesses said that the officers, who were working undercover for the department's gang unit, failed to identify themselves as policemen when they confronted Tatum with their guns drawn. Tatum, perhaps mistaking it for an armed robbery, drew his own weapon, and the officers fired, leaving Tatum with eleven gunshot wounds and permanent paralysis.[47] The *Los Angeles Times* coverage of cases like these suggested, first, that the use of excessive force was standard practice for the LAPD, and, second, that victims of police brutality were disproportionately black. Without immediate intervention, the newspaper warned, an unbridled culture of racism and violence inside the LAPD was certain to result in more tragedy, and it would be a pox on the city. LA's reputation as one of the nation's most progressive societies was at stake.[48]

For the Coalition Against Police Abuse, these cases, among others, only reinforced what members already knew to be true: that Los Angeles police flagrantly abused their authority and did so, all too often, with tragic results. Having spent nearly five years collecting reports from local citizens, CAPA had the evidence that Love's wrongful death was no anomaly. Nor were black residents surprised. John McKnight, an appliance deliveryman and father living in the Watts Nickerson Gardens housing project, complained that the police were turning neighborhoods like his into war zones. McKnight recalled half a dozen police shootings in 1979 alone, and countless violent arrests. Those who carry the badge, he said, "think a black man's always dangerous until he's handcuffed and laying on the ground."[49] Local teachers, pastors, council-members, and the black press heard testimony from Mc-Knight and other community members, young and old, who had experienced frightening encounters with law enforcement. As the *Los Angeles Sentinel* put it, citizens told their own harrowing stories in "meetings, demonstrations, rallies and clandestine rap sessions."[50] "We have lost too many of our citizens at the hands of police officers," an editorial in the paper declared, "and it must come to an immediate end."[51] Meanwhile, Maxine Waters took it upon herself to remind the white public that police violence against black victims was "not unusual." Then in May, in the midst of a concerted campaign to raise consciousness about police misconduct, cops shot Carlos Washington, another South Central resident. The fifteen-year-old black boy was gunned down while scaling a fence, fleeing from officers who suspected him of stealing a car.[52] As the *Sentinel* noted, Washington was an innocent young boy, a "typical junior high student" who followed the rules and generally steered clear of "trouble." He was the twenty-third person shot by Los Angeles police in a four-month period.[53]

In response to the May shooting incident, the *Los Angeles Sentinel* printed a two-part exposé on violence and bigotry in the Los Angeles Police Department. In the report, former LAPD officer Glen Wood told the *Sentinel* that racial biases pervaded police training, police policies, and police practices out in the field. Wood, whom the paper identified as white, noted the frequent use of the term "nigger" among his fellow officers, and he described a hypermasculine culture in which his coworkers frequently bragged about "kicking ass" and firing at suspects. He recalled one time when his partner, while they were patrolling South Central, got aggravated when he spotted a young black man washing his car in front of his home. The officer ordered the man inside, telling him, "Get out of the street, nigger, you don't own it yet." On another occasion, Wood witnessed a fellow patrolman pull alongside a car full of black youths, with windows down and bass thumping loudly from the speakers. The officer warned the driver, "Turn that f——jungle-bunny music down, nigger. Everybody don't want to hear that shit."[54]

Black boys and young men attested to being marks for hot-tempered cops. "General" Robert Lee, founder of the LA Brim Blood Army gang, an early incarnation of the Bloods, was thirteen when a Los Angeles patrol officer first threatened to kill him. In 1969, he and his friends were pulled over while cruising slowly in the Vermont Harbor area just west of South Central. As the cops questioned the passengers and Lee began laughing nervously, one angry patrolman demanded silence by shoving his shotgun in Lee's mouth and daring him to "smile now, nigger." Jimel Barnes, a Crip, summing up his similar encounters with the police, said, "I was treated . . . just like I wasn't human." He described being pulled over and hearing from a cop, "We're going to play this game . . . . Watch this." Then the officer would take an unregistered "throwaway gun" out of his boot, load a bullet in the chamber, and "put it to my head and burn the trigger."[55] Both Lee and Barnes learned in childhood to be wary of the police; Lee believed "the police started killing ten- and eleven-year-old young brothers; they were blowing their heads off." They and their peers feared the LAPD as if it were just as ruthless as any street gang, and more sinister, to boot. "When the devil pulled up," Lee said of the LAPD's frequent unwelcomed visits to social gatherings in his neighborhood, "brothers that didn't even do a thing were breaking their legs, tearing their pants, and jumping over cars to run away."[56]

Even those young people who made it a point to avoid associating with local gangs complained of racial profiling, brutality, and harassment. O'Shea "Ice Cube" Jackson learned at a very early age to fear men in blue uniforms. He said that even as a little boy, the police accosted him regularly, teaching him contempt for those who patrolled his stomping grounds. "When you in the hood, they get you early," Ice Cube explained of his memories growing up in LA in the late 1970s. "They'll pull you off your bike, make you put your hands on the hood. You'll be sitting on the grass, just played football, and these motherfuckers swoop up and fuck with you." From Ice Cube's perspective, the police neither protected nor served any purpose other than terror, and they treated all black boys the same: "Fucking with you if you're bad, fucking with you if you're good—don't matter."[57]

In the wake of the Eula Love killing, efforts to shine a spotlight on rampant police misconduct caused black Angelenos, who had generally approved of the manner in which the Los Angeles police enforced the law, to lose faith. A citywide poll conducted by the *Los Angeles Times* in 1978, the year prior to Love's death, had revealed that most African Americans viewed the LAPD as an institution that functioned to safeguard their lives and their property. By the end of 1979, however, similar polls showed that the vast majority of black respondents had concluded that the force did not operate to improve their quality of life, but instead degraded their community by prejudicially abusing its members. Latinos polled in late 1979 expressed similar views, with two-thirds citing the Love shooting as a clear act of brutality and 40 percent agreeing that African Americans in the city bore the heavy weight of police misconduct. Even white residents asked to reflect on the honor and integrity of the LAPD began to grow skeptical.[58]

At the tail end of his second term, Mayor Tom Bradley offered a careful statement acknowledging the public's growing misgivings about local law enforcement: "There is widespread feeling—which I share—that the [Love] shooting might have been avoided."[59] Bradley promised to have the Los Angeles Police Commission, a five-member board he appointed himself, review police policies and procedures.[60] For a growing chorus of police-reform activists, who demanded that citizens rather than bureaucrats guide oversight, this was a meager effort to effect change. Worse, it was a gesture undermined by the mayor's declaration of full support for Police Chief Gates amid calls for his dismissal. In defense of Gates's leadership, Bradley cautioned his critics against inflaming tensions between the police and the black community. One minister responded by accusing the city's first African-American mayor of having an "LAPD mentality."[61]

Eula Love had become a cause célèbre for police-watch advocates in Los Angeles. For organizations like CAPA, it seemed this one tragedy on South Orchard Avenue would catalyze the creation of city-sanctioned citizen police-review boards—precisely the kind of change that had eluded civil rights groups and black revolutionaries in the 1960s and 1970s and that might facilitate real, systemic improvements in criminal justice. As Paul Hudson, president of the Los Angeles branch of the NAACP, said, "I think that this very well may be the straw that breaks the camel's back."[62]

Rather than pressure the police department, as groups representing Puerto Ricans and African Americans in New York City had done with little success, and rather than entrust Mayor Bradley or the Police Commission to curb misconduct, activists focused their efforts on the 1980 election.[63] The Campaign for a Citizens' Police Review Board (CCPRB) set out to collect the 150,000 signatures needed to place an initiative on the ballot that would amend the Los Angeles City Charter to require the creation of such a board. In addition to CAPA, which did much to spearhead the campaign for a citizen police review board, CCPRB included dozens of progressive groups, including activists from the Campaign for Economic Democracy, the NAACP, and the ACLU. As the CCPRB ramped up its petition drive in the spring of 1980, the *Economist* reported on California's "gathering storm of protest" aimed at restraining "the enormous power of the Los Angeles police."[64]

But the campaign failed. Deep divisions within the CCPRB grew over the organizational details of the proposed board, including its planned budget, salaries for appointees, and needs for administrative staff. As a result, some allies withdrew their support, while others abandoned the drive to collect signatures. A fractured CCPRB was ultimately unable to meet its summer deadline and the initiative did not appear before voters that fall. While activists agreed that the defeat was a result of infighting, some suspected the LAPD of helping to sow the discord. Long after the summer deadline for qualifying the initiative had come and gone, advocates for CAPA and the ACLU uncovered evidence suggesting that undercover police officers had infiltrated the CCPRB and stoked internal divisions. By some accounts, police spies had also stolen scores of collected signatures. Chief Gates called all ac-

cusations of dirty policing and election meddling "garbage,"
even as discovered documents revealed that the LAPD's Public Disorder Intelligence Division had spied on an extraordinary array of city and state officials, including Los Angeles
City Council members, Mayor Bradley, the state's attorney
general, and Governor Jerry Brown.[65]

Thanks to an expensive and highly effective public relations
campaign, Chief Gates and his police department emerged
from the tumultuous events of 1979, 1980, and 1981 reinvigorated and emboldened. By the early 1980s, the Los Angeles
Police Department under Gates had demonstrated how impervious it was to crisis, and, more importantly, how resistant
it could be to any storm of protest. Local police-watch advocates, including CAPA, remained vigilant, but the broadly
organized movement that had churned in South Los Angeles
began to dissipate as the Reagan era opened.[66]

■  ■  ■

In the midst of the controversy surrounding the police shooting of Eula Love, Chief Gates told a meeting of Los Angeles
County Bar Association members that tragic incidents like
Love's death were "inevitable." South Los Angeles was, he
reasoned, plagued by urban crime and bloodshed, and budget issues had forced a reduction in the number of uniformed
officers: "In that kind of climate, where there is that much violence, you are going to have police violence."[67] Not long after
the failed review board movement of 1980, many in South Los
Angeles, including some who had been outraged by Gates's
flippant rationalizations for his officers' use of fatal force in
the Love case, began to agree with him. A broad coalition of
activists had stood in opposition to the most powerful law

enforcement agency in the nation, revitalizing a long tradition of protest against policing in South Los Angeles. But within just a few years, many of those same leaders were encouraging their communities to "stand behind" the police department.[68] Vociferous cries about abuse of authority, and uncompromising demands for community-centered solutions to counter bad policing, gave way to pleas for tougher cops and more of them.

The early 1980s saw a shift in the consensus about juvenile crime. For over two decades before that, black communities housing active street gangs had refused to be complicit in what former Los Angeles police chief William Parker defined as the city's "war on juvenile delinquency." Through the 1950s, the LAPD had launched a series of outreach programs designed to enlist the support of black Angelenos in the department's campaign against "unbridled hoodlumism."[69] Its professed dedication to "housecleaning" and "fairness to minorities"—for instance, Parker vowed to punish corrupt officers and promote black patrolmen—warmed some black citizens to the idea of assisting law enforcement in its efforts to stem the tide of juvenile crime. But even through the 1960s, as violent incidents blamed on black car clubs and gangs became the "major problem" about which the *Sentinel* warned, the onus had remained on the police to answer for its excessive use of force within these neighborhoods.[70]

In the years before and after the 1965 Los Angeles uprising, local black leaders conceded, and even lamented, that there were wayward teens in their communities, but still cited discrimination rather than delinquency as the critical public safety issue.[71] Black juvenile crime may have been on the rise, but even LAPD officials admitted that this reflected a spike in crime across the city. African-American youth advocates particularly took note of the racial disparities in policing. After three violent confrontations between citizens and police in a predominantly black area of town, an administrator from the neighborhood's Manual Arts High School offered an explanation: "The climate of today is an explosive one. The [community] knows that vice, prostitution and gambling are participated in by other communities which are overlooked by the police. [So] they respond explosively when the vice squad raids Central Los Angeles."[72]

In the 1970s, youth crime had become more brazen, and citizens of the communities of South Central, Watts, and Compton started to cooperate more with those possessing the tools and the authority to keep that crime in check. The flashpoint was bus violence. As reports issued by the Southern California Rapid Transit District (SCRTD) laid bare, bus drivers and passengers navigated virtual combat zones on downtown Los Angeles routes, and while traveling through the Central Avenue corridor just west of the Harbor Freeway and running from South Central to Compton. A slew of witnesses identified "Male Negro juveniles" as perpetrators of property destruction, theft, and violence against drivers and passengers. Some hurled rocks and "missiles" at bus windows; others robbed drivers of transfers and fares; women riders endured verbal harassment and sexual assault; and victims, young and old, came forward with harrowing stories of "unprovoked attacks."[73] In response, SCRTD installed silent alarms, hired undercover security agents to ride the buses, and improved radio transmitters for drivers to communicate with law enforcement. In 1976, a suggestion that SCRTD partner with the LAPD was met with enthusiasm from bus patrons, the majority of them black residents of South Los Angeles neighborhoods who had to travel outside of the community for work and city services. SCRTD's manager of operations applauded this partnership, predicting a new era of cooperation between city agencies and the people of South Los Angeles. It was a pairing he suggested might be "the answer to eradicating . . . criminal activities."[74]

By the end of the decade, even as a chorus of local African-American activists demanded justice for Eula Love and a say in police reform, LA's black "gang problem"—a phrase that had once reflected only distorted fears of benign school rivalries and teen car clubs—had become quite real. County officials determined that, over the last few years of the 1970s, gang participation in Los Angeles had snowballed. By the early 1980s, the region housed more than fifty thousand gang members sorted into as many as four hundred sets and subdivisions, tripling the highest estimates recorded in any decade prior.[75] The chance for local notoriety, the promise of fellowship, and access to material and social resources were powerful incentives for new gang recruits, particularly as youth employment opportunities and recreational programs tied to diminished federal funding were shuttered. Recruits also sought the protection street organizations offered, a critical benefit particularly as the underground market in narcotics and guns emboldened neighborhood gangs to stake claim to turf and then to defend it with lethal force. As the *Los Angeles Times* reported in 1980, gang-related killings had doubled within just three years. This unprecedented and "staggering" crisis prompted California state legislators to pass a bill funding a Gang Violence Suppression Program in 1981. The alarming spike in violence, those officials recognized, was only fueling gang recruiting, as young people living in the ganglands felt compelled to join or otherwise pledge loyalty to neighborhood cliques for self-preservation.[76]

Along with gang membership growth came the proliferation of satellite networks of young people who were not "active" in gangs but who "affiliated" or "associated" themselves
with local gang sets. Once a street gang embedded itself in a
neighborhood or school—through a process that sociologist
Steven Cureton calls "gangster colonization"—it began absorbing unpledged peers who promised to respect its authority.[77] These gang-adjacent youths enjoyed the privileges of
gang protection as well as the social benefits of fellowship,
yet they avoided the drug running and violent crime typically
demanded of full-fledged members, or "bangers." As a Pueblo
Blood member explained, those who merely associated with
gangs greatly outnumbered bangers: "If there are one hundred people in a so-called gang, you may only have five of
them that are really gang bangers. I mean really active. The
other ninety-five will just be kickin' it with the crew."[78]
Whether "really active" or just "kickin' it," these young men
were viewed by police, prosecutors, judges, wardens, school
administrators, and community leaders as hoodlums, just
the same. This conflation of active gangbangers with the
people who socialized with them likely had a number of consequences, by bloating the county's gang-member tallies, and
recasting almost all black juvenile transgressions as "gang-
related" crime. Even more generally, by the 1980s, it meant
that all young black Angelenos, whether involved with local
gangs or not, bore the racialized stigma of the "gangster."

With gangs multiplying and violent crime surging, black
youths—the most common victims of police abuse—earned
less and less empathy, even from those with a history of protesting civil rights violations. When, in 1980, LAPD officers
shot two black teens suspected in a robbery, the incident
failed to stir much concern in the local black press about

overly aggressive police procedures and instead served as a
reminder about the "crisis" of gang-related crime. The editors of the historically progressive *Sentinel*, while emphasizing that "community residents will not tolerate shootings like
Eula Love," allowed that they were "up in arms about the
hoodlums running rampage [sic] in our community making
it unsafe for our women, children and businesses." In this
case, the paper argued, the police were surely justified; officers should continue to crack down on such youths. "Don't
give them an even break."[79]

At one time, the deployment in South Central of police
strike forces, as in the Community Resources Against Street
Hoodlums (CRASH) program, might have provoked organized protests about systematic racial discrimination and harassment. But with narcotics and military-grade weapons
flooding the region, driving a disturbing rise in "drive-by"
shootings and other grisly killings, many in gang-controlled
communities welcomed the expanded police presence. Some
even welcomed militarization, if that is what it would take to
rid communities of "hoodlums and thugs." Seeing city and
county law enforcement agencies invest heavily in a new,
more aggressive war against juvenile gangs came as a relief to
black business owners, homeowners, school administrators
and staff, church leaders, social workers, parents, and others.
While many black residents continued to harbor distrust and
even contempt for Los Angeles law enforcement, their fears
of "youthful criminals . . . murderers and felons" caused them
to accept a form of police occupation. In a choice between
two evils, as the *Sentinel* described it, it was clear that gang
violence posed the greatest threat.[80] Juvenile gangs had to be
driven out of the African-American communities of Los An-

geles, the paper proclaimed, "while there is still a community for which to fight."[81]

Through the 1970s, South Los Angeles residents had been frustrated by the effects of gang-related crime on their day-to-day lives, their businesses, their home values, their schools, and the lives of their children. What was already considered a crisis came to a head in the early 1980s, with the arrival of rock cocaine on the streets. Still, community support for what promised to be a protracted war against local gangs came with reservations. Undoubtedly, many remained unenthusiastic about cooperating with police, and many worried about the price they might pay if gang members perceived them doing so. Most, however, put aside their apprehensions and elected to align themselves with LA's oldest "gang in blue" to gain protection from the others.[82] They found themselves clamoring for more beat cops, for neighborhood patrols, and even for the establishment of police-enforced curfews to curb juvenile delinquency.[83] "There was a time when Black people said there were too many police officers in this community," a *Los Angeles Sentinel* editorial noted. "But the simple facts of the matter are that only the criminals who wish for their crimes to go undetected are saying there are too many police officers in South Central Los Angeles."[84]

CAPA chafed against this new alliance between the black community and law enforcement in Los Angeles. The group continued to demand checks on specific police procedures that, it argued, were unnecessarily brutal and put lives at risk. Most notably, CAPA collected data on the "control holds"—the "bar-arm" and the "carotid" hold—routinely used by LAPD officers on suspects resisting arrest. CAPA discovered that both kinds of choke holds, by cutting off the flow of blood to the brain, had on multiple occasions proved lethal. Between 1975 and 1982, LAPD choke holds were to blame for the deaths of fifteen people in police custody, eleven of them black. (Of the other large urban police departments that employed the choke hold, including New York, San Francisco, Chicago, and Dallas, each reported only one death over the same period.)[85] After one of his officers choked twenty-year-old James Mincey, Jr. to death during a traffic stop, Chief Gates responded indelicately. At a hearing called by Mayor Tom Bradley to address concerns about a spate of bar-arm choke-hold deaths, the question was posed of why most of the victims were African American. The chief shared his "hunch": "We may be finding that in some blacks when it is applied, the veins or arteries do not open up as fast as they do in normal people."[86] With the Los Angeles branch of the Urban League calling for Chief Gates's suspension over that remark, CAPA successfully pressured the police commission not only to ban the use of the bar-arm hold altogether, but to forbid the use of all choke holds in "any situation other than one in which the use of deadly force is authorized."[87]

It was a win for police-reform advocates intent on protecting the lives of young men, which included those targeted by gang task forces. Like the Los Angeles Black Panther Party before it, CAPA pursued checks on police practices to improve the well-being of all black citizens, but especially those young people most likely to be casualties of police brutality. Through the early 1980s, when the consensus around juvenile crime shifted, CAPA remained committed to this cause. The problem for groups like CAPA, however, was that their ability to succeed in putting checks on the police, establishing new review mechanisms, and reining in the power of the chief hinged on public outrage. Because the case of Eula Love generated so much of that, it brought civil rights leaders, labor leaders, political leaders, the press, and South Los Angeles residents together in a concerted effort to amend the City Charter and enfranchise citizens in the process of police oversight.

Love was something of an anomaly; as a middle-aged woman and a mother, she was not representative of Los Angeles police abuse victims in general. The tragedy of Love's shooting, however, presented an opportunity to advocate for all victims—at least, as long as her story remained in the news. CAPA founder Michael Zinzun had learned that he could not count on enduring support from more mainstream black leaders for his fight against police abuse. Years later he would tell the *Los Angeles Times* that, up until 1992, "you couldn't even get them on the phone."[88]

In early 1985, Chief Gates and the LAPD faced what was, by then, a familiar problem: the threat of a public relations disaster connected to its overuse of force. The first voyage of the department's battering ram, in an African-American neighborhood in Pacoima, was a failure that resulted in several wrongful arrests, three traumatized children, protests, and a stack of lawsuits. In an effort to deflect public outrage—especially as news outlets reported that there had been kids eating ice cream in the house when the ram plowed into it—police officials worked to cast the February 6 raid as a mere misstep that revealed, more than anything else, how wily rock dealers could be. The chief, perhaps annoyed by what he viewed as naive complaints, noted that the house was outfitted with steel bars and a set of double steel front doors. Police Captain Noel Cunningham suggested that "there might be a strategy to put children and women in these locations to make us act a little more civilized, so to speak." A department spokesperson offered assurance that "knowing that children are in the house will not necessarily preclude us from making a safe entry." Gates elaborated on the point. "We strongly believe," he said, "that if dope dealers get the impression that you can make a rock house into a sanctuary by having children inside, you can then be assured that children will be inside every one of them."[89]

In spite of the protests following early reports of the Pacoima debacle, there was not, in fact, consensus among black citizens in Los Angeles against the battering ram and what promised to be a more militaristic approach to future policing in their communities. Chief Gates and his captains were able to exploit that ambivalence. Department officials were well aware of amplified concerns about gangs and gang-related violence, in part because citizen demands for more patrols and better solutions to youth crime in gang-controlled neighborhoods flooded LAPD offices in 1983 and 1984. They had also seen the *Sentinel,* the most prominent voice of black Los Angeles and a paper that had in the past condemned the police, again and again, for discrimination and abuse, calling vigorously for more cooperation by African-American citizens with law enforcement and more adequate policing of crime-heavy places like South Central (Fig. 1.2). Quite aware of the growing approval for his force among black Angelenos, Gates spoke over his critics. As he and his surrogates stressed, law enforcement was at war, defending the very fabric of Los Angeles society. The same LAPD spokesman who had expressed willingness to ram houses with children in them warned that if the police were not able to use the tactics they saw fit, "rock houses will be in every neighborhood. Not only will they be in the south-central area of Los Angeles and in Pacoima, but they will be in your neighborhood and my neighborhood."[90] Local black leaders Leon and Ruth Washington echoed the urgency in the spokesman's prediction in a public statement to their fellow concerned citizens (a statement Gates would praise as an example of "community introspection and wisdom"):

> If we are to sustain any kind of a livable society, we are going to have to get the drugs out of our midst, and while the battering ram has become an instrument of controversy, when used properly, no one can dispute its effectiveness . . . . Let us be mindful that unless something of substance is done, we will have to turn over the reins of our community to the young drug dealers.[91]

Gates had the public mandate he sought. Rather than yield to a handful of lawyers and activists who would have liked to see the chief immediately retire the battering ram and admit wrongdoing, he could double down. A comment he made after Pacoima made that clear: "This was just the beginning."[92]

■    ■    ■

By the summer of 1985, the LAPD had used the infamous blue battering ram a total of four times. This included its ignominious debut in Pacoima and three additional runs in South Central, including one in late April that was considered a significant victory in LA's drug war. In marked contrast to the outcry in Pacoima in February, the *Sentinel* reported popular support for the April raid, which targeted a "blatantly conspicuous" rock house located near a school. Parents of students at Jefferson High School and residents in the surrounding neighborhoods watched with "expressed delight" as the ram smashed down a drug operation that had reportedly recruited local children as drug runners.[93]

Fig I.2 A series of cartoons in the *Los Angeles Sentinel* in 1984 illustrated shifting ideas about crime and policing in South Central LA. An accompanying editorial statement advised: "This is our community and we are responsible for what happens to us." Reproduced from California State Library.

After the April *tour de force,* however, the battering ram remained eerily absent from police raids around the city. The LAPD disputed rumors that it had buckled under legal pressures stemming from the Pacoima blunder. Although lawsuits indeed remained to be settled, the battering ram was, as the captain of the department's Narcotics Task Force said, "simply the victim of its own success." The vehicle was a display of military-level power, designed to literally raze the lives of rock dealers who had, until the introduction of the ram, managed to successfully adapt their operations to elude arrest. Within one year of its dramatic debut, Chief Gates's

LAPD boasted that it had generated widespread "fear of the ram" so effectively that "police don't *need* to use the ram. It's gotten the message across."[94]

In late 1985, the LAPD announced it had retired its modified V-100, the first military armored vehicle to be used by an American police force for routine crime enforcement. In its three-month campaign against LA's rock houses, the battering ram had elicited harsh criticism. As with the deadly force used against Eula Love in 1979, Angelenos leery of discriminatory law enforcement viewed it as setting a dangerous precedent for the militarized policing of their communities. But the ram also drew widespread support within these same neighborhoods, especially among those concerned about an escalating gang crisis. Growing support for Chief Gates and the LAPD in the early 1980s, however surprising, ruptured what had historically been a broad consensus among black Angelenos with regard to police brutality. It may have been a flashpoint for some civil rights organizations like CAPA and the ACLU, but the LAPD's battering ram was roundly embraced by citizens inside South Los Angeles who saw in it hope to save their city from "urban terrorism."[95]

■   ■   ■

When Toddy Tee recorded his "Batterram" rap, he said he had one key objective. He wanted to make music "about what was going on" in Los Angeles from his perspective as a Compton teen, and to deliver those stories via "the hardest street tape" LA had ever heard. His goal was to connect with all his peers looking on, like him, as the war on drugs rolled across their television screens and into their communities. The Los

Angeles Police Department's battering ram was the ideal medium for achieving that end, embodying as it did both the ravages of rock cocaine and the oppression of militarized policing in South Los Angeles. Add to that, too, the mystery of where it and the SWAT unit would strike next—a constant topic of rumors, anxiety, and intrigue among young people not much older than the three children who had watched it smash into the Pacoima home. In the spring of 1985, Toddy Tee's "Batterram" street tape, which opened with a sample of a rumbling engine and a hushed warning—*"It's coming!"*—captivated local listeners with allusions both awful and familiar.[96]

Making "the hardest street tape" was about tapping into raw controversy linked to drug violence and police brutality, but it was also about gaining approval within an emerging regional rap scene. Toddy Tee craved local fame, something that had mostly eluded him in his role as the lesser-known half of a Compton DJ duo. He and his partner, Frank "Mixmaster Spade" Williams, a mix DJ who cut his teeth in New York's hip-hop circles in the early 1980s, played music for South Los Angeles house parties. As a small, mobile DJ outfit, Spade and Toddy Tee were part of a youth-based "mobile dance scene" or "street scene." This predominantly black subculture was driven by entrepreneurial mix DJs who depended upon access to rentable venues and their own (or their parents') record collections. It rested on the patronage of young local partygoers and support from KDAY radio. And it also depended, for better or worse, upon young financiers, promoters, and talented artists linked to local gangs and drug-trafficking enterprises.

This social network was emerging alongside the very "gangster" entities that both police and community leaders viewed as contemptible. Within the fellowship of the scene, however, there was no shame in welcoming those, like Spade, who lent time, money, and talent to the game. Indeed, the music, in its production and distribution, often leveraged those illicit relationships. Mixmaster Spade and Toddy Tee were regular performers in the dance party circuit, but it was Spade's side hustle that drew the most attention. In part to promote his mobile DJ business, Spade recorded "practice" mixes at home, featuring songs popular with neighborhood party crowds dubbed and blended together. He gave these "street tapes" out free to friends, who in turn helped generate the buzz that drew customers willing to pay cash for them on the street. In Los Angeles in the early 1980s, Mixmaster Spade later recalled, "everybody was on the corner making them dollars." He would set out with shoeboxes full of cassettes and soon they would be gone, all sold to people who knew him from the local dance scene, many of them gang members and dope dealers operating on the same turf. "So I was with them," he said of Compton's outlaw salesmen, "making them dollars too." His homemade tapes, which could sell for as much as $20 per unit, provided Mixmaster Spade with cash to supplement the income he and Toddy Tee made entertaining party audiences.[97] More importantly, street tape sales earned him name recognition, transforming him into a celebrity among his peers. "Everybody had Spade tapes in Compton, just everybody," Toddy Tee remembered.[98]

Piggybacking on Spade's following, Toddy Tee put his rhyme talent to work, crafting a song mix of his own with locally inspired content that might appeal to the same customers. Choosing as his instrumental tracks three recognizable hip-hop hits, he delivered his own rhymes in a cadence and tone that mimicked the song's original vocals—essentially the same template used by pop parodists like "Weird Al" Yankovic and KDAY's own funnyman Russ Parr. Toddy Tee transformed UTFO's hit "Roxanne, Roxanne," a favorite in the Los Angeles freestyle scene, into a lyrical drama about rock cocaine dealers called "Rockman, Rockman."[99] Over Whodini's 1984 single "Freaks Come Out at Night," he recorded "The Clucks Come Out at Night," another comical, expletive-laced tale told from the perspective of a womanizing dope dealer. To the tune of a lesser-known East Coast release, "Rappin' Duke"—a satirical anthem about a hip-hop cowboy—he delivered "Batterram."[100]

By the time KDAY's music director, Greg Mack, got hold of a "Batterram" tape in the summer of 1985, Toddy Tee had already achieved the local celebrity he coveted. The cassettes he hawked from the trunk of his car had earned for him what his partner Spade had: brand loyalty. That spring, Mack remembers, he fielded a flood of requests from young people on air and at KDAY-sponsored dances: "The kids at every school that KDAY did events at were all asking me, 'How come y'all don't play that Toddy Tee?'" From those teen audiences he learned that "every kid in LA already had a tape of 'Batterram,'"—and that he, a programmer revered for breaking new music, was behind the curve. Determined to seize on a trend catching the interest of the very listeners he targeted at KDAY, he tracked down the Compton rapper and asked for a version of "Batterram" clean enough for radio play. Toddy Tee provided him with a copy free of expletives, and Mack put the track into heavy rotation. As the fans promised, it was an instant hit for the station.[101]

Through the summer of 1985, as some local black community members and leaders formed a complicated partnership with the LAPD in its fight against gangs, the region's youth embraced one Compton rapper's defiant narrative about the police department's most notorious weapon. Young listeners flooded KDAY's call lines with requests, elevating Toddy Tee's rap song to a street anthem. It "exploded on the airwaves," remembered Robin D. G. Kelley, a UCLA historian who "rocked to the rhythm" of KDAY.[102] As Compton native and rapper Aaron "MC Eiht" Tyler noted, Toddy Tee enjoyed a special status in South LA's ganglands, as a "neighborhood favorite" among those most affected by street gang culture and the police surveillance it drew.[103] Using the same kind of portable recording technology and cheap blank cassette tapes Spade and Toddy Tee relied on to make their music, fans disseminated dubbed copies of "Batterram" and taped recordings of KDAY radio shows throughout Los Angeles County. Among the many kids hearing it booming out of cars rolling through their neighborhoods was a Long Beach thirteen-year-old named Calvin Broadus, Jr.—later to become famous as Snoop Dogg. As a product of another gang stronghold and a frequent target of police harassment, Snoop Dogg was inspired to hear a Compton kid deliver "an LAPD takedown."[104] For those who understood that in Los Angeles one's associations with gangs and dope dealers were not always the result of bad choices but sometimes just a by-product of where one resided or attended school, Toddy Tee's music was a rare reflection of their lived reality. For those who appreciated that anti-gang crusaders targeted all South LA black youths, regardless of whether one was "active" in a gang or simply grew up around one, the "Batterram" tape provided an early soundtrack for resistance.

Toddy Tee Howard and the young fans that made his "Batterram" song a summer hit recognized a crisis in Los Angeles, in which the police, not black kids, wreaked real havoc. The battering ram was only the most obvious demonstration of that. Using it as a metaphor for extraordinary police power, Toddy Tee's rapped lines articulated how ominous the threat was for black poor and working-class neighborhoods throughout the county: *"The Chief of Police says he just might / Flatten out every house he sees on sight."* His lyrics denounced not only Chief Daryl Gates for deploying the battering ram but also the most powerful black political leader in LA, Mayor Tom Bradley, who *"musta been crazy or half-way wack / To legalize somethin' that works like that."* In verse, he urged the archetypal dope dealer "Mister Rockman" to give up his trade lest he be forced to reckon with the six-ton hellhound on his trail, and, as the song's innocent bystander who becomes a victim of the battering ram himself, Toddy Tee delivered a cautionary tale for all those in the path of the beast because of their race alone. In rhyme, he contended, *"We all look the same"* to the LAPD, but *"I'm not the one slingin' 'caine / I work nine to five and ain't a damn thing changed."* When, in the summer of 1985, the LAPD announced that the blue armored vehicle would be decommissioned after getting "the message across," Toddy Tee's street anthem continued to resonate, warning of the eventual return of the sleeping giant: *"And if you didn't see the Batterram cross your line / Honey boon, I'm telling you—give it time."*[105]

Through the 1970s and the early 1980s, a growing body of evidence—including police choke-hold deaths, high-profile police shootings, the LAPD's infiltration of a citizen-led police reform movement, the introduction of tools of war for the purposes of civilian policing, and the success of an expensive public relations campaign designed to justify misconduct— added up to a picture of a Los Angeles Police Department with vast, impenetrable power. By the time Daryl Gates de-

buted the battering ram in 1985, his LAPD was the most notorious law enforcement agency in the nation. As Robert Lee
of South LA's Brim Blood Army put it, the police were "the
biggest gang"—the Crips and Bloods networks were no match
for their rivals in blue.[106] In the early 1980s, even communities that had long organized against over-policing were beginning to forge a precarious new partnership with law enforcement to combat the growth of gangs and gang violence close
to home. Black Angelenos remained vigilant in calling out police abuses, with CAPA as the most prominent example of enduring activism. The voices of traditional leaders, however,
especially in the Los Angeles black press, demanded greater
protection against the gangs who, they argued, terrorized
their neighborhoods and threatened the future of black LA.

This meant that black youths in LA were doubly marginal-
ized. Toddy Tee's "Batterram" spoke to the young Angelenos—
especially black teens—who were most vulnerable to police
violence. Whether they were directly involved with a gang,
peripherally affiliated, or altogether detached from gang activity, they were subject to it. Forsaken by many traditional
activists, yet buoyed by rap music and elaborate social networks tied to dance parties, young people developed their
own methods for addressing LA's urban crises. "Batterram"
and the enthusiasm for it anticipated the growth of a regional
music aesthetic dependent on two things: recognition of LA's
unique gang culture and direct engagement with police
power. In other words, "Batterram" foretold the future of Los
Angeles gangsta rap.

# CHAPTER **2** · Hardcore LA

▪ **"Please!"** On August 17, 1986, Whodini's frontman Jalil Hutchins stood on the Long Beach Arena stage, urging concertgoers to settle down. The thousands of music fans in front of him were gathered for a sold-out hip-hop showcase, waiting to see the act at the top of the bill, Run-DMC. As the reigning kings of rap made their way to the venue, and as the revelry devolved into commotion, Whodini strained to finish its set. Throughout the group's performance, arena security guards worked to contain scattered fistfights and shoving matches, but when one of these spilled onto the stage, the show stopped. Stagehands switched on the bright house lights and Whodini's DJ, Grandmaster Dee, quieted the music, stalling the show to let Hutchins make his appeal: "This is a place to party. This is a place to hear music."[1]

The abrupt break from the thunderous bass thumps of Whodini's "I'm a Ho" only focused more of the crowd's attention on the violence erupting around them. Extra light worsened things, emboldening some to rush their targets while others scrambled toward the exits.[2] Outside, as security worked to clear the hall, the pandemonium spilled into the parking lot. Long Beach police squad cars swarmed in, an LAPD helicopter hovered above with its searchlight trained on the action, and officers in tactical gear made arrests. *Billboard Magazine* later reported that "an estimated 300–500 gang members" had shown up for the "Long Beach fracas" that left dozens arrested and forty-two people injured (three critically). It brought the concert, one of the last on Run-DMC's *Raising Hell* tour, to an abrupt end before the trio even had the chance to take the stage.[3]

All efforts to prevent the melee from unfolding that night had failed. Arena officials, anticipating at least some gang presence, had hired dozens of extra staff, including off-duty Long Beach police, who led ticketholders through metal detectors and performed pat-downs, confiscating an assortment of guns, blades, and pipes—an arsenal which, in the possession of arena security, might have briefly reassured concert organizers but ultimately portended trouble. Once the throng outside had been efficiently funneled through entryways and checkpoints, guards and ushers left their posts in the lobby and moved inside to chaperone the sellout crowd. In the seating areas, the signs of mayhem came early.[4]

Rumors that hundreds of Los Angeles gang members were on site began swirling before the music started. As retired detectives working security spread word that some in the crowd had "disguised their 'colors' under jogging suits," crewmembers backstage placed calls to the Long Beach police requesting extra protection for the talent. But, by then, fights were already breaking out among concertgoers, some dressed in red and others in blue, and spilling over to bystanders and uniformed security guards.[5] In spite of the venue's security procedures at the ticket gates, some had managed to smuggle guns and knives to their seats. Others broke bottles, smashed metal folding chairs, or stripped fire extinguishers from walls to wield as weapons. The show began, but the scattered brawls made for a frustrating entertainment experience that became increasingly hazardous as the night progressed. Young rap fan Chris Baker said the scene made him "scared for my life."[6] By 10 PM, warm-up band Timex Social Club had finished its set, and Whodini was trying to get through its own songs. Police had already gathered outside, outfitted in riot gear.[7]

Chino, an LA Blood who recognized rival bangers in the crowd immediately upon arrival, later told a reporter, "I knew there was going to be trouble, there had to be." A teenager calling himself Mafia Dick explained that any concert that attracted youths from all over LA's ganglands was bound to be a tinderbox: "We don't get along outside, so we're not going to get along inside, and when you put all these groups together, you're lookin' for trouble." One detective who was present that night told *Rolling Stone* the violence was inevitable: "There are long-held grudges between these gangs, and when they converge in one place, the paybacks will come."[8]

In a word, it was "crazy," according to Run-DMC's Jason "DJ Jam Master Jay" Mizell. As he and his fellow band members arrived at the venue, they witnessed what was happening inside, then watched from backstage as event organizers and security proved wholly incapable of preventing a mass exodus. "It was like a stampede," Run-DMC front man Joseph "Reverend Run" Simmons recalled, "chairs coming up in the air, panicked kids in the crowd." He, like other witnesses that night, blamed gangs. "They just took over," he said, citing hundreds of predatory kids roving through the building "beating and robbing." Describing what sounds like a scene from the apocalyptic 1979 thriller *The Warriors*, Jam Master Jay described a hoard of people "dressed the same, with bandannas on their heads" who roamed the floor "walking as one, chanting, screaming the names of their gangs." As events unfolded outside, Run-DMC huddled backstage in a dressing room, joined by a few VIPs and stagehands. There, the young men broke apart a clothing rack to use the pieces as weapons while a staff member's walkie-talkie broadcast ominous updates from somewhere out on the arena floor: "We're losing it! We're losing it!"[9]

Sponsored by an AM radio station in LA, KDAY, and promoted by the county's most prominent mobile DJ crews, the Long Beach Arena concert in August 1986 promised to be two things. First, it was touted as Run-DMC's climactic show on the West Coast leg of *Raising Hell*, the group's first big tour. The sixty-four-date, multicity tour represented a milestone for the trio from Hollis, Queens, and the group's final sellout show on the other coast, in Southern California, was to help certify its move from local success to national fame.

Second, the Long Beach event had the potential to be a game-changer for hip-hop. Through the mid-1980s, rap music was synonymous with New York artists, New York fans, and New York venues. The East had incubated hip-hop for nearly a decade and guarded its creation closely. Bill Adler, publicist for Russell Simmons's label, Def Jam, later recalled the era: "Not only did New York dominate rap, but there was almost nobody else involved." Bronx rapper Chris "Kid" Reid put it even more strongly: "Any other place didn't even exist."[10] But music industry insiders predicted that the regional insularity of early New York hip-hop would spell its early demise. Run-DMC defied that expectation. The *Raising Hell* tour included a string of California gigs, culminating with the Long

Beach showcase; if it succeeded, that would do a lot to prove hip-hop's appeal to a broad consumer market. A sold-out Long Beach Arena rap concert would constitute an answer to the critics trying to dismiss this music movement as ephemeral, and pave the way to its future.[11] Run-DMC took their act to California hoping on some level to usher in a new era of hip-hop, break the music free from its East Coast shell, and let it evolve as both an art form and a pop phenomenon. The 1986 Long Beach Arena concert helped all of that happen, but not in the way anyone anticipated.

The *Los Angeles Times* called it the "rap riot," showing a headline writer's preference for short words, but also coining a label that neatly yoked hip-hop culture to unrest. Both Southern California and Run-DMC were immediately pulled into ongoing national debates about the connections between youth music and social disorder. The lurid news of a rap riot played into an established narrative about riotous behavior being set off by rock concerts. The early 1980s had seen plenty of reporting by entertainment trade publications, popular music magazines, and newspaper "lifestyle" sections about "hardcore" music subcultures and the antisocial behavior they encouraged—just as rhythm and blues music in the 1950s and rock 'n' roll in the 1960s had caused their own cultural panics. In that context, the Run-DMC concert looked to some like more evidence of the causal links between music and society's ills. Music journalist Frank Owen later called it "perhaps the worst rock 'n' roll riot in history," but at the time it also looked like part of a pattern.[12]

Southern California—particularly LA County and Orange County—was, in fact, the epicenter for the worst of the eighties "rock riots."[13] Early in the decade, violence had become the hallmark of punk rock performances throughout the region, not only in Long Beach but also in Newport Beach, Costa Mesa, Santa Ana, Huntington Beach, Fullerton, and Los Angeles. Police officials and city leaders railed against events featuring punk music because it was a youth trend that, as the Santa Ana police chief argued, was "conducive to violence." News of bloody clashes, drug use, and other "hardcore punk" behavior inside rock music clubs and concert halls fueled the public's fears. In 1983, *Billboard* quipped, "Just when you thought it was safe to go to a punk rock show in Los Angeles . . . along comes another 'punk riot' to fan the flames of controversy." The *Los Angeles Times* reported that "a recent concert featuring skin-slashing, furniture-smashing and window-breaking was not unusual for punk rock."[14]

No wonder punk rock shows in Los Angeles, featuring provocatively named groups such as Suicidal Tendencies, the Vandals, Social Distortion, Lost Cause, Verbal Abuse, Black Flag, and Agression, invited police attention (Fig. 2.1). City leaders, including those in Long Beach, worked closely with law enforcement to put punk-friendly venues "on notice," using existing fire safety codes, occupancy limits, and rules about loitering to tamp down the thriving scene. The tactics tended to work primarily by spooking insurance companies, which frequently denied punk venues and event promoters access to liability insurance—a critical buffer against the financial losses resulting from property damage or personal injury lawsuits. Rather than pass legislation barring punk rock concerts altogether, a move likely to be found unconstitutional, city leaders worked with existing laws in an attempt to, as one councilmember put it, "accomplish what we want."[15]

Public campaigns to police radical youth music scenes in the 1980s were not exclusive to Southern California, and nor was punk music the sole target. In fact, by the middle of the

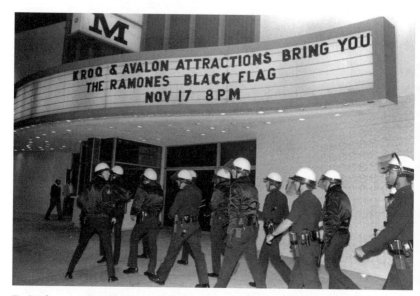

Fig 2.1 A group of LAPD officers in riot helmets patrol outside the Palladium in Hollywood, the site of a punk rock showcase featuring Southern California's own Black Flag, November 1986. Photograph by Gary Leonard, Los Angeles Photographers Collection / Los Angeles Public Library.

decade, heavy metal had become the bigger bogeyman for the anti-obscenity activists across the country reigniting the culture wars of decades past. On the national stage, in 1985, then-Senator Al Gore's wife, Tipper Gore, cofounded the Parents Music Resource Center with three other DC-based women. The group sought commitments from US record companies to place warning labels on albums with violent, sexually explicit, or otherwise morally abhorrent content. This and other forms of pressure in what has been called a time of "Satanic panic" were mainly targeted at heavy metal artists, including Judas Priest and Black Sabbath's former front man Ozzy Osbourne. But in Southern California, where punk bands flourished, moral crusaders targeted metal and punk with equal fervor. City leaders, local parent groups, school administrators, police, and youth counselors deemed heavy metal and punk rock to be essentially the same, despite the musical and philosophical differences their fans saw in them. In the eyes of concerned citizens, both punk and metal artists modeled dangerous and addictive behavior for their young, middle-class, white fans. Kids in the suburbs of LA and Orange Counties abused drugs and alcohol, disrespected authority, and engaged in violent, self-destructive acts, and musicians were to blame. At "Spikes and Studs," a one-day conference held at an Anaheim hotel in February of 1985, 130 people gathered to learn about "heavy metal and punk and their influence on children." Family counselors from the Back in Control Training Center warned about the associations between this "extreme" music and high levels of anger, violence, satanism, and "damage to both property and animals."[16]

Long before the rap riot in Long Beach, "punkers and metalers" were those most associated with event violence in the region, so much so that Southern California venue managers, promoters, police, and performers braced for it. In June of 1986, just two months prior to the Run-DMC show, police had responded to another flood of emergency calls about a sold-out event at the Long Beach Arena—this time, a heavy-metal concert featuring Ozzy Osbourne and Metallica. There, the Long Beach police made dozens of arrests, mostly for drug possession and assault, after four concertgoers jumped or fell from a balcony into the crowd below, one of them to his death. In an interview following the incident, the convention center's general manager said it was "not unusual" for an arena event of such size to devolve into chaos.[17]

Organizers of Run-DMC's *Raising Hell* tour may have been too nonchalant about problems at shows prior to the one in Long Beach, along with the police in various locales who

monitored the summer's events. In Pittsburgh, Cincinnati, Detroit, and Atlanta, law enforcement agencies reported no more
than "some bizarre conduct" following Run-DMC's appearances. In New York, police did make two dozen arrests outside
Madison Square Garden. But the group's tour promoter, Jeff
Sharp, explained the trouble as inconsequential: "When you
have a sold-out show at Madison Square Garden and only 24
arrests, that's not a problem. That's reality." NYPD officials
agreed, noting that at such events police always "anticipated" a
little misbehavior.[18] In Atlanta, a gunman fired into the crowd
during a July show at the Omni Coliseum, wounding an eighteen-year-old fan. But Atlanta police downplayed the shooting
as a fluke, underscoring that no one had been seriously injured
and that the lone suspect had been charged.[19] Violence in the
streets of Pittsburgh after the Civic Arena show prompted the
city's public safety director to issue, by then, a familiar warning
about "provocative and pornographic" songs poisoning the
culture. In spite of the occasional trouble inside and outside its
concerts, Run-DMC's sixty-four-date tour rumbled along, with
the group and its handlers largely unperturbed. "Of course, the
tour had been prepared for some trouble," as Def Jam publicist
Bill Adler would later recall. "Most of rap music's millions of
fans are teenagers, and there's always the possibility of unruli-
ness when thousands of teenagers get together." Russell Simmons, the group's manager, summed up the occasional "un-
ruliness" this way: "It was no problem."[20]

The Run-DMC show in Long Beach in the summer of
1986 reminded city officials and anti-obscenity crusaders
that popular culture could push bad people to do bad things.
Reacting to the concert violence in Long Beach, Tipper Gore
chalked it up to "angry, disillusioned, unloved kids united behind heavy-metal or rap music, and the music says it's OK to

beat people up."[21] Or, as observers on the other side of the debate noted, concert violence in 1986, predictably, drummed
up hysteria around the arts, which served to distract the public from other pressing social and economic crises. According
to *Melody Maker*, 1986 marked "the year that Run-DMC
joined AIDS, crack, and Colonel Gaddafi as yet another me-
dia-generated threat, a bogus disturbance designed to outrage all right-minded people and enhance the legitimacy and
cohesion of a rapidly crumbling social structure."[22]

Still, rap music by 1986 had become far more than simply
a proxy for other, whiter youth cultures that provoked public
anxiety and spurred cultural conservatives to take action. In
the aftermath of the "Long Beach melee," as *Billboard* called
it, debates about youth music trends began to center on the
topic of race. As the story of the disastrous Run-DMC concert riveted the popular press and intersected with news of
LA's ungovernable juvenile gang problem, the narrative
shifted from tabloid-style commentary about the "bizarre
conduct" of "headbangers" and "knuckleheads" and, instead,
turned to breathless reporting on LA's "ghetto toughs." In the
music press, in particular, the consensus was that the 1986
Long Beach show exemplified the "rap violence" that appeared to be a product of hip-hop's "gang war," and, in this
context, it was fair to cast LA's rap fans as "gangsters." Dog-
whistle terms like these reframed what was, for the 1980s,
otherwise run-of-the-mill concert violence that struck indis-
criminately in terms of genre and race. And they suggested
that the Long Beach "rap riot" would have more ominous implications for hip-hop, for Run-DMC, and for Los Angeles.[23]

■　■　■

In 1983, three years before the Long Beach Arena rap riot drew attention to "rap violence" in the Golden State, African-American filmmaker Topper Carew went west to find out whether hip-hop culture had gained much traction in Los Angeles, the entertainment capital of the world. The young, Washington, DC-based auteur understood the insularity of New York hip-hop, which was still in its infancy, and was thus curious when he heard rumors that the music had taken root in California. Los Angeles offered Carew the opportunity to test his theory that hip-hop was a more impactful cultural force than music critics in the early 1980s were willing to concede.

The product of Carew's research was a documentary film entitled *Breakin' 'n' Enterin'* (a reference to breakdancing, the dance style most commonly associated with hip-hop at the time). From the opening scenes, which included images of cars slogging along ribbons of freeway, palm trees towering above manicured lawns, and the weightlifters and roller-skaters of Venice Beach, the film marked LA—and its youth culture—as wholly distinct from New York. It helped that Carew recruited local hip-hop artist Tracy "Ice-T" Marrow to guide his cameras around town. Ice-T, a regular performer at a colorful downtown hip-hop nightclub called The Radio, gave the filmmaker intimate access to what the rapper described, in rhyme, as a singular regional "*movement*" marked by "*graffiti turning ghettos into art*" and "*kids who dance on the street and in the park.*"[24]

Carew's effort to showcase a distinctive rap culture in Hollywoodland nevertheless revealed a youth music scene subject to East Coast influences. From the multiracial break-dance crews to the colorful graffiti murals decorating the nightspots Topper Carew chose as backdrops, *Breakin' 'n'*

*Enterin'* presented New York hip-hop trends grafted onto Southern California landscapes. California came through, sometimes to the point of cliché. For instance, LA rappers and dancers honed their skills not on concrete basketball courts or in schoolyards but instead inside palatial ballet studios. In front of ranch-style houses, on long driveways and freshly cut lawns, kids exhibited "top-rocks," "freezes," and other dance moves learned, notably, from young Bronx migrants. As New York-based performer Suga Pop explained in the film, he and other breakdancers came to LA in the early 1980s for work opportunities, which, it turned out, included offering step-by-step dance tutorials to locals. Even Carew's well-connected local tour guide had East Coast roots; Ice-T had been born and raised in New Jersey, and his creative sidekick Charles "Afrika Islam" Glenn was a recent Bronx transplant.[25]

The Radio, the downtown nightclub featured in the film, was itself a kind of New York import. A French immigrant named Alex Jordanov ran the place, filling the venue's event calendar by tapping his Manhattan connections. Jordanov turned The Radio into one of the few after-hours establishments in Los Angeles, adopting a dusk-to-dawn schedule reminiscent of New York City nightlife norms. It was also one of the first LA dance clubs to provide New York's newest recording artists with West Coast gigs. Plus, Jordanov commissioned colorful faux graffiti murals for the stage. In a city in which street graffiti was mostly single-line, monochrome "tags" and Old English lettering written to designate gang territory, The Radio's vibrant, bubble-letter backdrops were an unusual sight, calling to mind MTA subway cars rather than the LA River's concrete tunnels.[26] Chris "The Glove" Taylor, a local DJ who sometimes performed at The Radio, recalled the scene as "a piece of the East Coast hip-hop scene right in the middle of LA," with its "spray-can art," "dance battles," and guest hip-hop performers from New York, including DJ Derek "Grandmixer D.ST" Showard, and the Queens trio Run-DMC.[27]

Other local entrepreneurs tacked in the same direction Jordanov did. In Hollywood, for instance, New Yorker Matt Robinson booked parties at the Rhythm Lounge, emulating the hip-hop showcases he had frequented at the Roxy in Manhattan.[28] At Club Lingerie, another popular Hollywood nightspot, punk rock devotee Brendan Mullen scouted bands and hip-hop talent for his line-ups, seeking to do for LA's music culture what new-wave princess Blondie, Brooklyn artist Fred "Fab 5 Freddy" Brathwaite, and hip-hop trailblazer Afrika Bambaataa had done for New York's Midtown. One of Mullen's most ambitious projects was a 1983 show at Club Lingerie billed as the "South Bronx Rap Party," starring Bambaataa and the Rock Steady Crew, and featuring local punk band Black Flag and the Red Hot Chili Peppers, a little-known group at the time.[29]

Through the mid-1980s, few paid much attention to Los Angeles rap. This was in part because reductive interpretations like Carew's documentary portrayed LA's post-disco youth music culture, at best, as tribute to New York City's hip-hop arts scene, and at worst, as an absurd imitation of that scene. As *Los Angeles Times* music journalist Al Martinez put it colorfully at the time, New York hip-hop "spread to LA and was eventually adopted by apple-cheeked Beverly Hills teens who rapped in the air-conditioned comfort of their Porsche Targas."[30] *Breakin' 'n' Enterin'* offered evidence that Southern California diluted hip-hop, turning a street-based urban music style created by poor black and brown kids into something palatable for a whiter, more privileged, California crowd. In

the film's concluding scenes, Carew's cameras captured a pair
of platinum blonds in pastel party dresses who appeared at
ease surrounded by graffiti murals and minorities. "It's fun to
try out new clubs and stuff," they beamed. Two other white
teenagers from the well-to-do suburbs of Pasadena and Arca-
dia said they took frequent trips to The Radio "because we
like the music here," and "it's a different crowd," sounding quite
like the white, thrill-seeking flappers who traversed through
black Harlem in the 1920s.[31]

Topper Carew's earnest attempt to capture the essence of
early 1980s Los Angeles hip-hop cast doubt on the notion
that Southern California youth were architects of their own
culture. For all of its focus on local color and its engagement
with West Coast dancers and partygoers, the film ultimately
suggested that all the artists and fans were mere disciples
of the New York scene. The film, one of the first to document
hip-hop culture, neglected important regional idiosyncrasies
and offered only a rough sketch of music-making within the
scene. As Ice-T later said of his own starring role, "I was the
only rapper that they could find."[32]

Plus, by adhering to the utopian characterization of hip-
hop culture promoted by the genre's forefather, Afrika Bambaataa—that the culture was a vehicle for racial harmony, to
"grab that black and white audience and bridge the gap"—
Carew fixated on multicultural crews and white, wide-eyed
clubgoers, somehow missing that there were predominantly
black networks of locals, far removed from the Hollywood
scene, building, financing, and consuming LA rap in its infancy.[33] But his characterization stuck; the film's portrait of
multicultural bliss in LA's street dance scene inspired TriStar
Pictures in Culver City to market a pair of B movies, romantic
dramas entitled *Breakin'* and *Breakin' 2: Electric Boogaloo*,

centering on a friendship between a white ballet dancer and
two pop-lockers from the 'hood.[34]

Casual observers were, like director Topper Carew, trans-
fixed by evident parallels between the hip-hop avant-garde in
New York and LA's "trendy crowds," between the Roxy and
The Radio, and between the two coasts' industry insiders and
entrepreneurs promoting a multiracial, "four elements" arts
movement tied to the aesthetics of punk. Mesmerized by the
East Coast cultures that buzzed in Los Angeles's Downtown
and Westside, many overlooked the lively youth dance scenes
that thrived outside those orbits. In the predominantly
African-American communities of South Los Angeles, including Compton and Long Beach, black youths were shaping a
musical landscape of their own, often by casting aside the
New York mold.[35] In the heart of LA's ganglands, far removed
from "aerosol can" murals and white "art school crowds," creative innovation flew under the radar as young people focused on building a regional dance-music scene they could
claim as their own.[36]

Through the early 1980s, the growth of hip-hop depended
upon a handful of independent labels based in New York, including Sugar Hill and Profile Records. These enterprises
discovered talent and showcased their signed artists inside a
thriving, industry-driven New York nightclub circuit. Here,
DJs played supporting roles, spinning records to serve the
needs of labels and the acts they represented. Most early New
York DJs, including DJ-cum-rapper Bambaataa, were supporting actors for talent scouts, the true stars of the city's
nightclub circuit.

In Los Angeles, the scene operated quite differently. With
the exception of hot spots like The Radio and Club Lingerie,
which tended to function as West Coast appendages of the

Manhattan scene, Los Angeles nightclubs in the early 1980s were a virtual wasteland for contemporary urban music and for the record companies seeking to expose crowds to it. In 1983, Steve Buckley, a promoter for Capitol Records' black music division, noted a dearth of venues for funk, electro, and rap, which struck him as counterintuitive considering LA's size and population density. "A much more active club scene in this community," Buckley told the *Los Angeles Times*, "would be important." African-American musician and Los Angeles native Leon Chancler said that, for black music, LA offered barely any of the kinds of live entertainment venues set up for discovering talent. While industry-intertwined music events were integral to New York's nightlife, Chancler lamented, "It's not part of the black culture here."[37]

Without the kinds of high-profile nightclub gigs and exposure opportunities afforded to their New York counterparts, Los Angeles DJs crafted their own scene, a do-it-yourself alternative to industry gigs. Rather than rely on the patronage of record labels or booking agents at venues, artists and entrepreneurs rented their own spaces, including garages, school gyms, hotel ballrooms, and conference centers, for "mobile" dance parties all over Los Angeles County. Black Angeleno youths with business savvy and carefully curated vinyl record collections organized themselves into "mobile DJ" crews and "mobile sound systems." Crews pooled their resources to book event spaces, hire security, recruit talent, purchase new records, and promote dances. Mobile DJs served as hosts and performed as top-billed acts with the kind of name recognition that could draw thousands of cover-paying partygoers. Developing their keen insight into the discriminating tastes of their LA peers, mobile DJs earned loyal fans. Indeed, they became some of the most influential tastemakers in Southern California, and

Fig 2.2 A 1982 promotional photo for Uncle Jamm's Army mobile DJ sound system shows the group's original members. Standing, left to right: Razor Sharp, UJA founder Rodger "Mr. Prinze" Clayton, Lester Malone, Troy, Muffla, Mr. No Good, and Egyptian Lover. Seated in front: Tomcat, Gid Martin, and Bobcat. Photograph courtesy of Egyptian Lover.

captains of a predominantly black-run, grassroots entertainment industry. These were thriving, vertically integrated businesses created by young African-American virtuosos who dominated the dance party circuit in Los Angeles County through the early 1980s.[38]

Chief among these Los Angeles institutions was Uncle Jamm's Army (UJA), the preeminent mobile DJ sound system of the era.[39] Rodger Clayton, UJA's founder, cut his teeth in the mid-1970s, spinning records for parties in his father's garage and collecting fifty cents from each guest, an early business venture that netted the teenager "good-ass lunch money." The neighborhood performances eventually earned

Clayton better paying gigs in Compton, Crenshaw, and Torrance, including a coveted booking with LSD, a local party
promoting group that managed to draw thousands of teens
to many of its events. When LSD refused to pay him for his
work, however, Clayton assembled his own full-service entertainment crew of DJs, dancers, security guards, and able-
bodied helpers (Fig. 2.2). Clayton also deployed friends and
fans as street promoters, who roamed the southern half of
LA County plastering posters and distributing fliers in their
own neighborhood haunts. With this network, plus a dozen
hulking Cerwin Vega speakers, twelve power amplifiers, four
turntables, fog machines, and professional lighting, Clayton
not only aimed to compete with LSD but hoped to reign su-
preme.[40]

By 1982, Uncle Jamm's Army was unrivaled. Clayton's
events, regularly filled to capacity, graduated from house parties in Compton and Torrance to large rented spaces throughout the county, including the Biltmore Hotel in downtown
Los Angeles, the Veteran's Auditorium in Culver City, and a
popular Mid-City skating rink called World on Wheels. At
much larger venues, like the Los Angeles Memorial Coliseum
and the Long Beach Convention Center, UJA's elaborate
shows drew thousands. Sometimes Clayton invited funk and
R&B heavy-hitters like Cameo, Cheryl Lynn, Lakeside, and
Midnight Star to take the stage, but usually it was only UJA's
elite DJs who filled the bill.[41] These upside-down event ros-
ters, which featured major label artists as openers and local
DJs as headliners, caught the attention of Greg Mack, the
newly hired music programmer at KDAY. He later recalled
being stunned by how Clayton's crew "could fill the LA Sports
Arena with 8,000 people for a 'dance'. . . . just DJs."[42] It was
evidence of a kind of DJ empire that Mack had never before

seen. As DJ Lester Malone boasted, "We had the whole market. There was nobody in LA but us."[43]

That did not remain true for long. Just as Clayton had built his enterprise in response to LSD, the Army's remarkable success galvanized other aspiring DJs and promoters, including original UJA members, to develop their own mobile sound systems. As Clayton demonstrated, mobile parties generated local fame, respect among peers, and a steady income for their organizers and talents. These were especially valuable for young black men contending with declining employment opportunities and the fast-growing influence of street gangs, fueled by cocaine trafficking in the region. UJA's achievements were notable in the context of the early Reagan Era—when, as Long Beach native Calvin "Snoop Dogg" Broadus remembered, "things started changing in the 'hood' and none of us could exactly put our finger on the why and whatfor of it all."[44] Clayton resisted the allure of the illicit, and with Uncle Jamm's Army he provided a blueprint for a legitimate—and lucrative—trade. He showed peers how to make ends meet by building a sound system, assembling talent, designing promotional materials, and stuffing milk crates with the funk and electro records local kids loved, by bands like Funkadelic, One Way, Morris Day and the Time, Prince, Zapp, Maze, Art of Noise, Kraftwerk, and others.

After UJA opened up the Los Angeles dance culture, other intrepid youths sought to make their marks on the scene. Greg "G-Bone" Everett, for instance, founded the Music Masters, a small mobile crew that aimed to provide the UJA experience but at a lower ticket price. To cover steep overhead costs, Everett teamed up with another group of DJs, Knights of the Turntables, to form Ultrawave Productions. They were unable to wrest control of LA's black teen market away from

UJA, but they did manage to earn accolades for community service. Thousands of partygoers attended Ultrawave dances at the Veterans Auditorium, where Everett's team collected canned goods to be distributed to South Los Angeles residents in need. "We were being like the Black Panthers," Everett said.[45]

In Compton, Frank "Mixmaster Spade" Williams and "Toddy Tee" Howard partnered to corner the house party market, promoting their services by distributing street tapes with a sampling of the blended song mixes they played for backyard barbecues and garage gatherings. The dubbed cassettes, which ultimately netted them more cash than did their modest mobile events, helped the two earn the local stardom they sought. Most significantly, the mixes gave Toddy Tee a foundation for promoting his "Batterram" tape in the summer of 1985, with its raps about rock cocaine, loose women, dope hustlers, and the Los Angeles police. These homemade tracks became the most requested songs at the kinds of dance parties he and Spade once worked to promote.[46]

Several other DJs emerged from the "teen scene" that Uncle Jamm's Army monopolized through the early 1980s. Among these was Alonzo "Grand Master Lonzo" Williams, one of UJA's first DJs, who split from Rodger Clayton in 1983. Lonzo made his move at the height of the mobile party craze, when most black youths shunned private discos and nightclubs. As Williams told the *Los Angeles Times*, "There were no clubs in the city that provided entertainment that catered to them."[47] Even The Radio, Alex Jordanov's all-ages spot depicted in *Breakin' 'n' Enterin'*, focused on the who's who of the New York-based music industry. DJ Afrika Islam described the typical crowd he saw at The Radio as "99 percent white and international," mostly affluent and "trendy" out-of-towners like Jordanov himself. The few black youths spotted at the club were performers, he noted. The Radio was not, in other words, a venue custom-made for LA's African-American youth.[48]

Lonzo, a staple of the local party circuit, understood how removed "hip" clubs like The Radio were from the flourishing South Los Angeles mobile dances. While Jordanov honored the Roxy model, Lonzo seized the opportunity to give mobile dance party patrons a more permanent home, and one located not on the periphery of South LA but deep within. Lonzo ran Eve After Dark, a small nightclub for sixteen- to twenty-one-year-olds on South Avalon Boulevard in Compton. There, he showcased his own DJ supergroup, the World Class Wreckin Cru, featuring Lonzo himself and three others handpicked from his Compton neighborhood: Marquette "Cli-N-Tel" Hawkins, Antoine "DJ Yella" Carraby, and Andre "Dr. Dre" Young. With Lonzo's clout among the UJA faithful, and thanks to the Wreckin Cru's dynamic shows, Eve After Dark often drew full-capacity crowds.[49]

Texas native Greg Mack might not have had the insider's perspective on the local mobile scene that Lonzo enjoyed, but he learned to respect, and later replicate, Clayton's business. In early 1983, when Mack began his stint as a music programmer for KDAY, the low-frequency radio station that served much of South Central Los Angeles, he recognized that his listeners were the very same local kids who filled the Uncle Jamm's Army mobile events. It was clear to Mack that Clayton's command over LA County's black teen party scene was a product of careful attention to the eclectic and ever-changing tastes of his crowds. As an *LA Weekly* piece would later put it, when Clayton was at the turntable, "the 'strength of street knowledge' was in the building."[50]

Mack's early career in Texas radio and limited experience as a party DJ predisposed him to recognize the powerful influence of South LA's DJ teams. He quickly realized that he would make better progress in his own mission to revitalize KDAY by understanding what was happening at the mobile dances around town.[51] Mack was impressed enough with Clayton's program that he sought to join forces with him. It was a relationship that Mack, who also made many advertising choices at KDAY, proposed as mutually beneficial. But the UJA founder ultimately rejected his offer of partnership. Mack remembers Clayton claiming, "We don't need radio," perhaps emboldened by the fact that hip-hop music label representatives, including executives at New York's Profile, Sugar Hill Records, and Def Jam Recordings, made a habit of rushing promotional copies of new records directly to him before reaching out to local radio disc jockeys like Mack.[52]

Rebuffed, Mack approached two other DJs his scouting had identified as the most promising in the county—namely, DJ Yella and Dr. Dre, the top-billed talents at Lonzo's Eve After Dark. In his role at KDAY, Mack could give Yella and Dre on-air spots to showcase their mixes and promote the nightclub's events. He also invited the two Compton DJs to moonlight as members of his own mobile sound system, the Mixmasters—the only DJ crew at the time harnessing the power of live radio. By 1984, over KDAY's airwaves, the Mixmasters broadcast some of the region's most popular dances, including those at LA's two largest skating rinks, World on Wheels and Skateland USA.[53]

The young Eric Wright was a frequent patron of Eve After Dark, and it gave him the idea to form his own mobile dance business. Later he would take the name "Eazy-E" and refashion himself as a hardcore rapper, but Wright's early foray into lawful, sustainable work was with his own mobile DJ dance business. Under the moniker High Powered Productions, he scouted backyards and garages around Compton and hired his friend Dr. Dre to DJ. Wright ultimately decided his financial future should not depend on promoting barbecues and house parties, but the experience gave the young businessman useful insights into black youth music culture in South LA and the trends that propelled it.[54]

Rodger Clayton, his collaborators, and his many competitors tailored their mobile DJ party businesses for their Los Angeles peers, and they did so with two significant and related results. First, events thrown by the "high priests" of the mobile scene drew together the party faithful from LA's most marginal communities. The *Los Angeles Times,* in a 1983 profile of Clayton and the UJA, noted that for local black teens "these rented-hall dances are the only game in town." Clayton's sister Adrienne recently recalled one UJA fan's devotion. "I met a gentleman a few years ago . . . he said, 'Yeah, you know, I didn't eat lunch all week so that I could save my $5 for the dance on Friday.' I said 'Really?' He said, 'You don't understand, you had to be there on Friday night or you were nobody, because everybody was at school talking about it on Monday.'"[55] Second, the leaders of LA's mobile DJ dance scene created the scaffolding for an alternative community-based economy. By the early 1980s, when the drug trade offered the promise of fast money even to those with other employment options, rented-venue dances created work opportunities that were both meaningful and legal.

One characteristic of the early Los Angeles hip-hop scene that did make it a New York analog was its birth in hardship. In the 1970s and early 1980s, recession and government reforms disproportionately disadvantaged blue-collar urban communities, particularly African Americans and immigrants in inner city neighborhoods where stable, salaried jobs were limited and municipal public services were as vital as they were scarce. Wage gains failed to keep up with rising inflation in the cost of living, and unemployment soared; according to the US Labor Department, some 11.5 million Americans lost jobs due to plant closings, abolitions of positions or shifts, or slack work between 1979 and 1984. These economic conditions, combined with cuts to some publicly funded social programs aimed at youth recreation and work training, took their toll on working-class black neighborhoods in Los Angeles just as they did in the predominantly African-American, Afro-Caribbean, and Latino regions of New York that had first spawned hip-hop culture.[56] The era also brought a greater and growing divide among African Americans, between upper and lower classes. The civil rights wins of prior decades had created more potential for African Americans to make significant economic, social, and political gains, and with greater access to higher education and growing demand for black talent in the professional fields, the proportion of black households earning middle- and upper-class incomes was expanding. Work by lawyers and activists to tear down racial barriers in housing meant that, by the 1970s, more upwardly-mobile black families in the decaying inner city had options to relocate to newer, safer, more affluent neighborhoods. As many did, those for whom the economic changes of the era were most burdensome were left behind.[57]

By the early 1980s, the concerted efforts of national leaders to stimulate the economy by slashing taxes for businesses and top-earners, cutting welfare spending, and shrinking federal regulations on banking (which paved the way for predatory lending), had come at a high cost to low-income communities.

These policies were particularly devastating to the families of the inner city—in places like the Bronx, Brooklyn, South Central Los Angeles, Compton, and East Long Beach—who already bore the brunt of wage disparity and urban flight. On both coasts, youths contending with revenue-deprived schools, scant recreational options, and challenging job markets used the resources they had to build and then capitalize on new music trends.

In Southern California, the plight of those living in low-income inner-city neighborhoods became especially acute in the early 1980s, when Proposition 13, an initiative passed in 1978 that placed a strict two-percent limit on annual property tax increases, caused state and local governments to slash spending on roads, parks, schools, libraries, and fire, paramedic, and police departments. In the wake of the tax revolt, Los Angeles County leaders put forth proposals for levying new local taxes to protect and expand public services, but those efforts mostly failed. This meant that those families already confined to the poorest neighborhoods by low wages and limited employment opportunities saw public schools deteriorate further and municipal services like public transportation become increasingly unreliable. The shifts coincided with, and resulted in, the further expansion of local street gangs, the rise in violent crime, and the spread of illicit industries, including guns and narcotics trafficking. These were devastating changes that gave the county's police agencies leverage to demand a larger proportion of public funds for crime control at a time when city budgets were in the red. By the early 1980s, residents in the most economically vulnerable regions of South Los Angeles County were struggling to adapt to deteriorating public services and worse job options—and also an increased police presence marked by "gang sweeps," rampant racial profiling, and a level of militarization extending to the infamous "batterram."

The most popular mobile dances of the first half of the 1980s worked precisely because, in this context, they delivered the entertainment that kids from places like South Central, Compton, Carson, Torrance, and Long Beach sorely needed. "We're giving them somewhere to go," Clayton explained of his parties, "where they can forget they don't have a job or that their parents aren't working."[58] One regular on the scene, Mark Luv, later reflected that he and his friends were saddled with the day-to-day challenges to "survive the Reagan era" while also enduring the dangers that pervaded the neighborhood. "People got jumped on the bus over shoelaces and jewelry or the wrong color Kangol," Luv said, crediting Uncle Jamm's Army events for offering everyone in South LA "a break in their lives."[59]

According to UJA's Egyptian Lover, the pleasures of mobile DJ dances—the music, the opportunity to meet someone new, and the chance to escape burdens on the outside—tended to draw as many gangbangers, pimps, and drug dealers as young people who considered themselves "law-abiding" and who were only peripherally associated with street gangs. Mark Luv insisted that all kids, no matter "their dirt," needed a social outlet. That was especially true, he thought, for the ones who were "selling, banging, seeing their homies get killed."[60] Plus, as one member of South Central's Pueblo Bishop Bloods explained, any black youth from a poor district of South Los Angeles could be considered a gang "associate" simply because, based on his address and school, he was tied geographically and socially to at least one neighborhood street clique.[61] Dividing active "gangbangers" from "associates" and "affiliates" was difficult, if not impossible. And for Clayton, any attempt to exclude the former would mean cleaving the social connections people had outside the dance, which he wanted to replicate inside. His curation of all-inclusive community dances was driven by the unique population he served even as it performed "a great service keeping a lot of people off the street" and out of trouble.[62]

By contrast, trendy nightclubs on the Westside and in Downtown LA, including Alex Jordanov's The Radio, enforced strict rules for entry that were intended to deter suspected gang members and others deemed dangerous. The dress and conduct codes inevitably affected black youths broadly. Citing security concerns, nightspots like The Radio, Club Lingerie, and the Palace granted entry only to those in "designer" fashions while regularly turning away kids in Levis, khakis, and T-shirts.

Whatever their ambitions for keeping young people off the street, the architects of the mobile dances came to depend upon gang members and drug runners as drivers of the scene. As loyal participants (partygoers, dancers, DJs, and rappers) and as party planners and staff (security guards, street promoters, and even financial backers) these "troublemakers" proved key to the success of mobile dances and the livelihood of their organizers. The Glove, who also DJ'd for Uncle Jamm's Army, recalled "more gangstas" than any other sort of partygoer on the dance floor.[63] Clayton's former partner Lonzo Williams acknowledged that "some of Uncle Jamm's Army's biggest clientele were Crips," particularly members from one of the gang's largest sets, the Rollin 60s. New York DJ Henry "Hen Gee" Garcia was so struck by the differences between the Los Angeles mobile scene and East Coast hip-hop culture that he took to referring to the electro and funk music blasting out of the speakers at Compton dances as "gangbanging music."[64]

By 1984 and 1985, LA's most popular skating rinks became known as the stomping grounds for the county's two most notorious black street gangs, thanks to their patronage of mobile DJ sound systems. The Crips claimed Mid-City's World on Wheels and the Bloods chose Compton's Skateland USA. When Craig Schweisinger opened Skateland in 1984, Compton police warned him that his business would attract gang youth. The rink, after all, stood in the cradle of LA's Blood territory, two blocks from West Piru Street, birthplace of the Piru Bloods. Schweisinger was unmoved, determined to provide all of Compton's black teenagers with a neighborhood alternative to Mid-City's World on Wheels. But the rink owner was also wary of riling police officials, so he paid to install a metal detector at the entrance and hung a placard outside that warned "NO CAPS—NO COLORS." Schweisinger dutifully hired venue security, as well—yet, to the utter horror of Compton police, he gave those jobs to known gang "affiliates" from the neighborhood who rarely enforced the dress code and allowed "a sea of red" inside the spot.[65] As Los Angeles rapper Michael "Microphone Mike" Troy (who later became "Myka 9") recalled, on any given night in the mid-1980s, the rinks were filled with gang members simply hanging out, "skating and playing video games."[66]

There were, of course, risks to such a communion. In a dance scene bound to warring street gangs, violence was a constant threat. Even the hint of trouble created significant practical challenges for event planners, performers, and partygoers. This was particularly true for the dance circuit's most popular crew, Uncle Jamm's Army, whose showcases became as notable, by 1984, for "gangbangers going crazy" as for "fresh" music. In spite of the confidence Clayton expressed that partygoers, no matter their hustle, would check all drama at the door, many from specific gang sets brought hostilities in from the outside and postured on the dance floor. To manage the unpredictable, Clayton spent extravagantly on "high-visibility" security patrols, and many of his hires, like those at Schweisinger's Compton roller rink, were tough kids from South LA's ganglands.[67] He also warned his DJs not to abruptly stop the music if they saw a fight, because it only drew more attention to the commotion and exacerbated the anxiety in the room. Instead, he instructed DJs to play Parliament's "Flash Light," a track with an uncanny ability to calm conflict and reenergize the dance. Most venues employed similar strategies, with varying levels of success. From 1984 to 1988, Schweisinger's Skateland reported two shooting episodes, and violence at World on Wheels, Skateland's Mid-City competitor, was even more common.[68] Clayton's UJA events, in spite of his best efforts "to stay on top of it," became popularly associated with gunshots and fleeing crowds. By the mid-1980s, audiences had grown used to bracing for danger.[69]

Still, participants in the DJ dance scene tolerated the uncertainties and resisted barring anyone from the scene, including those active in LA's most violent street gangs. In fact, some saw the benefits of folding these groups in. DJ Egyptian Lover, who parlayed his UJA gig into a career as a recording artist and label owner, later acknowledged that the gang economy had facilitated his success: "Drug dealers sell drugs, buy cars with big speakers, and then buy my records."[70] Mixmaster Spade told a story about hawking homemade tapes on the streets of Compton, and having a drug dealer approach him: "Man, dude, I been looking for you, man. How many you got?" When Spade showed him about thirty, "he said, 'Man give me all of them,' and pulled out a big wad like this. He said, 'Now make me some more,' and gave me a deposit." When enthusiastic customers like this played music in their opulent cars' powerful audio systems, they also became effective advertisers. For better or for worse, these were exalted, deep-pocketed, and culturally influential young men. To shun their support would be to reject a vital source of income and exposure.[71]

The fact is that gun-toting gangbangers, and the thousands of young people who were peripherally affiliated with them, were integral to the core mobile dance demographic that so many young strivers depended on to succeed in Los Angeles County in the 1980s. O'Shea "Ice Cube" Jackson, who grew up just west of South Central, remembered that he, like most of his peers, managed generally to abide by the law. But they accepted gang members in their communities as if they were the troublesome relatives in an extended family.[72] Tracy "Ice-T" Marrow, the breakout star of Topper Carew's documentary, offered an explanation: since virtually all of South Central operated "under the jurisdiction of the gangs," young men like him had to cultivate bonds with those who wielded the most power in "the Avenues." He was never a "frontline soldier," but in high school, Ice-T socialized with the Crips in his neighborhood. "I was more what I considered a 'gang affiliate.' I wore my colors," he recalled, rather than take the risk of being "a one-man team coming into school, with no backup."[73]

Gangs were a social reality woven into the Los Angeles mobile DJ dance scene in the early 1980s. Indeed, gang members and those who affiliated themselves with gangs gave the scene much of its shape. Any effort to exclude this part of the youth culture in South Los Angeles County might unravel the whole fabric. The mobile DJ sound systems that governed LA's post-disco, black teen music movement knew better.

■ ■ ■

This was the hidden Los Angeles dance scene that Run-DMC managed to captivate. By the mid-1980s, the three teens from the suburbs of Queens were beloved in Los Angeles as "heroes of the street."[74] Run-DMC's manager, Russell Simmons, knew it was significant to get this kind of validation from so ripe a market on the West Coast. As a young New York party promoter, he had rejected the early Manhattan hip-hop club scene and its reverence for "industry insiders" and bohemian white kids. Simmons looked to LA, instead, with its mobile party giants like Uncle Jamm's Army and Greg Mack's Mixmasters. He was particularly interested in the fact that, in Los Angeles, the dance scene's gatekeepers were black DJs and street promoters from the 'hood rather than white nightclub managers and record-label executives from the hills.

The distinction was crucial for Simmons, who believed Run-DMC's brand of hip-hop would thrive in the Los Angeles market. The group's embrace by black partygoers in LA, however, was not immediate, in part because mobile party kings like Clayton and KDAY's chief tastemaker, Mack, had few incentives to give the group exposure. An LA fan following remained an elusive prize in 1983, even as Run-DMC's single "It's Like That / Sucker M.C.'s" climbed the *Billboard* R&B charts. "We were so on our own stuff," dance regular Mark Luv remembered, "we didn't give it up for them."[75] Clayton offered a simple explanation for his initial resistance to book the New Yorkers for his events: "We did not need them." Eventually, however, Simmons's persistence paid off and Clayton capitulated, allowing Run-DMC to play an Uncle Jamm's Army show at the Los Angeles Memorial Sports Arena in late 1983. The three young, green performers were stunned by the size of the UJA audience. "They had never seen so many people," Clayton remembered. "They were scared."[76] Although their hosts were skeptical of them, and although they earned a measly sum for their appearance, the show was a promotional win for Run-DMC. Radio hosts at KDAY began fielding requests for the group's music, and regional sales of "It's Like That / Sucker M.C.'s" took off. Soon, Run-DMC was in a position to successfully lobby KDAY's Mack for more spins in exchange for recording promotional spots for the station. Mack's own DJs, the "Mack Attack Mixmasters," added tracks from the group's debut album *Run-DMC* into their on-air and party set rotations.[77] With the aid of the city's original hip-hop pioneers, Run-DMC earned the adoration of a new generation of Los Angeles rap fans who, by 1985, were beginning to favor hard-edged, narrative-driven rap over the lyrically sparse freestyle and electro-rap dance productions popular just a few years earlier. The devotion in LA that summer to Toddy Tee's "Batterram" mix tape—the homemade rap recording reacting to, among other things, the new military-surplus vehicle the LAPD was deploying in its war on drugs—reflected the shifting preference in LA toward street tales backed by bass booms and claps.[78] And as regional mobile, radio, and nightclub DJs responded to evolving local tastes, they laid the groundwork for the "pure and uncut" music of Run-DMC, leaders of the new hip-hop vanguard.[79]

Joseph "Reverend Run" Simmons, Darryl "DMC" McDaniels, and Jason "Jam Master Jay" Mizell made precisely the sort of artistic choices that manager Russell Simmons believed necessary for making waves in "the streets." Guided since the group's inception in 1982 by Russell's vision, each rapper fashioned himself as "the common b-boy." (Breakdancers had come to be known as b-boys and b-girls.) These were streetwise kids who weren't ashamed of their gritty, urban upbringings but instead, in style and substance, embodied that environment.[80]

To this end, Run-DMC embraced the basics of b-boy street wear, the understated styles worn not only by breakdancers but also by DJs, MCs, and legions of poor and working-class Bronx kids who reveled in the impromptu neighborhood parties of the mid-1970s. By the 1980s, b-boy fashions had fallen out of favor with hip-hop's earliest, most promising performers, who were now winning high-profile bookings in New York's downtown nightclubs and recording contracts with Sugar Hill Records, the hip-hop focused label founded by disco star Sylvia Robinson and her husband.[81] Groups like Sequence, Funky 4 + 1 More, Grandmaster Flash and the Furious Five, the Treacherous Three, and the Cold Crush Brothers found themselves setting trends for an as-yet undefined music culture. In this role, most of these artists took on the flamboyant trappings of disco, electro, and even doo-wop; their wardrobes overflowed with capes, headdresses, fringe, gold lamé, brightly colored suits, and head-to-toe matching leather outfits embellished with fur.[82] With Simmons's urging, Run-DMC rejected the splash and the theater, and instead dressed in the uniform of the inner city. By opting for sneakers, jeans, T-shirts, bomber jackets, and black hats, they implicitly honored hip-hop's b-boy origins and resisted what hip-hop was becoming as it moved from the block and into tony nightclubs and recording studios. Recognizing what was artistically radical about that move in the early 1980s,

Fig 2.3 At a 1984 performance in Long Beach, Run-DMC members Joseph "Reverend Run" Simmons and Darryl "DMC" McDaniels wear the leather jackets and black fedoras that became the group's signature "street" style. Los Angeles Times Photographic Archives, Library Special Collections, UCLA Library.

when the glitz worked, John Leland at the *Village Voice* explained, "Run-DMC force you to confront them as people, not as fantasies" (Fig. 2.3).[83]

Run-DMC's music was similarly defiant. The trio managed to upend most early hip-hop conventions in their production choices, lyrical themes, and performance techniques. While their fashion choices harked back to b-boy days, their musical production moved radically away from the orchestral, sample-heavy, electronic sounds so popular in early hip-hop. African-American session musician and producer Larry Smith (and, later, punk artist Rick Rubin) provided Run-DMC with a stripped-down, drum-forward sound that captivated a younger generation of hip-hop fans. Their rap music was altogether new, divorced more thoroughly than ever before from hip-hop's disco roots. At the same time, Run-DMC brought the music back to the streets. As Leland wrote in the *Village Voice*, "With just beats and rhymes, they brought rap closer to its original state before the producers took it out of the reach of ordinary schmucks."[84]

Run-DMC's approach reinforced its "homeboy credentials" and set them completely apart from older hip-hop acts.[85] Brooklyn rap artist Shawn "Jay-Z" Carter remembered, "From the first listen, Run-DMC felt harder than the Sugarhill Gang or even Kool Moe Dee and other serious battle rappers of the time." In sum, he said, "Their voices were big, like their beats." As a kid growing up in a Brooklyn housing project in the 1970s, Jay-Z had been mostly ambivalent about early Bronx-based hip-hop trends. But with their macho swagger and vivid tales of the hustler's struggles and successes, Run-DMC reinvigorated hip-hop for him, giving him faith that rap music could "be real" and perhaps even have a "point of view" in line with his own. MCs Run and DMC sounded to him like rebels, and with a "raw and aggressive" flow these young black men were on wax archiving lived experiences that sounded like his. It was a revelation, he remembered, for his circle of friends to hear in Run-DMC's raps echoes of everything from "our aspirations and our crumb-snatching struggles, our specific, small realities (*chicken and collard greens*) and our living-color dreamscapes (*big long Caddy*)."[86]

Outside New York, too, Run-DMC attracted a younger generation of music fans. Dallas native and Los Angeles rapper Tracy "The D.O.C." Curry could recall first hearing Sugarhill Gang's "Rapper's Delight," hip-hop's first hit single and one of the first hip-hop songs to reach audiences beyond the five boroughs. The track was The D.O.C.'s initial exposure to "rapping" just as it was for most young people across the country. But he was not impressed until several years later when he first heard Run-DMC, and more specifically, the electrifying cadence of Reverend Run's raps. Run was young, black, and brash, just like him and, thus, helped him recognize how he, a street rapper from Texas, might fit within hip-hop. "Run had everything I had," The D.O.C. remembered. "He had the same vocal styling, the same command in his voice." The fact that Run was also unashamed—"Whatever the fuck he was saying, he meant that shit"—allowed him to command attention the way The D.O.C. believed rappers should.[87]

Instead of "message raps" that told moral tales, Run-DMC offered snapshots of personal hard times (*"Bills rise higher every day / We receive much lower pay"*), temptations (*"They offer coke—and lots of dope—but we just leave it alone"*), and race pride (*"I'll attack this matter in my own way / Man, I ain't no slave, I ain't bailin' no hay"*).[88] Biographical sketches of hardened b-boys were rich with allusions to material wealth, sexual conquest, and lyrical supremacy. (*"We slay all suckers who perpetrate / And lay down laws from state to state"* was one line, well chosen to appear on *Raising Hell* tour merchandise.)[89] While their bravado thrilled new fans like Jay-Z and The D.O.C., some branded Run-DMC's music as too "harsh" and "political," with its trappings of black militancy. For instance, in 1984, writers for the television sitcom *The Jeffersons* crafted an episode in which a gospel quartet performed a rendition of Run-DMC's "It's Like That" at an all-white honky-tonk, finishing their performance with fists raised in Black Power salute.[90] Even Run-DMC's own label mate Kurtis Blow found the trio's frequent use of the colloquial term *illin'* too radical. "Those lyrics are bad," Blow told

*Newsday.* "What Run-DMC is doing is perpetrating, acting like they're tough gangster kids." Amid the critiques, Run-DMC gained renown as genre innovators for unapologetically abandoning the early hip-hop canon. Years later, rap patriarch Curtis "Grandmaster Caz" Fisher identified Run-DMC's rise as "the end of our era."[91]

Russell Simmons wanted the group he was managing to shatter conventions. He put his trust in the popular appeal of urban authenticity and encouraged his artists to be "true to themselves." Most importantly, Simmons aimed for Run-DMC to be two things that the music industry had assumed were incompatible; his group would be both "street" and "pop."[92] Although he sought exposure for Run-DMC on the downtown New York club circuit, he refused to pin the trio's success to places like the Roxy, which seemed to take black music and "whiten it up" and "water it down" for a broader audience.[93] Plus, as a Queens-based promoter of a Bronx-born experiment that had become a Manhattan phenomenon, Simmons recognized the potential for hip-hop to earn audiences throughout New York City and, eventually, outside its boroughs. Like many rap music cynics, Simmons believed that the fledgling genre—mostly sequestered in the Northeast and stymied by the Sugar Hill Records monopoly—was at a crossroads in the early 1980s. Music writers might have expected hip-hop to fade into obscurity, just like disco, but Simmons envisioned the flowering of the genre. With careful cultivation, he imagined it maturing, earning new audiences from around the country, topping the music charts, breaking sales records, and ultimately finding a permanent place within the recording industry. As Reverend Run later reflected, Run-DMC wanted to ensure that hip-hop could no longer be "dismissed as a fad." He and his band, under his brother's management, intended to change the game altogether, "not by softening up but by being tougher than leather."[94]

Within a year of its first single release, Run-DMC was the only chart-topping, commercially successful hip-hop act in the world. This unrivaled position was the result of the trio's unique street appeal and Russell Simmons's hunger for broad market appeal—but there was also another factor. Cable television's newest phenomenon was music video programming, and while MTV's video jockeys spurned early rap pioneers— including Grandmaster Flash and Sugarhill Gang—because their videos "didn't look very good," they welcomed Run-DMC.[95] With the support of Simmons's label Def Jam, the trio managed to produce slick video shorts that fit the channel's edgy style, even earning a place on the mantel of MTV celebrity. In 1985, at MTV's second annual Video Music Awards, host Eddie Murphy introduced Run-DMC as the three Queens kids who saved hip-hop. Once the butt of music industry jokes, rap was now "going strong," Murphy declared, thanks to "the baddest brothers in rap."[96] Within a year, *Melody Maker* was echoing this assessment, stressing rap's pop potential, a notion once considered absurd. It praised Run-DMC as "the first rap group to be truly significant, the first rap group to speak in a major language . . . the first rap act to be successfully marketed as a pop group so that they now rub shoulders with Madonna, Bruce Springsteen and Michael Jackson."[97]

In addition to its MTV ascendency, Run-DMC shattered market expectations by becoming the first rap act to sell enough music to justify a multicity, multivenue concert

tour. Even hip-hop's earliest and most lionized star, Afrika
Bambaataa, failed to register on American music charts until 1985, the year he appeared on a compilation album that
also featured Run-DMC.[98] While Bambaataa and his group,
Soul Sonic Force, boasted an international fan base through
the 1980s, their shows in the United States, even at peak
career, were sometimes described as lackluster showcases
that drew small crowds made up of "trendies" and "older,
white rock critics."[99] By contrast, Run-DMC filled to capacity sprawling concert venues throughout the country, beginning in 1984, the year its debut album, *Run-DMC*, was released. The group's tours included many of the nation's
major cities, premier nightclubs including the Front Row
Theater outside Cleveland, Ohio, the Inferno in Buffalo,
New York, the Channel in Boston, and the Stardust Ball-
room (also known as the Mix Club) in Hollywood. In their
first two years on the road, Run-DMC also played major
performance spaces like the Warfield Theater in San Francisco, the Hollywood Palladium in Los Angeles, and the fif-
teen-thousand-seat Madison Square Garden arena in the
trio's hometown.[100]

By the summer of 1986, Run-DMC understood they were
unrivaled. They were certified hit makers, stars of MTV, and
veterans of the national arena circuit. But Run-DMC's *Raising Hell* tour, to promote its third studio album, promised to
amplify the group's relevance within hip-hop. That year, the
group's label, Profile, financed more concert dates, including
bookings inside arenas and sports centers in the South and
across the West. Run-DMC's most ambitious promotional
tour was planned as a sixty-four-date jaunt that featured
dates in New York City, St. Louis, Dallas, Atlanta, New Orleans,
Oakland, and Los Angeles.[101]

.   .   .

When Run-DMC kicked off its *Raising Hell* tour in 1986, the trio from Queens stood as hip-hop's only platinum-selling artists and the genre's standard bearers. The "baddest brothers in rap" also had an image problem, and they knew it. After a flurry of crimes following performances in June and July, which included robberies at Madison Square Garden and a shooting near an exit at Atlanta's Omni Arena, some media outlets concluded that Run-DMC's brand of rap was to blame for the lawlessness. The narrative dovetailed with existing concerns about violence plaguing heavy metal and punk rock shows, a moral furor that culminated in 1985 with the widely publicized US Senate Hearing on the dangers of "outrageous recordings."[102] In a cultural environment fraught with renewed anxieties around youth music trends and social disorder, Run-DMC and other rappers found themselves under pressure to defend their genre. Reverend Run blamed bigots who didn't understand the music: "just because it's black people, they think we ain't got nothing to do except bust somebody's head open." He was not the only one, he noted, being demonized on local television, in the pages of popular magazines and national newspapers, and in political debates: "All of us rappers get a raw deal." He wished the critics would "chill out and stop hassling us."[103] Convincing the public that rap was not derelict music became increasingly difficult with every new report of concert violence, and it was a particularly awkward mission for a group promoting such a provocatively titled album. As *Billboard* observed, the *Raising Hell* tour was living up to its name.[104]

The "rap riot" that erupted inside the Long Beach Arena that August made the difficult task of scrubbing hip-hop's

reputation virtually impossible. *Raising Hell* tour promoter
Jeff Sharp saw the Long Beach Arena fiasco as a terrible watershed. "I've been in this business eleven years," Sharp explained, "and I've never seen anything like it."[105] Critics were
quick to note that the violence in Long Beach could not be
shrugged off by the rap showcase producers because, unlike
earlier vandalism, theft, and bloodshed on the tour, it all took
place inside the concert venue. Before Long Beach, those intent on citing Run-DMC's music as the catalyst for crime had
to rely on arguments that the group could be blamed for arrests made *near* a rap venue or in the hours *following* a performance. In its reporting on the Long Beach violence, *Melody Maker* noted that media outlets "didn't need to inflate
and exaggerate the violence . . . it was there waiting for them,
preened for the cameras and very real."[106]

In the wake of the Long Beach Arena disaster, Run-DMC
pivoted in its campaign to defend hip-hop from moral crusaders. Rather than continue to buck those critics sounding
the alarm about troublesome youths, Run-DMC now joined
the chorus. The trio, their manager Russell Simmons, and
members of the Profile Records staff ran a public relations
campaign aimed at exoneration, fearing that the group's
brand had been irreparably damaged by the violence in Long
Beach. Run-DMC's publicists carefully promoted the final leg
of the concert tour, promising it would engage good kids in a
"safe activity" rather than delinquents "raising hell." And the
trio gave interviews with many of the very same mainstream
media outlets they had once disdained. The message, simply,
was that it had been gangbangers, not rap fans, doing the
fighting; they had "sabotaged" the Long Beach show.[107] Jam
Master Jay railed against those who had prevented his fans
from enjoying the music, blasting all the Crips and Bloods who

needed to "get their life together and grow up."[108] Reverend
Run insisted "These weren't our fans" and called the brawlers
"scumbags and roaches." Talking to a *Los Angeles Times* reporter, he blamed LA for letting things get to the point where
"gangs are running your town." The group had played other
tough towns, he pointed out, but in places like Detroit gangs
respected that, inside the show, they were on Run-DMC's
"turf." Seizing the high ground, he blamed lax security in LA
for letting the "gremlins" through the door and complained
that now, "our fans are probably so scared to see us, that they
won't come near our show. And I can't live with that."[109]

LA's own Rodger Clayton, who had promoted the Long
Beach Arena show in partnership with Mack at KDAY, also
spoke to the *Los Angeles Times*. Clayton conceded that rap is
"street music" that "appeal[s] to the masses." Among those
fans, he said, "you're always going to have a few fools," but
"that doesn't make the music bad." The press was wrong, the
mobile party titan said (just as Run-DMC once had), to
demonize hip-hop and the predominantly black kids who
consumed it. Determined to shield itself and the hip-hop
movement from blame, Run-DMC issued a statement saying
it would "refuse to play Los Angeles until police and the authorities take sterner measures to protect Run-DMC fans
from local gangs. The gangs stand for everything that rap is
against." With that last phrase, they disavowed any connection
to a key sect of the local hip-hop scene and, by extension, its
"associates" and friends. Having worked for years to gain
acceptance on the West Coast, the New Yorkers now positioned themselves against a major contingent of its Los
Angeles market.[110]

Unwilling to be put on the defensive, officials at the Long
Beach Arena in effect punished the Queens artists, refusing

to book them for future events. Venues elsewhere, including in New York City and Atlanta, did not cancel future shows on the tour, although law enforcement in many cities expressed urgent security concerns having seen what had happened in Long Beach.[111] That was not the case for the rest of the California leg of the tour. Immediately, officials at the Hollywood Palladium canceled the next night's sold-out concert featuring Run-DMC and the Beastie Boys, a white rap trio from Brooklyn.[112] A spokesperson for Long Beach Arena management announced in the same week that the venue would institute a "prohibitive booking policy," which would bar other hip-hop acts from performing on its premises. Arena officials stated in no uncertain terms that fans of rap music exhibited "a propensity to create situations likely to cause injury to other patrons."[113] Michael McSweeny, marketing director for Long Beach city facilities, issued a similar statement about criteria for future concert bookings. As he explained, "A band's track record," and whether "it looks like there's been a bad show," would guide entertainment decisions henceforth.[114] In September, event organizers for the annual city-sponsored Los Angeles Street Scene scrambled to make an announcement regarding Run-DMC, who had been booked months earlier as one of the festival's headliners. The Festival Committee, in conjunction with the Los Angeles Office of Public Safety, first proposed new conditions requiring that the group "bring along a couple of well-known 'mainstream' artists to stage a special performance condemning gang warfare and the drug 'crack,'" which Run-DMC accepted. Ultimately, however, the committee removed Run-DMC from the event program, citing "controversy."[115]

The coordinated drive to mend the Run-DMC brand and safeguard the group's revenues out west soon delivered the trio back to Los Angeles, a place the rappers had only recently fled and publicly criticized. There, they inserted themselves into a community-driven anti-gang movement spurred by a recent spate of drive-by shootings. New data revealed that gangs continued to proliferate in the Los Angeles region, with law enforcement estimating nearly fifty thousand members in the county divided into more than four hundred cliques. Violent crimes had jumped significantly since the prior year, breaking municipal and county records. South Los Angeles community leaders, including former gang members, responded by expanding outreach programs and seeking more creative strategies for reducing the bloodshed.[116]

In September of 1986, LA's anti-gang nonprofit Community Youth Gang Services Project (formed in 1981), in partnership with KDAY, seized on the national publicity following the Long Beach Arena "rap riot" to call for a "Day of Peace" among LA gangs. Hopes were high that with KDAY's ability to reach a young and loyal audience, the day "could lead to a season of peace in November and December."[117] Program Director Jack Patterson later reflected on why the station got involved: "The anti-gang thing really came from having people say that only gang members listened to us because we played all this gang music. We felt we had to put forth the truth about how bad gangs were."[118]

KDAY invited Run-DMC to participate, an obvious choice in the immediate aftermath of the August Long Beach incident, and also given the group's ability to influence young people. Run-DMC agreed to participate, viewing the invitation as an opportunity to reset. After Long Beach, the young stars were suffering the fallout from what one journalist would later call their "catchy, vaguely gangster-like image," and it was very unclear whether they would recover.[119] A prominent role in an anti-gang radio broadcast on South LA's most beloved rap station, hosted by revered DJ Mack, offered a potential lifeline: it could cast Run-DMC as anti-gang advocates while underscoring the street authority they believed they had. "The hardcore crowd *is* the Run-DMC crowd," Jam Master Jay noted, so who was more suited to perform these good works for that crowd than they were? "Kids listen to us before they listen to their parents or teachers," Reverend Run boasted during a news conference promoting the outreach broadcast. "Maybe we can help young people who are thinking of joining gangs, using or dealing drugs . . . to think of some alternatives."[120]

On October 9, all three members of Run-DMC joined KDAY's two-hour "Day of Peace" radio program alongside the gang project's leaders, Olympic boxing gold medalist and East LA native Paul Gonzalez, and singer Barry White—himself a former member of South Central's Slausons gang. With the panel at the ready, KDAY opened its phone lines and each of them started fielding calls from members of local gangland communities. Live on air, they responded to "frustration, fear, anger, helplessness," the *Los Angeles Times* reported, and beheld the "grim portrait of Los Angeles-area neighborhoods gripped by gang violence, drug sales, staggering youth-unemployment and disintegrating families." There were harrowing stories of relatives and friends shot dead, children caught up in the drug-running game, and prison sentences. Other music and sports celebrities called in to offer their own condolences, prayers, and advice for coping with a crisis they mostly witnessed from afar. Pop mogul Quincy Jones, best known at the time for his work with Michael Jackson and producing the platinum-selling humanitarian anthem "We Are the World," urged LA youths to "respect yourself."[121]

During the "Day of Peace" broadcast, the gang project nonprofit fielded hundreds of calls over its hot lines, including a few from young bangers who cited KDAY's show as the impetus for their pleas for help. They desperately wanted "to know how to get out" of the gang life, one counselor reported. Project Regional Director and South Central activist Leon Watkins was encouraged. It was "naïve" to believe that one broadcast could stop the violence, he cautioned, but "some will listen. There has to be a starting point." Run-DMC was more confident that their on-air public service mattered. "I feel good if I know I've helped some kids," Reverend Run said. "I think I helped a lot today because kids love us that much."[122] Indeed, dozens of local gangs announced a few weeks later that they would work toward a ceasefire. According to the *Los Angeles Times,* between eighty and one hundred gangs promised to hammer out the terms of a truce, and authors of the proposed "Our Peace Treaty" credited Run-DMC and the KDAY "Day of Peace" broadcast for inspiring the diplomacy.[123]

At the end of 1986, Run-DMC proudly accepted praise for its community service efforts in Los Angeles, a turnabout for a group of easterners that had so recently berated the "scumbags" out west. Although the trio had used their New York City roots to remind the press that they were alien to the crisis in Los Angeles and "don't have anything to do with what's going on out there," they also claimed their working-class Queens upbringing gave them rare insight into such inner-city struggles.[124] In doing so, they tapped into the notion of urban authenticity, a trait that was prized in the world of hip-hop and, as Run-DMC discovered, increasingly vital to commercial success. Ignoring all the contradictions in their many public comments about Los Angeles and its gangs, and relying heavily on their own "street" credentials, the band believed they had emerged from a devastating public relations disaster as honored heroes in Los Angeles's war on gangs.

Despite efforts to bury the past, however, the August 1986 violence continued to haunt Run-DMC through 1987, forcing the trio again and again to deny the extent to which their music and their concerts promoted violence and, worse, glorified the gangster image. Still barred from LA's major performance venues and dogged by questions about the Long Beach show, the group refocused on its *Together Forever* tour.[125] With a $600,000 security budget, the international concert tour featuring the Beastie Boys promised to "restore rap's image as a safe activity."[126] The black rap trio and the white rap trio both touted *Together Forever* as a cutting-edge, racially integrated line-up designed to draw diverse and civil crowds. As *Newsweek's* Bill Barol wrote, the highlight of this tour was "out in the audience [where] black kids and white kids stood together, rapped along, waved their hands in the air, had a great time." The promise of *Together Forever* was that its success would eclipse the "hysteria" around the Long Beach disaster. As Beastie Boys rapper MCA emphasized, *Together Forever* would help fans forget the "one isolated event" that represented nothing more than "a problem in LA."[127] To their perpetual frustration, reporters in cities across America and even in Europe refused to let up, interrogating all the rappers about gang-related violence. "We're not these psychopaths that they talk about," Beastie Boys member Ad Rock proclaimed on *CBS News Nightwatch*, visibly frustrated. "We're good kids."[128]

In Los Angeles, the gang truce that Run-DMC purportedly inspired failed to materialize. The South Los Angeles gangland wars, in fact, expanded and intensified that winter, with some cliques harnessing the media attention generated by the fallout from the Long Beach Arena show to attract new recruits. Even those groups tasked with drafting the treaty ultimately fell back into conflict. A police sergeant for Inglewood's homicide division reported "a tremendous increase in violent gang assaults" in the months following the celebrated "Day of Peace" broadcast. Moreover, by 1987, LA's black press began reporting on the "drive-by wars," a terrifying surge in targeted shootings from moving cars—a crisis blamed, again, on rock cocaine and escalating gang rivalries.[129]

The year ended with yet another widely reported "rap riot," this time at a UTFO concert, the first hip-hop show held in the city since the 1986 Long Beach Arena event. (UTFO, a New York-based group, was popular in Los Angeles largely because Compton rapper Toddy Tee repurposed its most popular singles "Roxanne, Roxanne" and "Bite It" for his street stories, "Rockman, Rockman" and "L.A. Is a Jungle.") Despite ample security at the Hollywood Palladium, including airport metal detectors, extra staff posted around the venue's perimeter, and screening for gang colors at the ticket gates, representatives from at least eight Los Angeles gang sets made it inside with weapons. Fights raged and shots were fired. In the aftermath, the local press reported on LA's "mood of paranoia" about "heavily armed" black youths who "spray bullets at anyone and everyone," and posed a question that had tormented Run-DMC and divided its fans for nearly a year: "Can rap music—with its aggressive, jackhammer rhythms and often hard-edged street imagery—be performed safely in Los Angeles?"[130]

■  ■  ■

That music critics and the entertainment press kept a spotlight fixed on Los Angeles and its "crisis" vexed Run-DMC
because it threatened to undermine the group's success. This
spotlight, however, worked in favor of the region's fledgling rap artists. Prior to August of 1986, hip-hop music was
represented as an exclusively East Coast phenomenon with
New York roots and New York sensibilities. Run-DMC's sudden and extraordinary commercial success in the mid-1980s
seemed only to reinforce the axiom that hip-hop was an artistic phenomenon inextricably tied to the boroughs of the
Big Apple. But the Long Beach stop on Run-DMC's 1986
*Raising Hell* tour hinted at a sea change coming.

A small cadre of Los Angeles rappers and DJs, most of
whom had risen to fame within the Southland's mobile dance
scene of the early 1980s, absorbed the music made out East,
yet remained fiercely loyal to art created within their own en-
virons. Often with little more than crude recording systems,
local patronage, and the support of the low-wattage KDAY
radio station, South Los Angeles talents like Mixmaster
Spade, Toddy Tee, Rodney O, Joe Cooley, DJ Pooh, King Tee,
The Compton Posse, Ice-T, Cli-N-Tel, Dr. Dre, DJ Yella, and
Ice Cube dedicated themselves, in lyrical content and in musical production, to engaging with the urban landscapes and
cultures around them. These artists recorded and performed
music that reflected upon and, in some cases, romanticized
LA's street cultures, including life experienced in proximity
to gangs, the allure of easy money, the pervasiveness of violence, and daily encounters with the police.

Many young purveyors of this distinctly regional sound—
eventually referred to as "gangsta rap"—emerged, not coinci-
dentally, in the wake of the 1986 Long Beach Arena Run-
DMC concert, the event that KDAY's Mack would describe as

"the straw that broke the camel's back."[131] The violent rap show shook the music industry and threatened to ruin the careers of Reverend Run, Jam Master Jay, and DMC. For some, the "rap riot" threatened to be the death knell not only for the Queens sensation but for the whole genre of hip-hop. With its dominion jeopardized, Run-DMC dealt with the media by snubbing Los Angeles area rap fans and by ridiculing gang-related groups who were, like it or not, part of the fabric of LA's regional hip-hop scene.[132]

The Long Beach show proved a critical juncture, but not exactly in the way New York's kings of rap feared. The more Run-DMC and its handlers took pains to disassociate themselves from Los Angeles, the greater the public's fascination with those "problems" out west and the power of rap to provoke them. This presented a window of opportunity for LA's own rap hopefuls, who recognized the value of the limelight, even when the light was harsh. They understood how to harness the negative attention to promote themselves as artists and, crucially, to draw attention to the Los Angeles they knew—a place that the eighteen-year-old aspiring rapper Ice Cube described in rhyme as *"Hardcore, LA not like the past."*[133]

**CHAPTER 3** · The Boys in the Hood
Are Always Hard



▪ **In the early years** of Los Angeles rap music, all roads
led to Hollywood. There, on Santa Monica Boulevard just
south of the historic Hollywood Palladium, a small record-
pressing facility minted local stars. Through the mid-1980s,
the hydraulic vinyl stampers at the Macola Record Company
hummed and hissed daily, producing boxes of records for
anyone with a master tape and a stack of cash. Amid the ace-
tates, vinyl pellets, and cardboard, independent labels were
born, too, most of them founded by the young entrepreneurs
that ruled LA's mobile DJ party scene and were the plant's
best customers. By providing support for record-publishing
rookies and, more importantly, the capital equipment for
manufacturing a product quickly and economically, Macola
became, as *Billboard* christened it in 1986, a "major force on
the independent music scene." For young black talents in Los
Angeles, in particular, the Macola Record Company offered a
vital back channel into an otherwise impervious music industry.[1]

Macola opened in 1983, the brainchild of industry veteran Don Macmillan, a Canadian immigrant who had spent over twenty years manufacturing blues, jazz, and pop music at LA's Cadet Records, a large custom presser and supplier on the corner of West Slauson and Normandie Avenues, within reach of the dozens of large record companies, labels, and music distributors housed in the region. Southern California was home to, among others, Mercury, MCA, Warner Brothers, A&M Records, Arista, Atlantic, Blue Note, Capitol, Columbia, Epic, and SOLAR. In the early 1980s, the Southland was the place for pathbreakers and chart-toppers like New Edition, Teena Marie, The Kinks, Whodini, Midnight Star, Klymaxx, Diana Ross, The Police, Prince, Thompson Twins, Janet Jackson, and Michael Jackson. This, plus proximity to the most productive film and television studios in the world, made Los Angeles a globally renowned recording mecca. Tracing the long history of LA's dominance in the music business, a long-time industry insider wrote in an 1980 issue of *Billboard* about the cluster of complementary elements that grew up side by side there. By the 1940s, he explained "the combination of sunshine, movies, radio, a booming nightclub business and a thriving record industry was too much to resist" and performers as well as music industry professionals flocked to the city.[2] It was an ecosystem in which a company focused wholly on record pressing could thrive.

When Cadet Records became mired in a counterfeiting investigation and subject to police raids in 1981 and 1982, Macmillan took the company's turmoil as his cue to leave.[3] He headed north to Hollywood, setting up his own small pressing shop. Even if he could not compete with the large-volume manufacturers who were "operating the scoreboard"—including

Rainbo Records with its thirty-thousand-square-foot plant, and his former employer, Cadet—Macmillan trusted that the region's frenetic entertainment culture created enough work to sustain another upstart business. Like many other entrepreneurial ventures in LA, Macola was established to cater not to those at the center of the commercial industry but to players on the periphery.[4]

Greg Broussard, the young DJ who would gain renown as "Egyptian Lover," helped Don Macmillan realize his company's potential. Before connecting with Macola, he had been mixing, dubbing, and selling homemade rap tapes to kids around the way. Egyptian Lover's association with the unrivaled Uncle Jamm's Army mobile dances helped him market and distribute his cassettes throughout LA, earning him local celebrity status and, in 1983, a prominent role in filmmaker Topper Carew's documentary *Breakin' 'n' Enterin'*.[5] With the money he earned from performing and selling tapes, Lover bought a Roland TR-808 drum machine—a digital device preferred by his favorite electro artists and a tool he considered vital for engineering original music. By the fall, he had recorded two tracks, "Dial-A-Freak" and "Egypt, Egypt," each inspired by Kraftwerk melodies, Cybotron bass lines, and the eroticism of artists like Prince, and each crafted for the Uncle Jamm's Army party faithful.[6] Betting on his own renown— the chorus of "Egypt, Egypt" was a looped self-reference— Lover took the tracks to KDAY radio. Music programmer Greg Mack, who respected the popularity of Uncle Jamm's Army and its DJs among the station's young listeners, put both songs in heavy rotation.[7]

To convert radio requests into revenue, Lover went to Macola. He knew he wanted his music on pressed vinyl to spin at gigs, to put into the hands of other DJs, and to hawk locally in the same way he had sold dubbed cassettes. At Don Macmillan's shop, the only pressing facility that accepted short-run jobs, he could get five hundred copies for $1,000. At that price, Lover was able to print units as needed, selling out his stock and then returning with cash profits to order more. Once he was confident in the music's appeal, he asked Macmillan about a distribution deal. Like other, older music industry veterans, Macmillan was skeptical about the viability of post-disco trends, including rap and electro. But he agreed to bolster Lover's exposure by sending extra copies of the records to the retail stores and radio programmers he knew outside of Los Angeles, including Jem Records in Grand Prairie, Texas, Stan "The Record Man" Lewis in Shreveport, Louisiana, and Select-O-Hits in Memphis, Tennessee.[8] Egyptian Lover presented Macmillan—a veteran manufacturer but a novice distributor—with a promising opportunity to leverage his professional connections, expand the business, and grow Macola from a manufacturing plant into a pressing and distribution service. By 1985, "Egypt, Egypt" had sold nearly half a million units nationally, and Macola had earned its place as the foremost pressing and distribution vendor to LA rap artists.[9]

Key to Macola's success was Don Macmillan's decision to focus on the artists' need to get their work on vinyl and into retail outlets. As his partnership with Egyptian Lover showed, he did not have to build and then staff up his own marketing department. Many of the young performers who sought his pressing services understood quite well the art of promotion and could find their own ways to drum up demand. Nevertheless, to support his young, unsigned clients' efforts, Macmillan provided onsite space for them to form their own labels, design their own promotional materials, book gigs, and recruit and manage other talent. Artists covered label costs themselves and operated with full autonomy under Macola's roof.

Most of Macola's early customers had already, like Lover, built local followings with dubbed cassettes sold from shoeboxes and car trunks. They were plugged into LA's flourishing mobile dance circuit, where partygoers often became repeat customers and even partners in promotion. Artists who patronized Macola in its first years, including the Uncle Jamm's Army DJs, the LA Dream Team, Lonzo's World Class Wreckin' Cru, and the Arabian Prince, were thus already well positioned for small-market success. Macmillan recognized that, for some of his customers, manufacturing was enough: "These kids from Compton were having records pressed and selling five thousand to ten thousand units just among themselves and by word of mouth."[10]

For much of the 1980s, affordable access to vinyl pressing machinery, a vital part of the music business infrastructure, kept South Los Angeles artists streaming through the doors of the Macola Record Company. Unlike the industry's producers and distributors, the company did not choose projects based on artistic considerations or sales forecasts; it simply sold manufacturing services in simple buyer-seller transactions. Artists paid money for stacks of saleable product. For aspiring rap acts who had no entree to LA's record producers—which was the norm, given that when it came to hip-hop the industry tended to dismiss anything produced outside New York—Macola offered a route to wholesalers, retailers, and radio airtime, and at least some pathway to achieving broad, national exposure. As Egyptian Lover later reflected, Macola gave him the means to develop Egyptian Empire Records, to be his own boss, and to become a celebrity, all by the age of twenty.[11]

In a town that had become the global epicenter for the music industry, the Macola Record Company was a beacon of hope for artists from the 'hood. Until 1987, it was the only record-making business with an open-door policy, welcoming all comers, connecting aspiring artists, regardless of their experience or polish or the content of their art, to the means of music production. Don Macmillan was a short-run presser willing to partner with local DJs and rappers on national distribution deals, providing them with a platform for attracting major label attention and, thus, more lucrative opportunities. At the same time, crucially, young black artists doing business with Macola retained ownership of their master recordings and full creative control over their music and their images.[12]

■   ■   ■

Macmillan's operation was well suited to young Eric Wright, a Los Angeles drug dealer seeking a more lawful, sustainable line of work. Wright was raised in a blue-collar household in a once segregated, lily-white eastern corner of Compton, an unincorporated city in LA County that was, according to a reporter from the era, awash in "polite bungalows fronted by porches and lawns" and comfortably removed from the "boarded-up businesses, disheveled lots, soiled fast-food joints and two-bit stores" further to the north.[13] Wright's parents, one a Montessori schoolteacher and the other a postal worker, labored to insulate their son from trouble. But it found him. He dropped out of Manuel Dominquez High, a school that was, at the time, fighting a losing battle to keep drugs and violence off its campus.[14] Free of school, Wright sold marijuana then partnered with a cousin to move rock

cocaine, a business that netted him a small fortune. But by
1984, Wright had lost his cousin to gun violence. Heir to tens
of thousands of dollars' worth of cocaine at a moment of spik-
ing demand for the drug, Eric was unnerved by the shooting,
and increasingly anxious about the threat of incarceration
and retribution. He had had enough of ducking police and
dreading enemies. About the stress he said, "I figured I could
do something else or I end up dead myself or in jail."[15]

After ruling out a career with the post office, Eric Wright
plotted a path into music sales. His muse was a Japanese-
American record vendor who held court at the Roadium
Open Air Market, a popular swap meet inside a North Torrance drive-in theater. Tucked inside the maze of 430 wooden
booths filled with antiques, used books, oil paintings, clothing, televisions and stereos, mattresses, and Ayatollah dart-
boards, Steve Yano's stall was a Shangri-la for young music
fans.[16] Each weekend, Yano and his wife Susan blanketed the
twenty-foot-wide wall of their rented space with album cov-
ers. They filled shelves with rows of cassette tapes—some
homemade and hand-labeled—and loaded folding tables
with dozens of milk crates stuffed with more vinyl LPs, singles, and EPs (Fig. 3.1).[17] Over a couple of loudspeakers, Yano
played samples from his highly eclectic inventory, collected
from garage sales, thrift stores, pawnshops, local DJs, and
small record distributors like Macola. He attracted customers from Hawthorne, Gardena, Carson, Compton, Crenshaw,
and South Central Los Angeles, many of them local DJs who
spent hours hunched over the crates, fingering through records, listening to Yano's selections, and purchasing the tracks
that elicited the most enthusiastic responses from the swap-
meet crowds. "If it was good," Yano recalled, "kids would start
to break dance right there in the stall." By 1984, LA's major

Fig 3.I Customers sift through records in Steve Yano's booth at the Roadium Open Air Market. Courtesy of Susan Yano.

labels were jockeying for his attention, hoping "the uncrowned king of a swap meet music underground" would stock their latest releases. Yano became, as he remembered, "for a while a very important guy" who regularly convened with promoters and distributers after hours, often arranging late-night meetings in parking lots to exchange cash for wholesale product. "It was like we were dealing drugs."[18]

Eric Wright viewed Steve Yano as a model of free enterprise—a self-made businessman who enjoyed flexible work hours, financial independence, workplace autonomy, and local notoriety. In a Reagan-era economy sharply divided between lucrative, white-collar careers for those with college degrees and connections, and low-wage service jobs that provided little in the way of dignity and opportunity for advancement, Eric Wright had first taken a dangerous, alternative path: the dope game. But Yano revealed to him yet another aboveboard option for making ends meet—and one built around music, no less. Even allowing for some parking-lot meetings and off-the-books transactions, record vending was a legitimate trade, and Eric Wright wanted in. "Don't do it. It's a bad business," Steve Yano told him, thinking of the slim profit margins as well as all the crate-hauling. Yano, who had dropped out of a psychology program at CSU Los Angeles to build his mobile sales business, warned Wright against making the leap. "I can show you how, but don't do it."[19]

The hard truth about Yano's business, in fact, echoed the disappointment Wright had experienced during his short stint as a party promoter. Spurred by the successes of South LA's mobile DJ luminaries, like Rodger Clayton and Alonzo Williams, Wright had attempted to form his own mobile dance business in Compton. He rented small event spaces around the city and hired his friend Andre "Dr. Dre" Young, a local DJ with a record collection and a Numark DM-1550 mixer.[20] Backyard barbecues and house parties kept the duo busy, but Wright ultimately concluded about event management, as he did about record retailing, that it did not offer any sure route to riches. Still, both experiences gave Wright precious insight into the workings of South LA's enterprising black youth music culture. With greater knowledge of the various institutions involved, he homed in on the independent record labels on display at the Roadium, and the Macola Record Company favored by the region's most influential DJs.[21]

"He wanted to run his own label," O'Shea "Ice Cube" Jackson remembered.[22] Lacking recording experience and naive to the ways of the industry, Wright tapped the knowledge of others in his circle. Repeat visits to Steve Yano's re-

cord stall exposed him to a slew of Los Angeles-based re-
cord labels owned and run by black entrepreneurs, including
Egyptian Empire Records, Fresh Beat, Dream Team, Party
Crew, and Kru-Cut Records, all of them using the Macola
Record Company for manufacturing and distribution. His
old friend Dr. Dre had experience and connections to share,
mainly from working with Alonzo "Grand Master Lonzo"
Williams. Dre had earned a recurring DJ gig at Lonzo's nightclub, Eve After Dark, and then an invitation to join World
Class Wreckin' Cru, the electro-rap ensemble Lonzo had
pulled together to make music for Kru-Cut, his own label.
Wright asked Dre to set up an introduction. As Lonzo remembered, the five-foot-five Compton kid who made a
habit of keeping rolls of cash stuffed in his white tube socks
came to him with "a pile of money as big as [a] bowl" and a
request to "put him into the game of how to make it happen."[23] The young man known around town as "Little Rat"
was a quick study, and within months he had launched a
record label called Ruthless.

Taking cues from Lonzo's experience with Kru-Cut,
Wright scouted Don Macmillan's Macola offices in Hollywood as a potential home for Ruthless, and eagerly drafted a
stable of artists he trusted to know "what the kids in Compton are feeling." Wright went to familiar haunts to find talent,
including the Southside Crips neighborhood he covered as a
dope dealer.[24] There he found Clarence Lars, a high schooler
who spun records under the moniker "DJ Train," and Lorenzo Patterson, a friend of Lars who flirted with the idea of
gangbanging but instead made "little street tapes" under the
name "Master Ren."[25]

True to his label's "ruthless" branding, Wright also poached
Kru-Cut's most gifted artist, Dr. Dre, the star of the label's

World Class Wreckin' Cru. As a drive-time DJ on KDAY's airwaves, Dre had become a celebrated tastemaker, outranking even the mobile DJ titans who had reigned in the early 1980s. With the Wreckin' Cru, he had even managed to secure a major label deal at Epic, the home of Grammy Award–winning artist Michael Jackson. Nevertheless, Dre had been dissatisfied. A skilled audio engineer and an experienced disc jockey with an ear for "what people will like," he wanted more creative control at Kru-Cut, and often fumed through recording sessions with his Wreckin' Cru bandmates. Dr. Dre was an aspiring rap-music producer tired of crafting electro ballads and performing dance moves in medical scrubs. "I wanted to get up outta that shit," he recalled. When Wright approached him about joining Ruthless, Dre accepted the offer.[26]

Asserting his own vision for Ruthless Records, Dr. Dre invited a fellow Kru-Cut artist to be the label's songwriter. Ice Cube had a knack for crafting verses that were "totally street, totally dirty"—a standout skill that landed him gigs at Skateland USA, performing for Compton's toughest audiences. With Dre playing instrumental versions of popular rap records, Cube rapped obscene parodies, including "Diane, Diane," a pornographic take on UTFO's "Roxanne, Roxanne," and "My Penis," based on Run-DMC's "My Adidas." The duo also performed "Dopeman," an explicit composition that Ice Cube wrote as a "kind of funny" tribute to the neighborhood rock dealer.[27] His performances delighted Skateland's discerning young partygoers, most of them clad in red, claiming gang sets, and "prepared to toss a bad act out." Together, he and Dre discovered a formula that made them Skateland favorites.[28]

Kru-Cut, however, censored Ice Cube. By 1986, his group Stereo Crew had secured their own treasured deal with Epic

Records. But Epic promptly dropped the trio after its bawdy single "She's a Skag" flopped.[29] Emancipated from big-label restraints, the group sought to reset, and Stereo Crew became Criminals In Action (CIA). But in renewed contract negotiations with Kru-Cut, Lonzo insisted that the trio embrace a softer image, do less of "the hardcore stuff," and drop "Criminals" from its name. Cube agreed to clean up his rhymes and rename his group "Cru In Action," but he did so grudgingly. At the label's direction, he found himself whitewashing his music and his persona—most literally when Dre asked him to copy the "loud and screaming" style of the Beastie Boys, the all-white group that was New York's latest rap sensation.[30] Feeling "out of character" at Kru-Cut, he found he was unable to do what he did best: write authentic street tales for and about the homeboys from around the way.[31] Dr. Dre knew Cube was unfulfilled at Kru-Cut and convinced the songwriter to join him at Ruthless.[32]

With the help of Dr. Dre and Ice Cube, and the financial resources from his shadowy past, Eric Wright built a Los Angeles music business that encouraged its artists to be "as hardcore as you want to be."[33] By the end of 1986, the year Run-DMC waged its publicity war against LA's "ghetto toughs" and "gangsters," he founded Ruthless Records, a business rooted in the reality that those same toughs and gangsters were LA's most loyal rap fans and the counterintuitive belief that their stories were marketable. As Ice Cube would say years later, Wright "made it okay for all artists to be themselves; you don't have to put up all the front. You can be as hardcore as you want to be and still make money like the bubblegum pop stars—and be just as famous as the bubblegum pop artists, who have to put on a facade to be that."[34] Because Ruthless Records urged its artists to "be what you

Fig 3.2 An early pressing of "The Boyz-N-The Hood," manufactured at Macola Record Co. in Hollywood. The label of the twelve-inch single features the LA-inspired Ruthless logo created by Los Angeles artist Darryl "Lyrrad" Davis under Eric Wright's direction. It also refers to "High Powered Productions," the short-lived mobile DJ partnership between Wright and Andre "Dr. Dre" Young. After creating Ruthless, the two repurposed the name for production credits. From the author's collection.

want to be, say what you want to say," the label became a plat-form for artistic experimentation, honest storytelling, and youth rebellion. For the region's so-called gangsters—kids in places like Compton, Long Beach, and South Central who collected mix tapes, filled dance clubs, and bought records—it set the standard for LA rap.

■    ■    ■

In the fall of 1987, KDAY's music director Greg Mack got hold of a record by a new artist named "Eazy E": "The Boyz-N-The Hood." The twelve-inch single's sleeve was imprinted with the Macola Record Company logo, like most locally pressed vinyl in the KDAY stacks. But the label visible through its circular cut-out was something altogether new. The red-and-black sticker featured a banner illustration by local flyer artist Darryl Davis signaling a hard-edged spirit. Flanked by a sketch of the Downtown LA skyline on the left and the iconic hilltop Hollywood sign on the right were the big, bold letters of "RUTHLESS," drawn as if made of chrome, steel, and brick (Fig. 3.2).[35]

Eazy-E was Eric Wright himself and "The Boyz-N-The Hood" was the first track released by Ruthless Records. It deviated from many of the records popular with KDAY listeners at the time. Compared to the up-tempo electro rap that Macola continued to stamp out by the pallet-load through the mid-1980s, "Boyz" was minimalist, bass-heavy, and sluggish. Its lyrics, written by Ice Cube, were plot-driven narratives, in contrast to the loosely constructed rap braggadocio that characterized most hip-hop records at the time. "Boyz" chronicled a day in the life of a young LA street hustler; its verses, each more cinematic than the last, included a run-in with an ill-fated drug addict and a violent encounter with a girlfriend's father. Eazy-E's character watches as LA cops arrest two friends, and, later, inside a courtroom, witnesses a wild scene involving a judge, a defendant, and an Uzi-toting woman named "Suzy." Ice Cube's story unfolds, in Eazy-E's squeaky timbre, as a lurid black comedy in which every reference to crime, vice, and violence further impresses on the listener that, as the chorus declares, *"the boys in the hood are always hard."*[36]

From a production standpoint, "Boyz" was not entirely groundbreaking. In the context of the stylistic and even philosophical shifts going on in mid-1980s hip-hop, it was more a tribute to that metamorphosis. The record's producer and engineer, Andre "Dr. Dre" Young, borrowed heavily from two sources: Russell Simmons's Def Jam Recordings catalog, and the rhythms of Queens musician Larry Smith. The latter, as mentioned in Chapter 2, had pioneered the stripped-down, big-beat sound associated with early risk-takers Run-DMC and Whodini. Dre arranged the music for "Boyz" by peppering Smith's thumping drum pattern in Whodini's "I'm a Ho" with samples from Def Jam artists Original Concept, LL Cool J, and the Beastie Boys. The result was a composite of edgy records, each one its own rebellion against hip-hop's Sugar Hill Records days and the genre's old guard.

"Boyz" leaned on the work of a generation of artists and promoters—especially Russell Simmons—who, by cleaving hip-hop from its disco roots, saved the music from becoming obsolete. The goal was to grow the audience, particularly among young, black listeners, and that is what happened on the West Coast. In Los Angeles, music fans had favored, to varying degrees, funk, new wave, and electro over New York's first recorded rap hits. Mobile DJs and their black audiences preferred, for instance, Prince, Zapp, Funkadelic, Yaz, and Kraftwerk to the repackaged disco that Sugar Hill Records marketed as hip-hop. The stripped-down, big-beat arrangements that Russell Simmons's producer, Larry Smith, created for Run-DMC's debut were a welcome departure from the sing-song rhymes and lavish melodies of the Sugarhill Gang—and they had another prized feature. With digital booms and claps that, just like the electric bass in early-1980s funk and electro, thumped aggressively, they were valued by a lowrider car culture in which car stereos were judged by how effectively they rattled trunks and turned heads.

Music critics classified this fresher iteration of hip-hop, exemplified by the production of Larry Smith and Rick Rubin, as "hardcore," echoing the language used to describe contemporaneous developments in punk rock. But pinned to hip-hop, the label was also, often, a reference to hardcore lyrics. With a 1982 hit record called "The Message," there was a dramatic shift in rap content. This bleak, cinematic tale from Grandmaster Flash and the Furious Five, produced by Sylvia Robinson's Sugar Hill label, depicted the city as "*a jungle sometimes*," filled with temptation and danger around every corner. The record was, compositionally, a standard, disco-inspired hip-hop track, but Melvin "Melle Mel" Glover's verses were atypical in their explicit references to grim subjects: urban decay, poverty, and crime, "*thugs, pimps, and pushers*," hostile "*bill collectors*" and vulnerable children. It was bold songwriting characterized by a kind of literary realism, which confounded the critics as much as it seduced hip-hop audiences, especially those who saw reflections of their own communities in the lyrics.

Rap artists after "The Message" did more than pick up the thread. They wove this new "street" aesthetic into the whole fabric of 1980s hip-hop. Los Angeles rapper Ice-T explained that he had his eyes opened to how LA style would depart from "the blueprint" laid out by New York rappers.[37] Seeing how audiences responded to LA artists "making records totally street" was a revelation: "It blew my mind." After that, he used "the whole West Coast player life" as both trope and tenor—a storytelling device and an attitude. Indeed, in the wake of Melle Mel's chart-topping rhymes about black dreams deferred, a whole crop of hip-hop artists started creating what Ice-T called "reality rap," telling stories of hard times and hardened characters. By 1983, hip-hop records leaned toward the noir, full of narration of the dangers lurking in cities. Over hardcore beats, they described crooks and suckers, gangsters and cops, and, a favorite topic after 1983, dope dealers slinging rock cocaine.

Harlem's "Kurtis Blow" Walker took part in this shift. Following early successes with his 1979 "Christmas Rappin'" and 1980 "The Breaks," he recorded "8 Million Stories" in 1984, a *Billboard*-charting single about *"the mean streets and the ghetto culture."* With suspenseful piano riffs, a grinding electric guitar solo, and a guest appearance by Run-DMC, the track described dysfunction inside New York—*"a crazy city, man."* Kurtis Blow recited his verses *"without pity,"* detailing the lives of losers, including a *"fresh kid"* turned *"freebase jerk"* who, in the end, *"lost his car, his house, his kids, his wife"* and *"his life."*[38] Run-DMC's debut single, "It's Like That," the 1983 record that spurred the group's commercial ascent, similarly employed the era's message-rap rubric. Emcees Run and DMC traded verses about the strivings of working people whose *"bills rise higher every day,"* the spread of poverty and disillusion, wars abroad, and *"street soldiers killing the elderly"* back home. Nearly replicating "It's Like That" in style and substance, Brooklyn-based Divine Sounds had a 1984 hit with "What People Do For Money," an electro-inspired street parable about straying from the straight and narrow.[39] By 1985, music journalist Nelson George was identifying this street realism as the genre's main theme: "You can call it rap, hip hop or street, but it really is a way of hearing music—and partying hard—

that expresses the experiences and attitudes of a great many inner city kids."[40]

But street rap quickly advanced beyond biographical, cautionary tales; within just a few years of "The Message," it was presenting unbridled outlaw anthems. It now celebrated inner-city heroes of every ilk, some of them based on actual people but most of them archetypes reflecting fantasies and aspirations. These were caricatures of Casanovas, Robin Hoods, braggarts, fly millionaires, and presidents. And there were gangsters, too. In 1985, Def Jam artist LL Cool J claimed the "hip-hop gangster" mantle. On the monster hit "I Can't Live Without My Radio," he flaunted street credentials—*"My story is rough, my neighborhood is tough"*—and claimed to be devastating both in bed and on the microphone—*"Pullin' all the girls, takin' out MCs."* Like any outlaw worth his salt, the Queens rapper also fashioned himself as a menace to society— *"Terrorizing my neighbors with the heavy bass / I keep the suckas in fear by the look on my face."*[41] Bronx rapper KRS-One played the sinsemilla-puffing vigilante, shooting down a crack dealer and a pack of thieves in the Boogie Down Productions single "My 9mm Goes Bang." Chuck D issued more warnings to *"suckers,"* hinted at homicide, and compared his artistry to an Uzi submachine gun in Public Enemy's debut single "Miuzi Weighs a Ton." In "I'm Fly," Kool G. Rap rode around New York in a *"Caddy Seville,"* defying traffic laws, skirting cops, and giving *"some money to the poor,"* all while basking in his outrageous wealth—*"my pockets resemble Manhattan Bank."* A teenage William "Rakim" Griffin emerged in 1986 on "Eric B. Is President," paying tribute to DJ Eric B. while proclaiming himself as the best rapper alive.[42]

Thanks to this hip-hop reboot, the genre was at last gaining traction in commercial markets and growing its fan base.

Reflecting on it later, however, Shawn "Jay-Z" Carter said there was something "missing" from the street canon. The Brooklyn rapper wondered how it was that these characters in the music "were stepping through the broken glass and into the Caddy." He was one of those real inner-city kids Nelson George alluded to, but there was little in hip-hop music that resonated with his own experiences and attitudes, growing up in a housing project where "crack was everywhere." In Jay-Z's world, selling dope just made sense if a family needed to pay bills or a kid wanted the privilege of wearing clean sneakers to school—but references to the illicit that were not cartoonishly allegorical were hard to find in early 1980s rap. The New York hip-hop vanguard offered up "hustler" characters as heroes and antiheroes, but, as Jay-Z noted, the music failed to humanize them.[43]

Outside the New York sphere, more authentically street-hardened voices were emerging, many of them aiming for something one music critic described as a "no-holds-barred" approach to revealing the "the grimier side" of life. In Northern California, East Oakland rapper Todd "Too $hort" Shaw amassed a local rap empire by recasting message raps and battle rhymes into "playboy" narratives crafted to resonate with the local pimps, players, and dope dealers who were his best customers. On his earliest independent records, including *Don't Stop Rappin'* and *Players*, $hort offered tributes to Oakland, the *"City of Dope,"* celebrating rather than decrying its reputation as the *"Wild, Wild West"*—a place where *"the strong control the fake"* and where one's *"game . . . controls the lane."* Too $hort offered autobiographical sketches about befriending *"dealers and crooks,"* and he bragged about the *"gangsta waves"* in his hair, his *"gangsta ride"* outside, and the *"gangsta rap"* he performed.[44]

Philadelphia rapper Jesse "Schoolly D" Weaver raised eyebrows in 1985 with a trio of similar hustler-inspired tracks, "Gangster Boogie," "Gucci Time," and "P.S.K.—What Does It Mean?" In "Gangster Boogie," Schoolly D boasted of his *"gangster lean"* and battled *"a sucker emcee"* while working *"on the corner, selling some weed."* Laced with expletives, "Gucci Time" had Schoolly D addressing the rhetorical question, *"How the fuck didja get so cool, man."* But it was "P.S.K." that truly tested the limits of what could be defined as hardcore. The explicit verses narrated a day in the life of a *"homeboy"* who takes pleasure in the art of *"makin' that cash money,"* gets high with his girl on *"some brew, some J, some coke,"* and then, in the rap battle, pulls a gun on the *"sucker-ass nigga tryin' to sound like me."* Most provocative, however, was Schoolly D's reference—in the very title of the song—to P.S.K., an acronym for the Park Side Killers, one of Philadelphia's most feared black street gangs, and a group in which the rapper himself claimed to be active.[45]

According to Schoolly D, the commercial hip-hop music of the early 1980s featured too much theater and too little reality. "Those [New York] rappers like Run-DMC and the Beastie Boys, they're just playing a role that their producers . . . put together for them," he complained to the *Los Angeles Times* in early 1987. "None of them are for real. They're just spoiled little rich kids that know how to act, basically." His indictment of so-called street rappers as fake—he even called them "corny"—added to Schoolly D's own credibility. He was an independent artist working outside the boundaries of New York, still the sacrosanct dominion of hip hop, but unlike all its stars, he was "for real."[46]

When Ice-T first heard Schoolly D's "P.S.K.—What Does It Mean?," he was spellbound by the thunderous bass and the emcee's relaxed cadence. "It sounded like you were high, the way the beats were echoing," Ice-T remembered, "and his whole delivery was so crazy." It bore little resemblance to rap's usual braggadocio, in part because it was so cinematic and because "nobody had dared make anything that violent yet."[47] For Ice-T, "P.S.K." was also notable for how it represented an urban landscape governed by gangs. Schoolly D's verses, in fact, sounded as if they had been pulled straight from rhymes Ice-T had penned about the Los Angeles Crips. Years before "P.S.K.," Ice-T, a Crip affiliate, wrote from the perspective of an active gangbanger navigating his weekend, first from the seat of his lowrider car—*On the way to the party I was scrapin' and hoppin' / 'Cause I knew by the end of the night there was gonna be some poppin'*"—and then in the thick of a developing street scene—"*I just walked to the corner and listened to them talk / And on the first James Brown record I jumped up and did the Crip walk.*"[48]

Steeped in the trendy, and largely white, downtown hip-hop club scene, Ice-T initially curated a rap persona to appeal to the West Coast Planet Rock crowds. "I was listenin' to New York rap and attempting to rap about that particular type of shit," he remembered. "It wasn't me."[49] But in 1985, he was exposed to Schoolly D, foulmouthed and cool, and as provocative as the stars of the Blaxploitation films he consumed. In "P.S.K." Ice-T found a rap style he liked and knew he could use as a vehicle for telling "that drama" he witnessed around his neighborhood. On his 1986 release "6 in the Mornin'" he did just that, taking inspiration from Schoolly D in the low-frequency 808 drums, the casual delivery, and the harrowing urban adventures. The result was a speaker-rattling track unlike anything Ice-T had recorded previously—a massive local hit about eluding the police and traversing through the streets of Los Angeles where *"The Batterram's rolling, rocks are a thing / Life has no meaning and money is king."*[50]

By 1987, the year Eazy-E's "The Boyz-N-The Hood" debuted on KDAY in Los Angeles, rap music characterized as "street" had become commercially viable. A diverse league of young artists, to varying degrees, were channeling Melle Mel and testing the lyrical and musical boundaries of hip-hop. The platform for such experimentation was an expansive, national fan base, which included budding markets for street rap in the West. As the genre's fandom ballooned in the mid-1980s, however, virtually all of those who reaped industry rewards—who picked up major label deals, who booked arena concert tours, and who earned entry into celebrity circles—remained moored to the Northeast.

Some, like Too $hort in Oakland, 2 Live Crew in Miami, and Ghetto Boys in Houston (later to be restyled as Geto Boys), chose to carve out space for themselves in hip-hop by focusing on local consumers. Others, like Ice-T in LA and Schoolly D in Philadelphia, took issue with New York's monopoly and defied it by making music provocative enough to yank attention away from the Bronx, Brooklyn, Queens, and Long Island.[51] Eric "Eazy-E" Wright and his partners at Ruthless Records managed to do both.

Conceptually, "The Boyz-N-The Hood" was as niche as Toddy Tee's 1985 "Batterram" mixtape. Both were dreamt up for peers within the same predominantly black South Los Angeles youth dance scene, created by artists who performed within that circuit and were, thus, intimately familiar with its patrons and their tastes. Just as the celebrated "Batterram" tape was a product of Toddy Tee's partnership with celebrated local DJ Mixmaster Spade, "Boyz" was an outgrowth of the famed Compton performances that made Dr. Dre and Ice

Cube hometown stars. Toddy Tee borrowed the instrumen-
tals of current New York hip-hop hits to create LA anthems.
UTFO's "Roxanne, Roxanne" and Whodini's 1984 hit "Freaks
Come Out at Night" were remade as "Rockman, Rockman"
and "The Clucks Come Out at Night," tracks produced exclusively for West Coast ears. In that tradition, "Boyz" appropriated some of New York hip-hop's most recognizable compo-
nents, including Larry Smith's bass-slapping production on
Whodini's "I'm a Ho" (the very song Whodini performed on
the Long Beach Arena stage in 1986 when violence broke
out). Like Toddy Tee, Dr. Dre pinpointed what it was that
made the latest in street rap palatable in places like South
Central, Inglewood, Compton, and Long Beach—and popular
enough to surpass the electro-rap that had been the bedrock of
LA black youth culture. New York rap served as a source of input to local music innovation and local kids' entertainment.[52]

Also extending the lineage of Toddy Tee's community-fo-
cused rhymes about rock houses and the LAPD's battering
ram, Ice Cube's own verses for "Boyz" were written in the LA
vernacular of drugs, classic cars, and police abuse, and engaged with topics relevant to the South Central songwriter,
his friends, and the people he observed around him. So alien
to out-of-towners were the references to, for instance, an *"Al-
pine"* (a type of car stereo system), *"makin' that GTA"* (Grand
Theft Auto), and *"my 6-4"* (1964 Chevrolet Impala) that
when Dr. Dre sent the song to a New York group to record,
they rejected it, under the assumption that no one would
understand the lyrics.[53] A mention of the *"Times front page"*
that referred to the *Los Angeles Times* and another to *"the
county jail,"* regional shorthand for Los Angeles County's
oldest and most notorious correctional facility, were further

clues to Southern California listeners that this was a track made for them.[54]

"Boyz" embodied the Ruthless Records project. The label was founded as a Los Angeles enterprise, staffed with LA talent, produced and marketed in LA, and meant to be representative of LA—a positioning signaled not only by its logo design but in its first release. "Boyz" was crafted to be a colloquial street-rap record, from Dr. Dre's Alpine-rattling production, to Ice Cube's use of local slang, to the familiar vocals of the hustler known around the way as both "Little Rat" and "Eazy-E." The hope was that the record would generate buzz in South Los Angeles County, with a little help from KDAY, local DJs, and the region's record distributors. Eazy-E's methods for promoting the record reflected this expectation. The Compton kid who seemed to know everyone relied, pragmatically, on all his old community associations, from LA gangs to local record sellers. He passed out cassette tapes of "Boyz" to gang youth and other street VIPs who, in exchange for the free music, promised to drum up demand; he drove around LA County in Dr. Dre's burgundy Suzuki Samurai hawking vinyl copies of "Boyz" stacked in the trunk; he parceled out freshly pressed twelve-inch records to music venders respected among local DJs; and he handed off a copy to LA's most trusted trendsetter, Greg Mack.[55]

Although it took months, the promotional game plan worked. By the end of 1987, "The Boyz-N-The Hood" had captivated Ruthless Records' target audiences in Southern California. For Steve Yano, the baron of the Roadium swap meet, just playing "Boyz" over the speakers in his stall turned the record into his best seller. KDAY's music director, Greg Mack, witnessed a similar frenzy after he debuted the track on air. "Within 24 hours it was the most requested song," he remembered. One of Mack's DJs, Julio G, who was well-versed in both regional and national hip-hop styles, was impressed by every aspect of the record, especially how it ventured into taboo topics like drugs and gun violence: "Nobody was doing it like that." It also seduced young black filmmaker John Singleton, an LA native who first heard "Boyz" as a student at the University of Southern California and later directed a film inspired by the track. Singleton was especially struck by the song's references to a Los Angeles rarely depicted in popular culture, and by allusions to "stuff that we knew about on the block." As an artist already committed to disrupting conventional, predominantly white, narratives about Los Angeles, Singleton was riveted to hear local black vernacular and the colorful language about car culture, street posturing, and LA law enforcement. "We loved it," he remembered, "because it would give a voice to . . . where we're from . . . what we're about."[56]

For all the energy funneled into local promotion for the "Boyz" record, few at Ruthless expected sustained success to come from it; they were not even sure, as Ice Cube said, that the group's music would "see the light of day."[57] Cube and Dr. Dre savored the process of building the track. (Later, the group recalled laughing as Dre coached a reluctant and awkward Eazy-E through every rapped line.) Much as they enjoyed the camaraderie and a degree of creative latitude lacking in past projects, they figured any hype around their Ruthless Records work would be short-lived. Initially, Eazy-E was just as bearish in his predictions for "Boyz" and for his own rap career. He had hoped simply to parlay whatever attention the track garnered for his record company into a spotlight for the label's other act, J.J. Fad, a female rap crew from Rialto, a small city in San Bernardino County.

By the end of the year, however, there were signs that "Boyz" had the potential to be more than a KDAY listener favorite or a springboard for another project. From Los Angeles, word about the Ruthless record began spreading via friend and family networks to other black music markets. In Houston, Cincinnati, Memphis, and other cities, small, independent shops rushed to stock the record. "As soon as we got 'em, we sold 'em," Memphis record distributer Johnny Phillips later recalled. Eazy-E, as part of his efforts to build brand recognition for his label, arranged a meeting with one of Lonzo Williams's Hollywood industry connections, talent manager Jerry Heller. Heller, who had worked with the Who, Marvin Gaye, and Black Sabbath, among others, listened to "Boyz" and came away convinced that it was "the most important song that I had heard in over twenty-five years." It was an example of honest rebellion, with "no apologies, no excuses," he said. To his middle-class, Jewish ears, it sounded like "just the straight undistilled street telling me things I had never heard before."[58] It was fresh evidence for Eazy-E that the future of Ruthless could be in gangster tales and car culture—a distinctly LA version of street rap.

Reaching audiences outside of California would, however, be a challenge. Three issues in particular threatened to stifle the success of LA hip-hop artists. First, within the New York dominated hip-hop industry, the Los Angeles rap music scene was still dismissed by most, scorned by some. In the early 1980s, a small cadre of rap's youngest and most progressive go-getters, including New York promoter Russell Simmons, recognized the potential in LA's sprawling mobile

DJ dance scene for artist exposure. Ignored as an incubator for rap talent by even the most perceptive East Coast industry figures, Los Angeles was coveted by these rap pioneers for its cultural infrastructure. It was a place where New York hip-hop could sell, and where East Coast artists could become as celebrated as they were as local heroes in places like Queens and the Bronx. The most savvy players in the early 1980s saw the path to rap stardom leading right through Los Angeles, and that theory borne out by the success of Run-DMC.[59]

The brawling at Run-DMC's 1986 Long Beach Arena concert seemed to threaten not only the trio's career but the very existence of hip-hop as a commercially solvent music genre. Punk music had been forced to the margins of the industry, and in the wake of the Long Beach debacle some anticipated the same fate for rap—or worse. The *Los Angeles Times* put the question in a headline that summer: "Can Rap Survive the Gang War?" To protect record sales and appease moral crusaders, Run-DMC condemned the LA gangs they blamed—along with the police and press—for the concert violence. In doing so, the Queens-based trio inserted themselves into a gang crisis they did not understand, and ultimately ceded a region that had helped make them the reigning kings of hip-hop. Indignant that gang youths—many of them loyal rap fans—did not respect the arena as the performers' turf, and quick to call for "sterner measures" to control them, Run-DMC and their handlers rejected Los Angeles as a barbarous town that did not reflect the hip-hop spirit. The Los Angeles rap music scene had earned a spotlight, just not yet for its talent.[60]

The Long Beach Arena spectacle produced sensationalized coverage of rap fan rioting. But by the end of 1986, the public fascination with black gang culture faded, and brief attempts at generating dialogue around LA's festering problems—the county's dispossession of poor black districts and the militarized policing of these communities being just two examples—gave way, once again, to a preference for La-La Land fantasies that emphasized the region's idyllic weather, wealth, and whiteness. And, once again, LA rappers contended with an "authenticity problem." The perpetual myth of Los Angeles as America's promised land ran counter to local rap artists' attempts to stake a claim within a genre of music predicated on hardship. Nelson George, the editor in charge of black music coverage at *Billboard*, noted in early 1988 that his fellow New Yorkers, even after all the hoopla around the Long Beach Arena riot, still "considered Los Angeles 'too soft' to be a factor in hip-hop."[61]

While Los Angeles fans and industry veterans like Jerry Heller appreciated the provocative lyrics in "Boyz," Los Angeles street rap was still a peculiar thing in the late 1980s. The concept seemed absurd to many who lived far from the area—and even to some inside LA. In the Reagan Era, hip-hop had become a national phenomenon but in the public imagination it was inextricably linked to the inner city, to hardship, and overwhelmingly to New York. By 1985, rap music had already reached the point of being venerated as the authentic poetry of the street. It was a product of housing projects, tenements, and subway systems. In the words of *Black Beat* editor Steve Ivory, "This kind of music, hard-edged and urban, breeds in close quarters." An A&R executive at MCA cited "environment" as key; hip-hop artists, he noted, earned currency in the market for their lived experiences, and the more harrowing the better. In that regard, Ivory thought life in LA was too comfortable. "We've got

ghettos and people starving," he allowed, "but it's still easier
when you've got palm trees and good weather." Many of LA's
rappers lived in neighborhoods canopied by both. Rudy
Pardee of the LA Dream Team mused that his group's roots
in "sunny Southern California" might be why its output was
"more musical, more up-tempo" than New York crowds preferred. Some people thought what LA produced was "hard-
edged," Ivory said, but it was "just limp compared to a guy in
the Bronx with no water and it's 30 below."[62]

The third disadvantage for budding LA rap enterprises
like Ruthless Records was that most emerged just at the moment when radio had begun snubbing independent artists.
As pop music journalist Patrick Goldstein reported in 1986,
competition for advertising dollars and concerns about a federal probe into illegal pay-to-play programming decisions
put radio on the defensive. The once-radical industry, Goldstein explained, had morphed into a model of "new conservatism." Program directors nationwide tightened playlists and
shied away from unknown, small-label artists. Like punk
rock and heavy metal artists, hip-hop acts tended to record
with independent labels, which meant fewer promotional resources and no built-in clout to influence the radio programmers who broke hits. "The bottom line," one radio industry
veteran explained, "is that the young groups are getting fro-
zen out—no one wants to touch them."[63] In Los Angeles,
young local artists had KDAY, a haven for independent black
music in the Reagan Era. But outside of that market, radio
exposure was elusive for most hip-hop artists.

The Ruthless team therefore had valid reasons to expect
that "The Boyz-N-The Hood" would be little more than an
exercise in conceptualizing and producing a song. Eazy-E
had funded an experiment with few predictable outcomes

beyond getting a professionally recorded track that he could stamp with the Ruthless Records brand, reproduce, and sell. But the Ruthless experiment generated something else: a provocation. Eazy-E's original goal for Ruthless was not the incitement of broad public outrage or curiosity, but both proved critical to the label's ability to surmount industry obstacles. And that ascendency was contingent upon the events framing the release of its debut rap record.

■    ■    ■

When 1987 came to a close, Los Angeles County officials tallied nearly four hundred gang-related deaths for the year. The news of this record number of homicides reminded Angelenos living in the region's poorest districts that Southern California, along with its "palm trees and good weather," played host to the most dangerous street gangs in the country. The statistic also helped municipal leaders in the city of Los Angeles and Compton secure funding for gang suppression and anti-drug campaigns, and fueled support for increases in spending on state corrections, including the expansion of California's prisons, at a time when the state had less to spend.[64]

Outside of LA's south side, however, the number did little to arouse public concern. The crisis, as observed by those immersed in it, was contained within the county's predominantly black and Latino districts. White locals and most municipal leaders—particularly those representing more affluent communities west of the Harbor Freeway—could regard LA street gangs as deplorable yet tucked away, out of sight, buffered from the rest of the region by socioeconomic and racial boundaries. As a young man coming of age in South

Central, Ice Cube was keenly aware of the public indifference. "Our friends get killed," he once told *Spin*, but through much of the 1980s, "nothing was said about that."[65]

Karen Toshima's death altered the narrative about LA's gangs. The Japanese-American woman was shot on January 30, 1988, while strolling after dinner in the Westwood Village. *Time* magazine has described this posh business district near UCLA as a "glittering enclave of restaurants, shops and theaters."[66] It is a predominantly white and affluent neighborhood bordered by the whiter and richer neighborhoods of Bel Air and Beverly Hills—but that night, two black youths, members of warring sets of the LA Crips, fired at one another across the busting Village sidewalks. That there would be a bystander shooting death in Los Angeles was not unusual, but the particular setting of this one was. It became a bombshell story overnight, with cable news reporters recounting the story of a brilliant and admirable young woman out celebrating her achievements, and the lurid details of Toshima's final moments. Among the national print headlines were "Gang Violence Shocks Los Angeles" and "The Price of Life in Los Angeles." Even the London paper *The Times* proclaimed "Gangs Invade Yuppie Haven." Feature stories like "Violence in Los Angeles" revealed a sudden sense of vulnerability among those Angelenos who, until that January night, had been comfortably insulated from the region's brewing troubles. A racially-charged narrative emerged about a city under siege, where, thanks to weak law enforcement and the failures of local leaders to address the root causes of juvenile crime, the invisible boundaries that separated havens of white, middle-class life from poorer neighborhoods had been breached by black teens armed with pistols.[67] Within weeks of Toshima's death, 1988 had been branded "The

Year of the Gang," and Los Angeles was deemed the foun-
tainhead of the crisis.[68] As Ice Cube remembered, a "girl
got killed in Westwood, a white neighborhood" and white
Los Angeles, along with the rest of the country, began to pay
attention.[69]

As had been the case in the early 1980s, some of LA's African-American citizens and their leaders responded to the
spike in violent crime by making appeals for greater police
protection in their communities. County Supervisor Kenneth
Hahn, a white public official beloved by his mostly black constituents in South Central, called for stronger law enforcement, emphasizing that people of Los Angeles "can't go to
church or stand on a corner without fear of some gang taking
an Uzi and spraying them all."[70] The editors of the *Los Angeles Sentinel* supported Supervisor Hahn's demand, reminding readers of the dozens of black innocents killed by stray
bullets in black neighborhoods. The paper expressed hope,
darkly, that the death of a privileged Asian woman inside an
affluent white enclave of West LA would draw more attention
to a crisis long neglected by city, county, and federal officials.[71] In concert with the black press, local citizen groups
such as the South Central Organizing Committee and the
United Neighborhoods Organization worked to use the spotlight cast on the Toshima tragedy to expose the civic divest-
ment crippling black communities like theirs.[72]

Karen Toshima's death and the public outcry it engen-
dered provided a powerful mandate for Los Angeles Police
Chief Daryl Gates in his years-long campaign to expand the
scope of his anti-gang programs. Even among black Angelenos and community leaders who had in the past castigated
law enforcement officials for racial bigotry and overreach,
voices arose in support of tougher policing. People wanted to

see "hard-nosed measures," "no mercy," and "no half-step-ping."[73] Gates also had the explicit support of municipal leaders, who scrambled to respond forcefully to the high-profile January shooting. Within days of it, the Los Angeles City Council voted to triple the number of patrolmen assigned to Westwood; it approved the hiring of one hundred and fifty new officers; and it approved a boost in annual funding for the LAPD.[74] Meanwhile, LA's city attorney sought a court order to prevent anyone suspected of associating with the Playboy Gangsta Crips, the gang set implicated in the Westwood shooting, from congregating in public spaces in groups of two or more, and from leaving home after 7:00 PM for a reason other than work. A Los Angeles Superior Court judge ultimately ruled the attorney's "vagrancy order" unconstitutional, but the message about the threat of black youth had already registered on the public.[75] In Sacramento, the state legislature also acted swiftly, crafting a bill to increase penalties—including new mandatory sentencing rules—for any felony committed by someone found connected to a gang organization, however loosely. The Street Terrorism Enforcement and Prevention (STEP) Act of 1988 was cosponsored by two Los Angeles Democrats (one of them being South Central Assemblywoman Gwen Moore) and it passed with bipartisan support. Governor George Deukmejian signed the STEP Act into law in September.[76]

With renewed support among city, county, and state leaders, Police Chief Gates gambled on shock and awe. He announced "Operation Hammer," an aggressive anti-gang program which the LAPD had been quietly implementing already in the months prior to the Westwood shooting. Now in the open, it expanded more loudly. As Gates told reporters, thirty Operation Hammer officers would be deployed to hunt

Karen Toshima's killer. But the unit's primary objective would be to round up as many suspected juvenile delinquents as possible, in what the chief referred to as "gang sweeps." The mission was, as he emphasized, to "make war" on all the "rotten little cowards" terrorizing the city.[77]

To this end, Gates resurrected his department's battering ram, the six-ton military-surplus armored vehicle customized with a fourteen-foot steel beam. The provocative LAPD vehicle had been retired in the summer of 1985 after only a few forays in SWAT operations. For two years, the only signs of the "Batterram" were in Compton rapper Toddy Tee's popular anthem on the topic and in the hard-to-suppress memories of those it was used against. But the infamous blue vehicle rolled out of storage in the spring of 1988, this time deployed for more than rock house raids.[78] Emboldened by widespread support for Operation Hammer and its gang sweeps, Gates broadcast a stern warning to the youths in South LA's ganglands, the hotbeds of the region's rap music: "The hammer is coming down, and it's going to come down harder and harder and harder."[79]

From February to March, the Chief deployed more than two hundred officers with instructions to "make life miserable" for anyone and everyone associated with gang life. Weekend after weekend, night after night, helicopter searchlights tracked patrol car clusters through "high crime" neighborhoods. Police arrested suspects en masse, issued stacks of citations, seized guns, and impounded cars. As the *Los Angeles Times* reported, "Any young man who flaunted red or blue rags around his head or waist or wrist, or who flashed certain hand signs to passing traffic, or who stood in a distinct slouching posture was fair game." In just four weeks, the Operation Hammer squads had scooped up 563 suspects and the county's Central Jail was filled to near capacity. Police officials boasted that law-abiding citizens of Los Angeles could celebrate the beginning of the end of gang-related violence.[80] The Los Angeles Police Department pointed to progress, at last, in its war on street gangs, but, as Chief Gates announced in early March to a gaggle of news crews, the gang sweeps had only just begun. "We are going to continue to do it over and over and over," Gates declared, promising to "hit them when they least expect it."[81]

In 1988, growing outrage over the "spate of slaughter" in Los Angeles provided the LAPD with the justification it needed to pursue a program of round-the-clock raids in the mostly black communities of South Los Angeles. This was a presidential election year fraught with racially charged rhetoric and featuring the candidacy of Democrat Jesse Jackson, a champion of the black freedom struggle. It might have been expected in such a time that the LAPD sweeps would trigger debates about profiling and civil rights abuses. Instead, Gates's department earned praise from both the right and the left. In support of Operation Hammer, the *Wall Street Journal* reported that, by the end of the spring of 1988, Los Angeles County had already tallied 387 gang-related murders, more than the number counted for the full calendar year of 1987. "To put that level of carnage in perspective," the *Journal* noted, "Chicago police counted 47 gang-related murders last year." In other words, Los Angeles was burdened by a murder rate nine times higher than that of "the nation's former gang capital."[82] Campaigning for president, Republican George H. W. Bush praised the by-all-means-necessary policing in Los Angeles that spring, and made his own pledge to treat the nation's gang members and drug dealers as "domestic terrorists."[83] Gerald Ivory, a probation officer from South

Central, expressed frustration that even local leaders who were "*supposed* to be serving my community" ultimately condoned Operation Hammer, which he saw as blatant abuse of power.[84] Michael Zinzun, founder of the community organization the Coalition Against Police Abuse, was similarly disappointed by liberal compliance. He warned that the unprecedented aggression of the LAPD's policing—which saw young people being tracked, searched, booked, detained, and in many cases abused merely for being young, black, and in close proximity to a targeted gang sweep—would leave "a stamp on the lives" of a generation of African Americans already burdened by the economic and social challenges of the era. Zinzun told *LA Weekly*, "When those kids are picked up during the sweeps, scars are left."[85]

Hollywood actor and filmmaker Dennis Hopper wanted his feature-length film *Colors* to reveal these scars and more. In the summer of 1987, as LAPD officials began comparing South Los Angeles to war-torn Beirut, Hopper embarked on his ambitious project. Known for his commitment to cinematic realism, the *Easy Rider* star envisioned an unconventional kind of buddy-cop drama, a poignant one examining the people in Los Angeles law enforcement and the young people they pursued. *Colors* would be no *Beverly Hills Cop*. Hopper insisted that his film would be "about real stuff," an honest exposition of race, masculinity, and power in Los Angeles.[86] *Colors* would "wake up some people" to an "all-too-real drama" too long ignored by the general public. Hopper admitted to the *Globe and Mail* that the setup was incongruous: " I mean, you got palm trees and the sun's out and you got violence."[87]

In his quest for cinematic realism, Hopper insisted on filming on location in Watts, where, he said, "these things are really happening." With guidance from his cinematographer,

Haskell Wexler, who earned critical acclaim for his work on a documentary about the My Lai massacre and for *One Flew Over the Cuckoo's Nest,* and with the support of the film's producer Robert Solo, who described black Los Angeles as "the wild west," the *Colors* film crew scouted gritty, sunlit, urban locations miles away from Orion Pictures' gated Hollywood sound stages. They opted for neighborhoods on the south side that, Hopper claimed, "even the police won't go into unless there's a body lying there."[88]

Hopper's crew also managed to solicit assistance from city and county police officials, who wanted to insure that the film accurately portrayed the work of their men and women in blue. The county sheriff's Operation Safe Streets gang investigation bureau and the LAPD's Community Resources Against Street Hoodlums (CRASH) crime prevention unit provided resources and statistics.[89] Robert Duvall and Sean Penn, playing the leading roles of LAPD officers, rode along with CRASH deputies during their patrols through Watts and South Central. CRASH also granted Hopper permission to use the task force's acronym to lend authenticity to the police teams in the script. In addition, county officials provided statistics on gang membership and gang-related crimes—numbers featured in the film's title sequence.[90]

In defiance of the law enforcement agents assisting him, however, Hopper also recruited help from the very criminal networks police targeted. He scouted acting extras who were, according to both police and casting agents, gangbangers. "If I was shooting in a Crip area," Hopper boasted, "I'd use Crips as extras. Shooting in a Blood area, I'd use Bloods."[91] The director also drafted Ice-T, who touted his connections to the Crips and vowed to tap them to deliver a "first-person gangbanging story" for the film's soundtrack.[92]

But by early 1988, before *Colors* was scheduled to debut in April, police officials were crying foul, protesting the film's use of genuine LA gang handles and colors, and referring to it derisively as "the gang movie." For Dennis Hopper, the Westwood shooting and the gang sweeps it spurred only raised the stakes of a project he viewed as "educational."[93] For Los Angeles authorities, *Colors* was an incitement. Wes Mc-Bride, the Los Angeles leader of the California Gang Investigator's Association, warned that Hopper's movie would surely "leave dead bodies from one end of this town to the other." Community leaders working directly with black youth in gang-occupied districts also prepared for the worst. One South Central activist warned black readers of the *Sentinel* that *Colors* "could have a hell of an impact on something that's already out of control."[94] In the days before the film's nationwide release, South Central's Community Youth Gang Service spoke out against Hopper's careless exploitation of real gang rivalries. A representative of the agency told the *New York Times*, "This movie is going to cause a war."[95]

*Colors* was a smash hit. The Orion Pictures production, which debuted in mid-April, grossed nearly $7 million in its opening week, aided by the sustained coverage of the shocking Westwood murder and the related controversy swirling around the film's untimely release. By its third week, *Colors* reached number one in national box office tallies, easily defeating Warner Brothers' blockbuster film *Beetlejuice*, which had opened on four times as many screens. At the end of its ten-week run in theaters, *Colors* had raked in over $46 million in domestic ticket sales, making it a top-grossing film for Orion Pictures.[96]

While Karen Toshima's death in January 1988 introduced the nation to the scope of gang violence in LA, *Colors* created a narrative about it. As Ice-T argued, that narrative did far more to compel the public to consider—and avoid snap judgments about—LA's gang crisis.[97] Film critics and moviegoers, many of them far removed from the urban drama portrayed on screen, celebrated the film's "authentic" glimpse of life on the mean streets of Los Angeles. One reviewer called *Colors* "genuinely three-dimensional and utterly enveloping."[98] Although Hopper had insisted time and again that he had not produced a documentary, and although gang experts disputed many of the film's details, audiences concluded that the movie provided them with rich insight into conflicts playing out inside one of America's most exalted cities. "All I can say is that I'm much more aware of what the residents of South Central LA go through on an everyday basis," said a West Hollywood lawyer. "I feel for them, I really do."[99] A New York moviegoer lamented the "painful, unavoidable implication [that] nothing can stop the gang mentality from perpetuating itself," while a writer for an Australian paper summed up his own response as "a profound sense of relief" that he lived on the other side of the world.[100]

Dennis Hopper's blockbuster, told from the perspective of two white cops, aroused in its audiences some sympathy for a police force locked in what appeared on screen to be a losing battle (an affront to the LAPD according to Chief Daryl Gates, who in the months prior to the film's debut was touting definitive progress in his war on gangs). But *Colors* treated most of its subjects—cop, citizen, and criminal alike—as flawed, driven by complex impulses and ills. For instance, the tension between the two protagonists, LAPD CRASH officers Bob Hodges and Danny "Pac Man" McGavin, was the by-product of their dangerous and demoralizing work; community leaders railed against young gangsters and vied for pro-

Fig 3.3 An Orion Pictures press-kit photo for the 1988 film *Colors* shows director Dennis Hopper and cast members. With many "throwing up gang signs," both real and fabricated, the film's "authenticity" is on bold display. Orion Pictures / Album / Alamy Stock Photo.

tection from local law enforcement while simultaneously protesting police abuse; and individual gang members, like eighteen-year-old Clarence "High Top" Brown, came across as otherwise typical kids navigating atypical social and economic obstacles. Meanwhile, promotional materials for the Hollywood film juxtaposed the necessarily imposing rule of law and the degraded boys forced to prostrate themselves before it.[101] Even where it indulged in overt caricatures, the film effectively tangled portrayals of good and evil, allowing some to argue that *Colors* humanized its young black subjects, others to charge that the movie glorified street crime, and still others to see Hopper's cops as do-gooders, albeit with some brutish tendencies (Figure 3.3). Ice Cube assessed the film as too sympathetic to the LAPD, thinking it did little more than "show the gangbanging from the police point of view."[102]

LAPD Chief Gates was not amused; he was adamant that sympathetic portrayals of gang culture turned thugs into celebrities. Even as he relied on press coverage of LA's gang crisis to justify his aggressive crime-fighting operations, he blamed it for popularizing gangsters. Gang experts, community activists, and former gang members themselves might tie the problem to youth unemployment, defunded social programs, and the influx of cocaine into poor black neighborhoods, but Gates was convinced there was a certain kind of young person who joined a violent gang because he wanted to be in the news, to "be a star." Gates's 1988 anti-gang initiative, "Operation Hammer," was therefore as psychological as it was material, with the LAPD employing terror in the hopes of combatting the growing allure of "gangster chic."[103]

Gates's aggressive tack ultimately helped to certify, however, that Los Angeles gangs were as pervasive as the Westwood shooting indicated and as the drama of *Colors* suggested. Along with news conferences, legislative sessions, and the chief's inflammatory comments about African-American men, the controversial Operation Hammer program generated national attention, drawing politicians, cable news networks, pop journalists, and filmmakers to Los Angeles, all of them riveted by what *Newsweek* called "a nightmare landscape inhabited by marauding thugs and hard-nosed cops." They came to witness an American "apocalypse."[104]

■  ■  ■

Dennis Hopper began his own hunt for reality in LA's notorious ganglands in 1987, at a time when the young people of those communities were making "The Boyz-N-The Hood" a smash local hit. These kids, who would later be portrayed in *Colors* as socially doomed, embraced "Boyz" as a song that, by honoring the local vernacular and nodding to hip-hop trends, saluted those ganglands. The Ruthless Records artists who came together to produce the record found a receptive audience for their West Coast twist on street rap. The response convinced them—and especially their front man and financier Eazy-E—that the bold provocation at the heart of the track, *"the boys in the hood are always hard,"* could define them as a group. The enthusiasm for "Boyz," as Ice Cube remembered, "told us we'd found our niche."[105]

The group became NWA. It was a simple label, and a purposefully opaque one that teased a defiantly provocative phrase, "Niggaz Wit Attitudes." The acronym (which the members deliberately avoided clarifying for music writers and other reporters, making for awkwardly-constructed, if not wildly racist, headlines) fit with the "Boyz" lyrics about living hard, acting hard, and fighting hard against those who *"come talkin' that trash."*[106] The members—including Eazy-E, Dr. Dre, Ice Cube, MC Ren, DJ Yella, Arabian Price, and, although he was not a performing member, The D.O.C.—adopted a brand name fitting for a group of Los Angeles artists angling for recognition within the bullish, yet still New York–centric, street-rap market.

In the late summer of 1988, after Orion Pictures' so-called "gang movie" had sent moral guardians into a panic, NWA released its debut album, *Straight Outta Compton*. The record was, as Eazy-E told a *Los Angeles Times* entertainment writer, rap music reflecting the "reality of [our] situation, no fairy tales."[107] The promotional run for *Straight Outta Compton* dovetailed with the public fixation on Hopper's film and

LA's urban crisis depicted in it. Indeed, although NWA had completed all recording before the April release of *Colors,* its members promoted the project as a response to the movie and, more specifically, as an effort to reclaim the narrative about their lives and about the things—including gang sweeps—that they, and not white Hollywood elites, experienced firsthand. Ice Cube told *Melody Maker,* "We're trying to show how it is on the other side, what it's like to have to deal with that kind of asshole cop in the movie on a day to day basis."[108]

*Colors'* impressive box-office performance and the chart-ranking success of the film's soundtrack—which featured LA rapper Ice-T on the title track rapping *"The gangs of LA will never die / Just multiply"*— affirmed that gangster antihero tales, once a fixture of Depression era cinema, were again in vogue. Moreover, black gangster narratives in particular, framed by real-time revelations in the news about urban crime and urban police, were a rising stock in American popular culture. NWA responded to this cultural shift. And they tapped into a market ripe for self-styled gangster storytellers who, unlike director Dennis Hopper, could paint from a palate of their own exclusive observations and experiences.

But the members of NWA also, more pointedly, represented themselves as "underground street reporters" with an intimate understanding of the problems that undermined long-standing myths of Los Angeles as a promised land. As Ice Cube told the *Washington Times* in defense of the violence in his lyrics on *Straight Outta Compton,* "It's a hard life out there, I'm sorry to say. I ain't the one who made it hard, but I'm the one that lived it."[109] Dr. Dre described the songs he produced for *Straight Outta Compton* as reflections of "real" life growing up in ways that subverted typical LA lore.

He might be a Los Angeles native, but as he explained to the *Los Angeles Times* in 1989, "I know what street rap sounds like. I've lived it. I stay in touch with it."[110]

More than anyone else in the group, Eazy-E claimed for NWA a reputation for authenticity. He did this, in no small part, by attacking "that phony stuff out there," including *Colors* and New York street rap. At the same time, he nodded to NWA's original fans, including the local kids who heard in his label's music familiar—even mundane—echoes of their own lives. "The stuff they were talking about was just shit about guys that I grew up with," remembered Lawrence "DJ Muggs" Muggerud, an LA producer who, inspired by NWA, formed the rap group Cypress Hill in 1988. *Straight Outta Compton* moved Muggs because the album's characters summoned up memories of "guys in my neighborhood like Big Hub, Madman, Baldie. That was their lifestyle." To his ears, NWA was simply "gangbangers rappin."[111] But *Straight Outta Compton* also mattered to locals because it sounded like black journalism about a place heavily cloaked in white myths of opportunity and tolerance. As the Ruthless Records founder told the *Los Angeles Times* in early 1989, "we're telling the real story of what it's like living in a place like Compton. We're giving them reality. We're like reporters. We give them the truth."[112] Recognizing the connection between the sensationalized coverage of the problems they navigated each day and the fast-growing interest in their music, the members of NWA seized on a mantra: "We just tell it how we see it."[113]

■ ■ ■

Independent production, through Eazy-E's Ruthless Records label and the distribution services provided by LA's small shop pressers like the Macola Record Company, allowed NWA to create freely. At Ruthless Records, Eazy-E encouraged his artists to experiment, without restraint. He built his label based on the belief that unfiltered expression would be marketable—even and probably especially if it was filthy. It was a faith nurtured by the Compton music scene, which embraced artistic irreverence, and by the enduring popularity of the raunchy routines of black comedians like Rudy Ray "Dolemite" Moore, Richard Pryor, and Eddie Murphy.[114] "We knew the value of language, especially profanity," Ice Cube explained of his original Ruthless Records partners. "We weren't that sophisticated, but we knew the power it had."[115]

Independence also allowed NWA to freely promote its music, outside the bounds of conventional marketing. With Eazy-E at the helm, and public dialogue about Karen Toshima, Operation Hammer, and *Colors* in the sails, NWA could embark on a new course. It would go on to blend fictional "street stories" with semibiographical "street reality" in ways that stirred controversy and seized the attention of the nation. It was a fortuitous time for NWA to emerge fully as ghetto truth-tellers—the most authentic reality rappers from LA's ganglands. The year 1988 marked the moment when, as the *New York Times* noted, "the gang member has become one of the prevailing images of the young black male on television and in the movies."[116] As KDAY's Greg Mack told the *Los Angeles Times*, things had reached "a turning point."[117]

## CHAPTER 4 · Somebody's Gonna Pay Attention

■ **In August 1989,** Ice Cube described to *Melody Maker* the concept for NWA's first music video, a video MTV had very publicly banned just months earlier. It was simple, he told the British magazine: it depicted a gang sweep. The video was a dramatization of the police raids that targeted young men like him and that had been, for years, commonplace in the black districts of South Los Angeles.[1]

First employed by the Los Angeles Police Department in the early 1980s, gang sweeps had become the centerpiece of Chief Daryl Gates's "Operation Hammer," an unprecedented show of force designed to combat gang-related crime throughout the city. In 1988, the sweeps began making national headlines both for their "successes" and for their violent excesses. Anxious to contain what police officials believed Dennis Hopper's film *Colors* had uncorked—one Los Angeles Sheriff's Department commander said the movie promoted the idea that "you can be a movie star if you're a gang member!"—Los Angeles law enforcement escalated the Hammer sweeps. LAPD Chief Daryl Gates led the charge, determined to lay to rest popular fears that his department had lost control of the city's now famous gang crisis.[2]

In August 1988, one particularly perverse and widely reported LAPD raid left two South Central apartments demolished, furniture smashed with sledgehammers, clothing doused with bleach, and graffiti scrawled on walls declaring "LAPD Gang Task Force Rules." During the police blitz, Dalton Avenue resident Jeannie Carter, in her third trimester of pregnancy, was handcuffed and forced facedown to the floor. Officers reportedly tormented another resident, young Hildebrandt Flowers, threatening to lynch the teen with the gold chain he wore and, then, with fence wire. Police also rounded up dozens of youths within a four-block radius of the Dalton apartments, and ordered the detainees to whistle the theme song from *The Andy Griffith Show* to avoid beatings. The so-called "Dalton Raids," which were so destructive they left four families homeless and drew the emergency relief efforts of the American Red Cross, netted just six ounces of marijuana, less than an ounce of cocaine, and one felony charge. In spite of legal threats and the public outcry from leaders in South Central, the LAPD followed up its August operations by partnering with the LA County Sheriff's Department and anti-gang task forces in Inglewood and Compton to ramp up the sweeps.[3]

Not long after the 1988 Dalton Raids, NWA filmed its video for "Straight Outta Compton." The point, according to Ice Cube, was to provide a different perspective on the ongoing battle in Los Angeles, one that reframed the narrative about cops, criminals, heroes, and villains. The rapper explained soberly to *Melody Maker* that NWA chose to recreate a gang sweep to reveal how Los Angeles County police "abuse their authority."[4]

The video opens with a group of young black men, including the frontmen of NWA, weaving through alleys and strolling down sidewalks. A series of carefully selected images— "Welcome to Compton" signage, a Bail Bonds awning, a Compton Unified School District mural, and the imposing facade of the Compton Courthouse, nicknamed "Fort Compton"— establishes the setting. Scenes of a mustached cop prepping a handgun, twirling a side-handle baton, and circling Compton on a map foreshadow the coming conflict.[5] Ice Cube delivers his lyrics, boasting of *a crime record like Charles Manson.* MC Ren follows, pointing provocatively at the camera, pretending to cock imaginary weapons (in line with his lyrics), and grandstanding about his gangsta *"rep."* Last up, Eazy-E declares himself *"ruthless, never seen, like a shadow in the dark,"* dodging police at every turn. From the passenger seat of a drop-top black Chrysler LeBaron, he delivers his lines, mocking the driver of a police van. Throughout the video, NWA performs a hard-core, and explicit, version of rap braggadocio, in which posture, tone, and content serve to taunt, defy, and humiliate the group's main foil: law enforcement.[6]

The short film, however, casts the song as an expression of powerlessness. Only police wield actual deadly weapons, and they use them, zealously, to round up NWA and their friends. The video's central drama, in fact, is the police chase, with filmmaker Rupert Wainwright imposing upon the audience the pursuing officer's perspective of black youths gathered on a neighborhood corner. They try in vain to flee the police, running down alleys and around dilapidated homes until caught, only to be forced to the concrete with shotguns pointed at their skulls and shoved into their shoulder blades (Fig. 4.1). By the end of the video, every rapper appears in

Fig 4.1 A still from NWA's "Straight Outta Compton" video, portraying the final moments of a gang sweep in an abandoned lot in a residential South Los Angeles neighborhood. Guns drawn, LAPD officers apprehend black youths, including an unarmed Ice Cube. Director Rupert Wainwright filmed much of the video from a similar vantage point, giving the viewer the police perspective. *Rupert Wainwright, Priority Records.*

handcuffs, sitting inside a police paddy wagon, with the exception of Eazy-E and his partner, still cruising in the Le-Baron. The final frame of the video features a close-up of a young black man with his cheek pressed against the hood of a patrol car.[7]

*Spin* magazine reviewed the "Straight Outta Compton" video as a "four-minute action pic" that "opens a wide gray area between right and wrong, then runs wild in it." Against the bleak urban backdrops, NWA's rap lyrics became "too black, too strong, too rock 'n' roll." An entertainment writer for the *Washington Post* went further, suggesting the video could be considered "incendiary." In the spring of 1989, not long after NWA made its debut on MTV, the cable video network officially refused to air "Straight Outta Compton," citing its depictions of guns and violence (without noting that, in the video, only police display weapons and use physical violence).[8]

These critical reactions came as no surprise to Ice Cube, however. They only reaffirmed his suspicions, first, that the popular press chose to ignore the pervasiveness of police abuse in black neighborhoods like his and, second, that it preferred to spin narratives about threats posed by young black men. He told *Melody Maker* that NWA recreated a gang sweep to challenge audiences in precisely the way most commercial rappers did not—by exposing them to the mechanisms of oppression that disrupted the daily lives of African-American kids. Ice Cube explained that the police operated on the assumption that they "basically have the right to pick someone up just because he's black and he happens to be walking down the street." The gang sweep gave them carte blanche to engage in racial profiling, a toxic form of abuse that remained unchecked because America's leaders "don't honestly care about what's going on." In his world, police ignored due process and devalued black lives, while those with the power to affect change did nothing. The only "problem" with the "Straight Outta Compton" video, Ice Cube suggested, "is that we're telling the truth" about police abuse and the public apathy that helps perpetuate it. He argued that media outlets like MTV feared the implications of NWA's popularity. As NWA's message pervaded the mainstream, packaged in the form of a music video, audiences would be compelled, finally, to reckon with injustice. "And that hurts," he said.[9]

By describing the premise of NWA's debut music video and the controversy swirling around it, Ice Cube was implicitly articulating his group's marketing plan: NWA would "show how it is on the other side" and welcome the furor that would inevitably follow.[10] It was a tactic grounded in a sophisticated sense of the public's growing fascination with dark narratives about 1980s Los Angeles. The release of Eazy-E's debut "The Boyz-N-The Hood" had, after all, coincided with the sensationalized coverage of Karen Toshima's murder—a tragedy that, because it occurred in affluent Westwood Village, ignited racially coded debates about whether black street gang violence posed an immediate threat to LA's white communities. The swelling popularity of "Boyz" in 1988 also overlapped with the theater run of Dennis Hopper's *Colors*, which, after the Westwood shooting, drew audiences like rubberneckers eager to glimpse a grim scene of inner-city crisis. The neo-noir stories coming out of Los Angeles in the late 1980s—*Newsweek* compared South Central LA to "the set for some B-picture about the world after a nuclear apocalypse"—captivated an American public that had previously thought of Los Angeles as an exemplar of economic and racial progress in the Reagan era.[11]

But Ice Cube's press tour, in which the rapper blasted MTV for censorship, also showed something of how his group fit into a rapidly changing media environment—particularly as it related to music production and entertainment. MTV's widely-reported decision to ban the "Straight Outta Compton" video from its programming came just at the time that the cable outlet was launching the first nationally broadcast program wholly devoted to hip-hop music. Like other rap acts, NWA heralded the introduction of *Yo! MTV Raps* as a watershed moment for their genre, which had struggled up to then to find real advocates in radio or television, and therefore remained an underexposed and underestimated counterculture. Here would be a powerful new platform for rappers and their labels, unconstrained by many established rules, and eager to engage in innovation, experimentation, and controversy. With the help of handlers and collaborators, NWA provided all three—first, by unveiling an infectiously musical album scored with obscene "reality" raps; then, by testing image-centered promotional strategies custom-made for the music television spotlight; and, finally, by deftly escalating a squabble over a rejected video to assert its cultural authority. All this made NWA a model of what Def Jam's Bill Stephney declared in 1989, the year LA gangsta rap broke from the margins: "The revolution will be marketed."[12]

．　．　．

NWA began work on its first studio album *Straight Outta Compton* in the summer of 1987. Dr. Dre took the reins in each recording session, coaching his emcees and engineering each track with the assistance of former World Class Wreckin' Cru bandmate DJ Yella. Ice Cube, along with MC Ren and Arabian Prince, penned lyrics, often with input from Dre's Texas protégé The D.O.C. The group's founder Eazy-E bankrolled the whole operation, providing occasional vocals while letting others mold his product.

Although it did not include Eazy-E's seminal song "The Boyz-N-The Hood," the album employed the single's winning formula, pairing a California version of street rap with trunk-rattling digital percussion, snippets of the Los Angeles soundscape, and an eclectic mix of funk, soul, and hip-hop samples. James Brown, Sly & the Family Stone, William

DeVaughn, the Pointer Sisters, and Kool Moe Doe punctuated lyrical accounts of turf wars, dope deals, drive-by shootings, police confrontations, and sexual conquests. It was not an entirely novel design. The album's producer and engineer, Dr. Dre, had been inspired by his contemporaries, including New York's Boogie Down Productions, Public Enemy, and Run-DMC, all of them pioneers of a hip-hop street sound that married modern ghetto themes with black music of earlier generations.[13] When *Straight Outta Compton* was complete, the consensus within NWA was that it would elevate the fledgling group to preeminence in Los Angeles, where each member had already earned a modicum of fame on the local black dance scene. Yet national commercial exposure still seemed a pipe dream.

Eazy-E, who footed the bill for recording, was more ambitious than the rest, and from the helm of Ruthless Records he set out to market *Straight Outta Compton* broadly. He solicited music manager Jerry Heller to shop the album to major labels. "This is what Eazy hired me for," Heller recalled, "for my Rolodex."[14] Both men, one an industry novice and the other a seasoned rock 'n' roll booster, anticipated varied, even visceral, responses inside boardrooms and executive suites. Indeed, most labels rejected Heller's pitch outright, citing NWA's image as unmarketable, its name behind its acronym— Niggaz Wit Attitudes—as obscene, and its lyrics as a legal liability. After a dozen rejections, only Capitol Records got back to Heller. The label's chairman, Joe Smith, whom Heller knew well, offered to buy the Ruthless Records trademark. But he refused to add NWA to his company's roster. Smith had sought to draft hip-hop artists to establish "a presence in rap" for Capitol so it could compete in the genre with other majors, including Columbia and MCA, who had recently begun distributing music for Def Jam and Profile, respectively. The chairman, however, did not want ownership of the "crap" his friend was peddling. Heller labored to demonstrate NWA's broader cultural relevance, particularly in its black radicalism and rock 'n' roll rebellion. "Joe, it's the Black Panthers," he stressed. "It's the fucking Rolling Stones." But Smith, unmoved by NWA's music simply responded, "I hate what they are saying." He questioned his friend's judgment: "What makes you think anyone is going to buy this garbage? Who's going to listen? Tell me who is going to play it? No radio station in the world."[15]

The fact was that American radio programmers had long snubbed hip-hop, with urban contemporary, crossover, and top-40 stations routinely treating it like a fad that could simply be willed away. At the point when Capitol's Joe Smith was questioning the prospects of NWA's music getting any airtime, hip-hop artists and promoters had already spent more than three years battling for playlist additions, or "adds" as they are called in the industry. The rise of street rap in the early 1980s defied the mainstream convention of whitening black music. Rap artists and their labels resurrected early hip-hop music, updated its style, refreshed its themes, and recast it for a younger, blacker audience—with the expectation that the changes would drive sales. The music was deliberately designed to be both "hard" and "pop," not one or the other—a tricky combination in the context of an entertainment market increasingly driven by top-40 radio, competition for ad dollars, and artistic compromises. The formula made little sense to radio program directors and label executives who viewed the popular mainstream as wholly synonymous with white consumer trends. By refusing to, as Def Jam's Russell Simmons put it, "water it down," street rappers like Run-DMC were proposing a new blueprint for giving music commercial appeal, one that most radio outlets and large record companies did not initially embrace.[16]

Through the late 1980s, radio program directors all but boycotted street rap, and, because major labels also refused to touch it, rap artists had little leverage to curry favor with stations that had hit-making power. Without radio plays, a key metric used by top trade publications like *Billboard* and *Radio & Records* to rank hits, rap songs rarely charted, which further justified the reactions of major label executives, like Smith, who characterized the music as unsalable "garbage." Yet street rap did sell records, and it sold them well even without radio support. Through the mid-1980s, healthy sales of rap albums, singles, and tapes featuring new "hardcore" artists, including LL Cool J, Dana Dane, Ice-T, and Schoolly D, demonstrated the resilience of a genre blackballed by traditional music media and supported by only a network of small, independent labels. Hip-hop was proving itself to be the kind of sleeper phenomenon that earns big returns for investors with patience. But even after 1986—a year in which Run-DMC, on independent label Profile, managed to shatter all rap sales records, saw its albums reach gold- and platinum-level sales, played to arena crowds on a sixty-four-date national tour, and earned a Grammy Award nomination— the music industry's traditional gatekeepers remained largely unwilling to commit.[17]

"We've never received radio play commensurate with our true popularity," Run-DMC's publicist Bill Adler complained in 1988, arguing that if radio truly reflected consumer demand, "there isn't an urban station in the country that would be playing less than 30% or 40% rap." Adler's frustration was with an entire nexus of urban radio outlets, including those with black and urban contemporary formats, that seemed disconnected from, even deliberately defiant of, market trends. When *Billboard* conducted a survey of program directors in America's urban markets that year, it found that most firmly refused to add rap titles to playlists even as they acknowledged the genre's sales. They cited listener distaste for rap and, in one respondent's words, the risk of "professional suicide."[18]

Prospects for hip-hop airplay were further diminished when, because of widespread reporting in the mid-1980s about major music labels' use of independent promoters to skirt laws regarding pay-for-play, two Congressional investigations were opened into "payola and possible mob ties" in the industry—and the major labels promptly dropped all use of promotional middlemen. This had the effect of cutting out what the *Los Angeles Times* described as "a key cog in the hit-making machinery—radio airplay for new artists." The newspaper quoted one industry veteran's explanation: "The loss of independent promotion . . . has hurt the artists who need the most help—the young, developing groups. Radio programmers have been so rattled by all the controversy over independent promotion that they're playing it very safe. They're only adding big name bands to their playlists."[19] Young rappers were not the only black artists affected. The Reverend Al Sharpton was quick to hold a protest against "the unilateral dismissal of all independent record promoters" because they were a critical resource for many black performers either recording on indie labels or not prioritized by their major labels' in-house promotional departments—and, as he pointed out, "black promotion men are not implicated in the allegations."[20]

The black program directors at urban contemporary format stations, however, seemed particularly averse to hip-hop music and wary of its tough tone and tougher content. Some stations even ran ads promising rap-free programming. "Outlets are really closing up," said Bill Toles, an advocate for the creative freedom of black musicians. Vernon Reid, the guitarist for Living Colour, a black rock band that was frequently—although mistakenly—categorized as a hip-hop group, said "black radio wouldn't touch us." Def Jam's Bill Stephney, first hired to secure radio airplay for the label's acts, defined the resistance in black radio, and eventually in black television programming, to rap as a missed opportunity to present audiences with a fuller, more complete picture of African-American experiences. When Robert Johnson, president of Black Entertainment Television, told him he "didn't see the importance of doing a rap show, that it wasn't applicable to his audience," Stephney lamented Johnson's blind spot and concluded that the BET brush-off was representative of a broader problem. "We understand the message on CNN is not going to be close to ours," he told *Spin*. "But if BET or black radio is going to position itself as having a so-called black perspective, it better be pretty close to what the people in my community are talking about. And it isn't." [21]

There were exceptions within black radio programming, and most of them, by the late 1980s, were on the West Coast and in the South. Small, local R&B and urban contemporary stations, including KPOO in San Francisco, KDIA in Oakland, WFXA in Augusta, KQXL in Baton Rouge, and WEAL in Greensboro, added hip-hop tracks often enough for entertainment journals to tally a smattering of playlist adds. Through the summer of 1988, a few rap songs broke through radio firewalls—most notably, Ice-T's "Colors," LL Cool J's "Goin' Back to Cali," and DJ Jazzy Jeff and the Fresh Prince's "Parents Just Don't Understand." All three of these tracks had the major label distribution others coveted, and "Col-

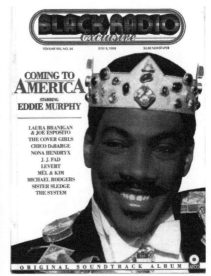

Fig 4.2 Full-page ads in *Black Radio Exclusive* promoting the soundtracks for *Colors* and *Coming to America*, both released in early 1988. Ice-T and J.J. Fad, two of the only rap artists added to black urban radio playlists that year, were linked to these high-profile, major studio films. *Black Radio Exclusive.*

ors" had the added benefit of being the title track for Dennis Hopper's acclaimed film.[22] Another breakthrough track was J.J. Fad's "Supersonic" (on Eazy-E's Ruthless Records), which was generating buzz in some radio markets in the South and the West thanks to its inclusion on the soundtrack for the blockbuster movie *Coming to America* (Fig. 4.2).

In the case of "Supersonic," it also helped that urban contemporary music programmers treated the song not as a rap track but as a dance record or, as *Black Radio Exclusive* described it, "up-tempo techno."[23] As an electro-inspired female trio, J.J. Fad fit seamlessly into a 1980s dance music market dominated by freestyle, electro, and R&B women vocalists including Neneh Cherry, Jody Watley, and Lisa Lisa, all of whom incorporated playful, syncopated lyrics into their bass-heavy music. Despite these notable examples of hip-hop artists succeeding in penetrating urban radio markets by various means, including genre bending, the industry's conservatism remained a well-known obstacle to most rap acts.

At a time when media markets held rap music at bay, KDAY in Los Angeles was the one truly remarkable outlier. Its hip-hop-heavy programming—described as "rap, rap, rap" by one disgusted Silver Lake resident whose house wiring picked up stray signals from the nearby station—emerged from Music Director Greg Mack's turnaround strategy for the struggling AM station.[24] Offering his unwavering support was KDAY's program director Jack Patterson, who Mack later recalled was himself an anomaly in Los Angeles in the early 1980s, when "all the radio people in LA *hated* rap. Program Directors hated it, the big record stores wouldn't carry it. They thought it was just a novelty and would go away."[25] Throughout the 1980s, Mack and Patterson provided a radio platform for hip-hop artists by tapping into the tastes of local DJs and relying on ad revenue provided by local businesses—including rap-friendly nightclubs and mobile DJ enterprises. During a decade in which national contemporary radio, in effect, froze out hip-hop, KDAY stood as an absolute exception.

In its liberal policy regarding playlist adds and its dependence upon grassroots support, KDAY served artists in much the same way rap-friendly independent labels did. Just as Greg Mack's success reviving KDAY was possible because of hip-hop experimentation and not in spite of it, indie producers similarly watched their influence expand and investments pay off as they cornered the rap market. Echoing Mack's approach to music programming, Delicious Vinyl founder Michael Ross asserted that the retail success of his small hip-hop label could be credited to his staff's privileging of local tastes—

"keeping its ear to [the] streets" rather than focusing on in-dustry charts, urban radio playlists, and market outlooks. Monica Lynch, president of New York-based Tommy Boy Re-cords, made a similar claim. Her company produced first-wave hip-hop artists, including Afrika Bambaataa, back when critics lampooned the newborn genre as a gimmick. By 1988, it boasted a full roster of profitable rap acts, including Stetsasonic, Queen Latifah, and De La Soul. "Rap put us on the map," she told *Billboard*. Similar strategies employed lib-erally throughout the second half of the decade—namely, ex-perimentation, a commitment to artist development beyond first releases, and local, grassroots promotion—made suc-cesses of Oakland rapper Too $hort's 75 Girls Records and Tapes, Luther Campbell's Luke Skyywalker Records in Mi-ami (later renamed Luke Records), and Eazy-E's own Ruth-less Records. Hip-hop also made Profile Records a force in music retail; by 1988, thanks to Run-DMC's record sales, it ranked as the most profitable indie label in the country. Against heavy odds, these indies thrived without the major labels' promotion and distribution advantages. Moreover, in an era when the music business was thought by many to be too risk-averse and wedded to yesterday's hit-makers, their support of artists that major labels shunned suggested that these small, marginal enterprises were curating the next wave of popular music. In 1988, *Billboard* referred to rap indies as "the artistic and creative backbone of the music industry."[26] They were beating the big producers at their own game.

In the 1980s, few independent rap enterprises were as well positioned as Bryan Turner's Priority Records. Turner was a Jewish kid from Winnipeg who had once worked for K-Tel International, a company best known for its as-seen-on-tele-vision consumer products, including the Veg-O-Matic, a food-processing device as popular for its utility as for its lengthy commercials that riveted viewers with "But wait! There's more!"[27] In the early 1980s, Turner served in the company's entertainment division licensing music, a position that brought him to Los Angeles. As a representative for K-Tel, he traveled between Los Angeles and New York, where he had a "light-bulb moment." After observing young bar patrons responding enthusiastically to even the hint of a hip-hop beat, he resolved to market the music. "There's definitely something going on, appealing to this young generation," he thought. "Something clearly parents wouldn't understand or really like." Banking on the very same rebel spirit that had once fueled the explosion of rock 'n' roll, Turner ventured to create his own music-licensing company. He, along with Mark Cerami and Steve Drath, colleagues who shared Turner's vision, left K-Tel in 1985, taking with them intact relationships with record companies that had partnered with K-Tel over the years. With seed money provided by Turner's uncle and father, they founded Priority Records.[28]

Priority was not created as a rap label. Turner, Cerami, and Drath set it up as a song-licensing company that mined and then compiled hit records. Priority took its cue from K-Tel's repackaging of music trends, with an initial focus on collections of fifties pop, rock, new wave, and metal. But Priority's hip-hop cassettes proved its bestsellers. The fact that young rap fans, as Turner discovered, were unusually "aggressive buyers"—perhaps by necessity, since few radio outlets played rap hits—meant there was strong demand for rap compilations. Plus, for rap consumers, these curated collections mimicked the dubbed "street tapes" that hip-hop DJs sold with ease in places like Oakland, Miami, Philadelphia, Houston, and Los Angeles. Priority's tapes, with titles like *Power Rap* and *Rap's Greatest Hits*, fit seamlessly into an already established youth-driven economy. The company's advantage was in its ability, as a licensed distributor, to put its products inside music retailers and some national chain stores—venues that were, of course, inaccessible to DJs vending bootlegs. As Turner noted, even Priority's first rap release, *Kings of Rap,* "sold heavily in the racks [at] Kmarts and Wal-Marts."[29]

K-Tel also paved the way for Priority's unorthodox approach to promoting its music products. In the 1960s, K-Tel's founder Philip Kives, a relative of Turner, developed the "infomercial," a long-play commercial with methodical demonstrations of product features. At K-Tel (short for Kives Television) the business model was to use television to amplify Kives's unrelenting door-to-door sales pitch and then, having drummed up demand for a product, direct viewers to the retail stores where they could purchase it. Unlike standard televised ad campaigns, which rarely lasted more than thirty seconds and aimed mainly to boost brand awareness, K-Tel's infomercials were often five-minute spots, produced to close the sale on an impulse purchase.

In 1987, Priority Records transformed the California Raisins, a set of Claymation characters popular in Sun-Maid Raisins commercials, into a platinum-selling Motown cover band. The concept worked without the kind of radio support that traditional labels relied upon. In fact, Turner deliberately sidestepped radio programmers and, instead, leveraged the popularity of existing California Raisin Advisory Board ads and related Claymation network programming to sell *The California Raisins Sing the Hit Songs.* "That was a K-Tel-oriented marketing idea," Turner explained, a nod to the way his former employer racked up gold and platinum records for its compilations by side-stepping traditional forms of radio promotion in favor of the long-form television pitch.[30] Turner's success stunned the record industry. Other labels' executives were aghast that, within just two weeks, the Raisins had sold over six hundred thousand units and were taking up precious space on the American pop charts. Priority Records also surprised music journalists, who nevertheless were quick to pun on the achievement—Dave DiMartino at *Billboard* marveled at this "new wrinkle" in the charts bringing the label "its most fruitful sales to date," while Stanley Mieses at *Spin* quipped that, by pushing the cartoonish group, Priority was committing "statutory grape."[31] The ridicule, however, seemed only to reaffirm Turner's own posture as an industry hustler whose schemes actually worked. In 1988, with his two-year-old company's coffers brimming with money thanks to anthropomorphic dried fruit, Turner could brag that he had a winning approach. Major labels "think about hit songs," he said. "I think about hit concepts."[32]

■   ■   ■

When Eazy-E began Ruthless Records, he similarly set his sights on hit concepts over hit songs. His Los Angeles-based label was initially set up as a vehicle for the promotion of an electro-rap girl group, J.J. Fad. The Rialto-based trio (Juana "MC J.B." Burns, Dania "Baby-D" Birks, and Michelle "Sassy C" Franklin) was Eazy-E's first big concept, developed in response to "Push It," a surprising—and surprisingly salacious—hit record from New York's female rap trio, Salt-N-Pepa. "Push It" was originally the B-side to Salt-N-Pepa's 1987 single "Tramp," a song that failed to gain radio traction. After San Francisco DJ Cameron Paul, best known for his thumping up-tempo dance mixes, transformed "Push It" from the long-play album cut that it was into a trimmed-down, drum-heavy, made-for-radio dance remix, "Push It" became a sensation. Salt-N-Pepa was not the first girl group to become a staple of 1980s dance radio; the Cover Girls, Seduction, Exposé, Company B, and Sweet Sensation (Salt-N-Pepa's labelmate) already filled the crates of the newest generation of radio tastemakers. But the crossover success of Salt-N-Pepa suggested to Eazy-E that the dance market was ripe for female rap groups and that Ruthless needed to have its own. J.J. Fad fit that bill. The group had already released an electro-rap song called "Supersonic" on the LA indie label Dream Team Records, to which Eazy-E had close ties. He recognized the crossover potential in "Supersonic," signed the group, and in 1988, J.J. Fad released *Supersonic* the album under the Ruthless Records banner. That summer, Ruthless banked its first certifiable pop smash. Boosted by its inclusion on the soundtrack for Eddie Murphy's comedy *Coming to America*, J.J. Fad broke into the top 30 on *Billboard*'s Hot 100 chart. As Jerry Heller noted, "Eazy's instincts were, as usual, right on the money."[33]

Yet, even with a winning record, Eazy-E and his new partner, Heller, could not convince the majors to bring Ruthless artists aboard. Even Atlantic Records, which helped distribute *Supersonic*, had no interest in hitching its wagon to Eazy-E's roster of LA street rappers. Ruthless Records had the option to go it alone. "The Boyz-N-The Hood" had been a boon for Eazy-E's fledgling label, driven by the Compton rapper's own tireless street promotion and hand-to-hand distribution. Los Angeles was awash in small record pressers, like Macola Record Company, that churned out thousands of saleable units quickly and without creative limitations, which meant that entrepreneurs like Eazy-E had direct access to the tools of the trade. Plus, the demand for "Boyz" in California and in certain black-music markets in the South demonstrated the potential for his label to continue to garner the kind of grass-roots support that, for instance, Oakland's 75 Girls and LA's Egyptian Empire cultivated through the late 1980s.

But, moving forward, Eazy-E wanted more for his own enterprise than niche popularity. He wanted J.J. Fad sales numbers, and thus he was determined to secure a formal distribution deal—if not with Atlantic, then with someone else. If the goal was mainstream exposure buttressed by corporate resources, NWA's music would be a tough sell, as both Heller and Eazy knew. They anticipated the slew of rejections Heller ultimately fielded, and both concluded that Ruthless would need an unorthodox sort of partner—one with enough capital and a measure of recklessness—to provide help.

Although Eazy-E was uncertain about whether he and his fellow members of NWA had the same kind of hit-making potential that J.J. Fad exhibited, he was confident in his group's design. He had Dr. Dre to create carefully layered and painstakingly engineered masterpieces, and Ice Cube, Ren, and The D.O.C. to craft rhymes. But Eazy-E believed that the greatest strength of NWA's debut *Straight Outta Compton*—and his own solo material on *Eazy-Duz-It*—was in its full mastery of the art of storytelling. Jerry Heller pitched NWA to possible distributors as a group that, in production, lyrics, and character, dramatized the lives of the very gangsters and hustlers sensationalized in 1980s popular culture. In the months leading up to the release of *Straight Outta Compton*, major media outlets continued to paint young black men from South Central and Compton as "marauding thugs," "cold killers," and "angry harbingers of a new Watts riot." These were the sorts of caricatures that stoked fear, particularly during an election year in which crime and punishment dominated the political debate, often with racial overtones.[34] But the attention, however negative, trained a spotlight on the ganglands of Los Angeles, one that Eazy-E, with the help of Heller, hoped to exploit. If the nation had become newly obsessed with South LA's "bad guys," then Eazy-E intended to position Ruthless Records to represent them. Ruthless would offer up a new, more cinematic version of hip-hop music that gave voice to the vilified.[35]

While still refining his reality rap vision, Eazy-E continued to run his company's production and distribution, reaping the benefits of his own relentless promotion on his Los Angeles home turf. His efforts had helped solidify the label's appeal in the county, with limited reach in Northern California and the South. Early on, Ruthless found its most enthusiastic audience within the KDAY broadcast range and, by 1988, had managed to earn young fans beyond the LA bubble with the help of a smattering of event bookings in the San Francisco Bay Area and retail connections in Texas, Louisiana, and Memphis. But it was Bryan Turner's Priority Records that proved to be a better conduit for connecting Ruthless Records' brand of street rap to the broader—and whiter—public.

Priority Records had an extensive catalog of record releases and, now, a fresh reputation for having manufactured a pop sensation with the California Raisins, but it did not make a habit of signing recording acts. In its first years of operation, it only licensed music. Just as their forebears at K-Tel had done for over two decades, Bryan Turner and Mark Cerami purchased the privilege to reproduce, cover, and sell copyrighted tracks, which were then folded into best-of compilations. It was a modestly lucrative strategy for selling records that steered the company away from dealing directly with artists and hepled it avoid the expense of building up a library of original music. The label had few incentives to offer recording contracts, and it had even fewer resources to gamble on unsigned acts.

By early 1988, however, sales of Priority's titles associated with the Raisins—"We sold millions of those stupid things," Turner reflected—drew the attention of artists seeking label representation and, at the same time, filled the company's war chest. In a position to venture into new territory, Turner and Cerami intended to follow in the path of hip-hop's first successful indie labels, including Profile and Def Jam, who Cerami defined as run by "entrepreneurs . . . who felt the excitement surrounding the music and saw the potential for it." Like them, Priority's young executives wanted to seize on the phenomenon "going on in the clubs and on the streets" that major label executives "were slow to recognize."[36] With both the financial resources and the desire to invest in rap, Turner and Cerami refashioned themselves as label A&Rs, poring over cassette tape demos and meeting with talent managers, including Jerry Heller.

"What impressed me about NWA and Eazy-E," Turner remembered of his response to Heller's pitch, "was that these guys lived the things they talk about." Rather than homing in on hit songs in the Ruthless catalog, he picked up on the Compton label's recipe: entertainment from the periphery or, more plainly, raw stories told by society's outcasts. Turner recognized that, as tabloid-like coverage of the drama in LA's ganglands created intrigue, the audience for NWA's brand of music would grow. Turner saw how NWA's reality rap could tap right into, and perhaps even inform, the feverish debate about black youth, crime, and policing being amplified by cable television news. "All I was hearing on the news was the perspective of the police," he said, but conspicuously absent from

the coverage were the voices of the black kids—the "outsiders."
Turner and Cerami struck up a production deal with Heller
for Priority to partner with Eazy-E and NWA. As Turner said
of his company's new investment, "It really hit me that their
side of the story is important to tell."[37] Over the objections of
some of Priority's most important retail clients, Turner and
Cerami dug in, betting on Ruthless as the wellspring of the
next generation of hip-hop.

Priority's wager was based first and foremost on Eazy-E's
edgy reality rap concept, that rappers could present their version of LA's "ghetto truths" to provoke audiences. Turner's
memory of first meeting NWA was that he said "Let's do it.
This is some scary stuff. It will scare some white people here."
After all, plenty of reporters, politicians, filmmakers, and
news anchors had piqued the public's interest by doing the
same.[38] Second, it was grounded in one specific market observation: as Turner saw, in spite of radio blackouts "everyone is into rap now, even 12-year-old white kids in Texas."[39]
And third, it was a partnership custom made for the harsh
reality that the traditional workings of the recording industry were stacked against hip-hop artists, and only by skirting those conventions could success be achieved. All of
these considerations grew out of the new, unprecedented
role for television in the marketing of music, a sea of change
happening in the 1980s that altered the very anatomy of the
recording industry, and in doing so, created new avenues
for Los Angeles rap.

■  ■  ■

To be sure, television had long played a role in music promotion. In the 1950s, for instance, the advent of television variety

shows hosted by the likes of Steve Allen and Ed Sullivan, and of course the *American Bandstand* program that would make Dick Clark such a force, gave recording artists the chance to seduce a national audience larger than any they could ever assemble on the concert circuit. Radio still reached more people, but television recalibrated listeners' relationships with musicians, magnifying the importance of the artist's visual image. Moreover, early television music programming taught record labels to privilege rather than merely patronize teenage consumers, who made up more and more of television's viewership with each decade. In the 1970s, popular syndicated dance shows like *Solid Gold* and Don Cornelius's *Soul Train* proved to television broadcasters and record companies just how fruitful, and lucrative, a cross-media partnership centered on a young demographic could be.[40]

The launch of MTV in the early 1980s complicated that alliance. Initially, it seemed a foolish idea for any television producer to forego road-tested variety and dance-show formats in order to screen prerecorded videos. That was especially true because virtually all videos first available were press-kit fodder—shorts created by labels at low cost to push new recording artists. Before the 1980s, music videos were cheaply made promotional videotapes, which might only play on loop during in-store appearances or be used for international publicity. Directors, artists, and talent managers considered them a "curiosity" at best and "lavatory paper" at worst.[41] The architects of MTV, however, envisioned a near future in which the videos would get better—and a fortune to be made by stitching them together just as radio DJs did with records. The young staffers on the MTV payroll, many coming straight from FM and college radio programming, saw no reason not to create a parallel to the radio market using these otherwise disposable short films. As founding executive John Lack recalled, "A video radio station—that was my dream."[42]

Rather than replicate the one-size-fits-all approach they saw inhibiting the producers of even the most daring, late-night network shows like *Saturday Night Live* and *The Midnight Special*, MTV's founders refused to design a channel "to please everybody." In 1981, in the midst of a national recession and a music industry slump, John Sykes, a founding member of the MTV team serving as promotion director, told a room full of skeptical record-label executives that the old broadcast networks had failed them. "We live in a very fragmented society which just won't support a mass appeal, network-style format anymore," he argued, touting MTV's "target audience" concept. MTV took its inspiration from the world of radio, in which a given station pegged its format to a particular music style and carved out a listening audience with specific demographics, whether based on age, race, region, gender, or class.[43] When it premiered in 1981, MTV was simply a visual iteration of FM radio in which a three- to five-minute film set to a song counted both as airplay (or, in industry lingo, a spin) and as powerful advertising for the artist. Jack Schneider, who had worked in radio and television before investing in MTV, stressed that, as novel as it might have seemed, the concept of music television was virtually identical to the radio station with its microphone, transmitter, and stack of records. "We are simply adding the video aspect to it," he said. Even the practical experience of turning on MTV was similar to tuning into a favorite DJ's program on a rock radio station. As Ann Wilson of Heart remembered, "You could just put it on and party around the TV."[44]

Even as they offered the reassuring parallels to radio, MTV's creators promoted their outlet as a unique and, more pointedly, a subversive force that would disrupt the entire media landscape. And, indeed, it did pull off the neat trick of having viewers like Ann Wilson not seem to recognize, or care, that they were watching long-play television commercials. The use of chyrons on music videos to identify the track title, artist, album, and label built brand awareness (a feature that set MTV promotion apart from marketing on radio, where DJs often neglected to mention any song information at all). MTV was, in essence, a twenty-four-hour infomercial for the recording industry.

Record labels, still trying to recuperate from a global decline in record sales, responded by hiring better directors, stylists, and film editors to showcase their products. Meanwhile, artists discovered—and sometimes bemoaned—a new obligation to develop an on-screen persona. "I hated making videos," Billy Joel recalled. "I became a musician because I knew I wasn't cut out to be a movie star."[45] A Capitol Records marketing executive conceded that, as MTV established itself as a media force, "the look of an act" became as important as talent, if not more.[46] Producer Rick Rubin, who worked with Run-DMC, agreed that MTV "changed what was expected of an artist. The job changed. It became a job of controlling your image."[47] By the early 1980s, the recording industry could already see how music television was revolutionizing American pop culture: visual concepts were suddenly essential to success in music.

Music television altered the way people consumed music, broadly speaking. But for rap music, the impact was mixed. It appeared to be the ideal medium for hip-hop, which was, from its creation, a visual music culture. Hip-hop coevolved with street art and dance; it was a genre that, like disco in the 1970s, had been incubated within party scenes dripping in provocative style and colorful innuendo. Over the course of the 1980s, it came to center on the theatrical appeal of the streetwise rapper—whose "hardness" appealed to suburban kids because it made him, in the words of cultural critic Jonathan Gold "an image of what their parents feared most."[48] While established rockers of the 1960s and 1970s initially "didn't get the point" and "didn't care" about shooting videos, most of the central figures of hip-hop's pioneering generation immediately saw the value.[49] In videos for tracks like Sugarhill Gang's "Rapper's Delight," Grandmaster Flash and the Furious Five's "The Message," and Afrika Bambaataa's "Planet Rock" hip-hop artists and their labels showed an embrace of a medium that, as a commercial force, was as improbable as they were.[50]

Hip-hop artists only stood to benefit from the fact that, already by 1983, video programming had begun to undermine radio's monopoly on music marketing. Music television was a brand new avenue of exposure—a way to break through for an entire genre that found the path to radio playlists blocked. Across the spectrum of radio outlets, from top 40 to urban contemporary, program directors ignored hip-hop throughout its first decade. The black stations that had traditionally been a refuge for African-American musicians unable to crack the white-dominated pop radio market were also loath to play rap. Even in the mid-1980s, when Run-DMC, LL Cool J, and other acts began booking stadium tours, some black radio outlets refused to include hip-hop on their playlists and even plugged this exclusion on the air. As MTV gained industry muscle, rap labels felt less need to spend energy and resources trying to win over these stations. "I'm tired of talking about black radio now," Def Jam's Bill Stephney commented. "Now kids are reacting to videos instead of radio . . . . The whole focus has switched."[51] Russell Simmons noted that MTV presented his artists with something black FM could not provide: access to large white audiences.[52] For Run-DMC in particular, Simmons coveted the success that a handful of superstars had enjoyed by keeping their black following while winning millions of white fans, too. *Billboard's* Nelson George wrote about this version of the classic "crossover," which he defined as "a strategy for growing your music-buying audience from a black audience to a larger white one," and credited Prince in particular with "leaping over the barriers that constrained most artists of color."[53] (Later, in the 1990s, "crossover" picked up a negative connotation in some circles as it was used to label commercially popular rappers as pedestrian—or worse, "corny." But back in the 1980s, the term could refer to black triumph over the music industry's color line.)

The problem was, for all of the potential advantages it offered hip-hop, MTV replicated, in its early years, the very conservatism that had historically pervaded both television and radio. Since the dawn of television, network executives and variety program hosts, highly attuned to sponsors' preferences and audience ratings had shied away from any artists perceived as polarizing. It was a position that, in practice, disproportionately impacted black musicians who did not reflect or were not familiar to overwhelmingly white, suburban network television audiences. This, of course, ran counter to the needs of established black-owned recording labels like Motown and SOLAR, but it was particularly disadvantageous to the younger companies trying to develop and market rookie black talent.

In the early 1980s, heavyweights like James Brown, Ray Charles, and Natalie Cole could secure guest spots on, for instance, Johnny Carson's *The Tonight Show* and NBC's *Saturday Night Live*—both of which had already featured many black artists. Black-owned record labels also carved out space for their artists in primetime specials, like *Motown 25,* and syndicated programming including Don Cornelius's *Soul Train* and *The Jackson 5ive* cartoon series. By contrast, the freshman class of hip-hop artists and their labels found virtually no support on network television. That remained true until the late 1980s, with just two notable exceptions. First, in September 1980, rapper Kurtis Blow appeared on Don Cornelius's Saturday morning dance program *Soul Train.* Cornelius, a founder of SOLAR Records, crafted *Soul Train* as a showcase of mostly African-American talents for whom network television invitations were elusive. By the 1970s, Cornelius was a nationally recognized star who, as Nelson George described, offered a window into "this entire other world of black style and black music."[54] But Cornelius, like his contemporaries in black radio, could not and did not hide his disdain for rap. He suffered through Blow's performance, obviously irked by the New York kid and his unmusical music. The other exception came in February 1981, when the Bronx ensemble Funky 4 + 1 More performed on *Saturday Night Live.* The group's appearance, often interpreted as a landmark moment in hip-hop history, was not due to a decision made by the show's talent coordinators; they were brought on board by the episode's host, Debbie Harry. The new-wave goddess, slated as both host and musical act (with her band Blondie), used her celebrity to expose the show's national audience to a piece of the edgy New York music scene she adored.[55]

When MTV premiered in 1981, it promised change—a leap toward a more enlightened future for the entire world of music entertainment. Its creators, Bob Pittman and Fred Seibert, cast MTV in the image of the NASA moon landing. As Seibert later laughed, "We were the most conceited, arrogant people. . . . We thought: We're gonna change the face of television!"[56] But by the end of MTV's freshman year, the self-proclaimed mavericks of television were being called out in many quarters for doing nothing to overturn the racial discrimination that had long plagued the medium. Frustrated record-label executives demanded that MTV's founders account for the exclusion of black artists from its video playlists. Singer Rick James was one of the first to publicly accuse the cable channel of "blatant racism," after it rejected the video for his hit record "Super Freak." Black Music Association Executive Director George Ware proposed taking the matter up with the Federal Communications Commission, to charge MTV with racially discriminatory practices.[57]

MTV's Sykes had little patience for the accusations, explaining, "We don't sit in a room and say, 'they're black, we won't use them.'" He stressed that MTV's programming was equivalent to a radio station with an album-oriented rock format—versus, say, a country, classical, or urban contemporary format—and reminded his growing chorus of critics, "We are going after a rock audience."[58] But disco star Sylvester (Sylvester James, Jr.) rejected MTV's format justification as disingenuous. The segmentation seemed a convenient means of exclusion: "You have to be either black or rock, with no merging between different types of music. And if you're black, you have to be r&b." Meanwhile, white R&B acts, like Hall & Oates, Culture Club, and The Eurythmics, all had videos accepted by the network's acquisitions

committee and each appeared in heavy rotation.[59] Even David
Bowie, one of MTV's earliest luminaries and a beneficiary
of its openness to white artists who played black music,
used an on-air interview at the station itself to challenge
it: "Why are there practically no black artists on the network?"[60] A few years later, Les Garland, the MTV executive
tasked with overseeing program content for the channel,
would say the problem had been a matter of supply: "simply stated, there were few videos playing by black artists
because few had been made." Yet, for every Donna Summer
and Tina Turner video MTV played, there were known to
be many others—including chart-toppers Rick James, Michael Jackson, and Prince—whose videos had been turned
down.[61]

In the early 1980s, the greatest hope black artists had to
overcome MTV's rejection was, ironically, that it would succeed well enough to inspire competition against it. The company was operating on a new business model and had yet to
turn a profit, but the model seemed workable enough to lay
the groundwork for other emerging cable channels looking
to hook new viewers. Even established broadcast television
companies seeking to revitalize stale programming followed
MTV's lead. And they all benefited from the fact that MTV
had not cornered the music video market.

Indeed, through the first half of the decade, television producers piled onto the "video music bandwagon."[62] Inspired by
MTV's experiment, television producers rushed to carve out
space in the cable landscape for their own vision of music
entertainment. The USA Network offered both *Radio 1990*
and *Night Flight,* a weekend series that featured music from
"outside the mainstream," including punk, reggae, and Latin
rock, along with music documentaries, concert clips, comedy,

and other material that, according to the show's creators, "has not been shown on other networks, but has a high entertainment value."[63] With *Chartbusters, Power Play,* and *Night Tracks,* the Turner Broadcasting System replicated MTV's more streamlined model, with hosts playing popular videos and little else.[64] Black Entertainment Television introduced its *Video Soul* series focused on "urban contemporary" music, a blend of R&B, dance, and pop that paralleled the breadth of black FM radio. The Nashville Network compiled country music videos in its *Country Clips* series. "Premium cable" and satellite television subscribers, still a tiny percentage of all television viewers, had a range of other options, as well, including *Album Flash* on Cinemax, HBO's *Video Jukebox,* and The Playboy Channel's *Hot Rocks,* which hyped its prerogative to play the videos MTV declared too obscene to screen.[65] Meanwhile, Miami Cablevision partnered with Southern Bell Telephone to create a remarkably lucrative twenty-four-hour video channel that was interactive; its programming was driven by viewers who called a 976 toll-call service and paid to have requests played on air.[66]

Cable television had no monopoly on early music-video programming. Because the vast majority of American households for much of the decade did not subscribe to any cable provider at all, MTV's inaccessibility to most music fans generated incentives for network television to design traditional, advertising-supported options. Clip shows, specials, and music channels proliferated on the networks, feeding consumer demand while also orienting the wider American viewing public to the phenomenon of music videos.

When NBC unveiled its *Friday Night Videos* series in July of 1983, the music press announced, "Viewers without cable can now get their fix."[67] NBC promoted the weekly show, scheduled to follow Johnny Carson's *The Tonight Show,* as a late-night companion to the network's *Saturday Night Live.* Certainly, like *SNL,* the new show could lean on NBC's historical ties to the recording industry to recruit A-list music talent. The ambition was greater than that, however. Promising not only top video clips from top stars but also exclusive "World Premieres," *Friday Night Videos* aspired to leave a mark on music culture as deep as *SNL's* influence on comedy.[68] Executive producer Dick Ebersol, noting in 1983 that "more than nine-tenths of the US has never seen MTV," also pledged to showcase "good rhythm and blues," committing to serve the larger market that MTV, with its overwhelmingly white programming, was ignoring. Although critics tended to see it as merely an "MTV clone" and derided it for airing fluff pieces—"It should just shut up and play the music," *Variety's* television reviewer declared—*Friday Night Videos* was an early ratings success.[69]

It was not alone. ABC scored its own late-night syndicated hit with *New York Hot Tracks.* By the mid-1980s, some eighty stations carried the program, and in the nation's biggest television markets, it competed directly with NBC's *Friday Night Videos.* According to producer Brooke Bailey, *Hot Tracks* was successful because it did three things that set it apart from other network video programs. It spotlighted neglected videos, with an emphasis on black artists; it flaunted the show's culturally renowned urban setting, regularly filming inside New York nightclubs and music venues, including the historically black-oriented Apollo Theatre; and it curated its playlists for a predominantly nonwhite viewership. Whereas *Friday Night Videos* occasionally played R&B, perhaps to avoid the bad publicity MTV had earned for "video bigotry," *Hot*

*Tracks* sought to be the broadcast networks' leader in black music video programming.[70]

Meanwhile, by the end of 1985, close to a dozen music video channels had cropped up in regional markets on UHF and low-power frequencies. While certainly lacking viewership on the scale of *New York Hot Tracks,* they could provide their audiences with what *Variety* described as "a cross between the MTV cable service and a local radio station that plays contemporary music all day and night." In this very practical way, small-outlet producers and programmers in cities across the country, including Las Vegas, Houston, Detroit, Los Angeles, Boston, and San Francisco, anchored music shows to local communities. Many aired "homegrown videos," interviewed hometown artists, featured call-in request shows, and even reported the local weather.[71] Viewers of Rick Kurkjian's Oakland-based California Music Channel were treated to San Francisco landscapes and ads from Bay Area businesses including the Oakland Invaders (a short-lived professional football team).[72] Lanny Ziering, the producer of KWHY-TV's *Video LA,* said, "We can't compete against services like MTV. But we can focus on local groups, focus on local events, local concerts, local acts, local hits."[73] John Garbedian of Boston's WVJV-TV explained the strategy more succinctly: "We've localized, localized, localized."[74]

By 1988, American television viewers had at their disposal over one hundred music video programs, most of them focused on pop, rock, and R&B. Furthermore, as *New York Times* music critic Jon Pareles observed, the "high-fashion, high-velocity visual style" of the music video had permeated everything from commercials to scripted dramas like *Miami Vice.* As music television saturated the market, top to bottom, Cynthia Friedland, creator of *Night Flight,* worried that overproduction of music programming was depressing consumer demand for it. "Video is no longer a novelty," she lamented. "Every time you turn on the TV set you've got another video, and if you switch the channel, you're likely to see the same one." As individual shows' ratings sank and advertisers began to flee, the music video industry was pressed to rethink the value of its principal product. Commenting on the rapid maturation of the market, *Night Tracks* producer Tom Lynch offered an analogy that must have sounded ominous to rock 'n' rollers' ears. Music television, he said, had become "like a middle-aged man."[75]

By the late 1980s, MTV was staring down the fate that haunted any programmer committed to an aging format: irrelevance. Thus, the original trailblazer of music video programming, and the catalyst for its proliferation, sought newer, bigger ideas. The most significant of those came from two New Yorkers in MTV's promotions department, Pete Dougherty and Ted Demme. Both men were fans of hip-hop with ties to New York's edgiest music scenes. Dougherty had spent his teen years going to punk and glam rock clubs like CBGB and Max's Kansas City, and he considered producer Rick Rubin and graffiti artist Fab 5 Freddy to be good friends; Demme was a dyed-in-the-wool rap fan who was, unlike his bosses at MTV, attentive to the growing popularity of hip-hop in spite of its lack of commercial exposure.[76] Both were adamant that rap music could rejuvenate the cable channel.

The idea was not a profound one. Years before Ted Demme began hounding MTV's general manager and bugging the company's entire music department about "the next wave of music," others within the recording and television industries were making noise about hip-hop and its unappreciated potential.[77] With strong sales numbers to bolster their case, Def Jam's Bill Stephney and Russell Simmons had labored mightily to convince cable networks to support rap artists and their music. Undaunted by rejection, they remained confident that rap programming, once adopted, would draw audiences across regional, racial, and class lines.[78] Hunting in the late 1980s for a bright spot in a dulled video television landscape, TBS's *Night Tracks* creator Tom Lynch concluded that rap music was "the only good thing that's happened" and that rap videos possessed "the fun rock used to have."[79] Priority Records founder Bryan Turner, of course, was another devoted hip-hop fan who, like Demme, was eager to create avenues of national exposure for rappers (and their labels). He told the *Los Angeles Times* in 1986 that it did not take extraordinary insight to see that white kids were rap's latest and most enthusiastic converts.[80]

*New York Hot Tracks* provided the proof to these arguments. When it first debuted in 1983, the late-night show was a scrappy "vidclip" series that featured not just black videos but hip-hop videos—lots of them. It was originally carried by just one ABC-affiliated station in New York, not far from the uptown nightclubs and street scenes that served as backdrops for the mostly low-budget rap shorts. Within a year, however, *New York Hot Tracks* was syndicated, carried by dozens of stations throughout the country and competing directly, in its regular timeslot, with NBC's *Friday Night Videos*. It was a baffling development at a time when virtually every other music and television outlet recoiled at the idea of playing hip-hop, assuming that audiences would be repelled by it. Just as astonishing was the fact that *New York Hot Tracks* frequently outperformed *Friday Night Videos*—the series that was meant to be as culturally transformative as *Saturday Night Live*. Unlike its bigger-budget competitor, *New York*

*Hot Tracks* did not mimic the MTV model, and its content was not geared for a general white viewership. Indeed, the show billing itself as "The 'Hottest' Late-Night Music Video Program in America" was, as rap promoter Monica Lynch said, "the great black hope."[81]

In the midst of their own company's scramble to refresh its programming, Demme and Dougherty seized on the opportunity *Hot Tracks* handed them. By pointing to its surprising national popularity, and years of impressive hip-hop sales numbers, they prevailed in their campaign to bring rap—its videos, its artists, and its visual culture—to MTV. In the fall of 1988, after airing a one-off hip-hop special that broke ratings records, MTV unveiled its new weekly series: *Yo! MTV Raps.* The program, featured music videos, but was equally defined by the kind of home-turf, venue-based segments that had set *New York Hot Tracks* apart from its competitors. The show's first host, Fab 5 Freddy, rejected the conventional in-studio "VJ" format and instead ventured out into the neighborhoods, homes, and hangouts of the rap artists he profiled to conduct interviews and tape video introductions.

*Yo! MTV Raps* stayed in its own lane as a television program distinctively committed to hip-hop culture and the varied perspectives of black youth, turning what Greg Mack had done for half a decade on KDAY radio in Los Angeles into a national phenomenon. For much of the 1980s, KDAY had been the only broadcast outlet defined by its hip-hop patronage; it was a kind of lone prophet on a media landscape that treated the genre as if it barely existed.[82]

*Yo! MTV Raps* took up that mantle, however, within months of its premiere—a profound shift, even for those in California within reach of KDAY's signal. "Now we had a national show dedicated to our music," Ice Cube explained. Years

later, Snoop Dogg would recall how MTV's new series amplified hip-hop, creating opportunities for exposure he had always assumed were exclusive to white rock artists. For him, as
a Long Beach teen entertaining fantasies of a music career in
rap, *Yo!* was a revelation.[83] Carlton "Chuck D" Ridenhour, the
politically outspoken front man for New York's Public Enemy,
said that hip-hop was "headline news," and that made *Yo!
MTV Raps* "the Black CNN." It presented black life, in stereo.
Just like Ted Turner's pioneering twenty-four-hour Cable
News Network, *Yo!* functioned as a revolutionary new platform for reflecting on the most captivating people and events
of the moment.[84]

Within months of its debut, remarkably high ratings
prompted MTV producers to move *Yo! MTV Raps* to a full-
hour timeslot, to produce it daily, and to rescreen episodes
during early-morning programming. By early 1989, *Yo!* was
airing twelve hours per week. As Def Jam's Bill Adler declared, kids of all backgrounds "have gotten a whiff of rap on
MTV and now they've begun to demand it."[85] For their part,
black kids throughout the country needed no "whiff" to draw
them to a genre they had been consuming for over a decade.
But what Bill Adler recognized, along with *Yo! MTV Raps* ar-
chitect Ted Demme and MTV general manager Lee Masters,
was that other young viewers—particularly white teenage
boys—were tuning in, too. Ironically, in light of all the charges
that had been leveled at the channel's discriminatory programming, *Yo!* put MTV on track to become an outlet dependent on a genre that was predominantly black, even as its
viewership remained mostly white.[86]

For host Fab 5 Freddy, the fact that MTV's audience was
largely white presented radical opportunities. "We know how
whites live," he explained of American culture in the 1980s.

"We don't have to think about it. Motion picture, television, they're all full of how white people live, act, how they kiss." But the introduction of a nationally broadcast hip-hop show, which orbited around black music, black art, black humor, black vernacular, and black individuality, and had a mostly white viewership, meant that "now things are swinging around a little bit."[87] Fab 5 Freddy, and the show's eventual in-studio hosts James "Ed Lover" Roberts and Andre "Doctor Dré" Brown, aligned their work with that of activists and artists across generations, from the nineteenth-century muckraking of Ida B. Wells and the pageantry of Marcus Garvey's UNIA to the literature of James Baldwin and the comedy of Richard Pryor. All of them took aim in their different ways at a national culture that perpetuated inequality by ignoring dimensions of black humanity. Thinking along the same lines, Doug Herzog, MTV senior vice president of programming in the late 1980s, claimed that *Yo!* was as instructive as it was entertaining, particularly for the channel's young, white viewers. "If you are seventeen years old and living in Des Moines, you're not going to pick up the *New York Times*," he asserted, but by tuning into *Yo! MTV Raps*, "you're going to learn a little more about race in America."[88] MTV's executive vice president Lee Masters, originally a hip-hop skeptic, was happy to admit that, within months of *Yo!*'s debut, rap had become one of his channel's biggest attractions in its history, on par with new wave and metal.[89] But on top of this, MTV's executives were saying that rap programming was healthy for America.

Commercial validation—that is, exposure via mainstream outlets that catered to white audiences—mattered to hip-hop artists, promoters, and rap recording labels. From its inception, hip-hop's inability to capture white audiences large enough to gain entry into the media mainstream had excluded it from commercial outlets and threatened its long-term viability. In this context, the launch of *Yo! MTV Raps* was a watershed event, particularly for those hip-hop leaders, like Def Jam's Russell Simmons, who imagined rap as broad-appeal "teenage music" rather than a race-specific dance trend whose time would quickly pass.[90]

But *Yo!*'s hosts did not simply view themselves as cultural ambassadors to America's heartland, and nor was their only objective to crack open pop markets for hip-hop. They were at least as interested in stitching together disparate rap cultures. By the mid-1980s, it was obvious that the genre was rapidly evolving, and no longer wholly defined by Bronx ingenuity, East Village exposure, and Queens style. Instead, hip-hop was flourishing as a set of regionally distinctive and innovative music scenes, each fostering homegrown talent and reflecting local experiences—more and more of them a long way from New York. Fab 5 Freddy was a globetrotting artist with music industry ties who had rare insight into rap's sweeping influence, and privileged access to all its geographically unique variants. As a painter steeped in the postmodern art movements of the era, he was a principled advocate of cultural blending who helped draw together New York's uptown street parties and downtown gallery scene. It was all part of what made him "the coolest person in New York."[91] Using his postmodernist insight, Freddy aimed to fuse together America's various hip-hop sects. Early in his tenure at MTV, he boasted, "I'm the king of synthesis."[92]

From its debut, *Yo! MTV Raps* did more than provide a platform for artists to promote their wares and court skeptical radio programmers; it became "the most important force in hip-hop" because it connected them, by offering a window into the far-flung reaches of American hip-hop and the many contexts in which it flourished. Between videos, *Yo!* was replete with artist interviews and hometown profiles. These segments, which often mimicked news reporting, introduced audiences to a patchwork of the creative styles and real lives rooted in such distinct locales as Bed-Stuy, Queens, Miami Beach, West Philadelphia, Houston's Fifth Ward, East Point Atlanta, Oakland, and Compton (Fig. 4.3).[93]

The *Yo! MTV Raps* platform was tailor-made for the West Coast rappers who already understood quite well that breakout success in the expanding, fractured, and increasingly competitive field of hip-hop did not come from music alone. Neither was it a simple product of radio adds or music video airings. Those things mattered, to be sure—but market demand hinged, more than ever before, on image and intrigue.

■  ■  ■

By the time MTV unveiled its rap programming, NWA and its handlers had already proven adept at spinning media attention into promotional gold. Inventive forms of marketing and distribution had defined the early experiences of the group, individually and collectively. These were self-reliant music makers who had paid cash for pressings and personally distributed cassettes and vinyl on the street, at swap meets, out of car trunks, and to local DJs. The key disadvantage of independence—the lack of advance financial support from a big business entity—spurred each to hone their marketing hustle. The K-Tel veterans at Priority Records who, by

Fig 4.3 Fab 5 Freddy (bottom row, left) pictured in Elysian Park in Central Los Angeles, with Compton rapper Anthony "Tone Loc" Smith, members of Oakland's Digital Underground, Eazy-E and MC Ren of NWA, and Michael Concepcion, a founder and former member of the Los Angeles Crips. All were featured in a 1990 *Yo! MTV Raps* segment on the video shoot for "We're All in The Same Gang." Jeff Kavitz / FilmMagic, Inc. / Getty Images.

contrast, did have rich investors in their corner, still banked on this type of promotional strategy to limit overhead costs while growing their nascent rap label. Bryan Turner's own "but-wait-there's-more" lineage informed his decision to sign Eazy-E and NWA, who promised to encourage "impulse buying" by raising eyebrows with cutting-edge production, taboo topics, and a rebel image. Plugging the talent on the Ruthless roster, he boasted, "[these] are guys who don't pull any punches."[94]

The Ruthless and Priority camps both operated on the premise that controversy was currency. With enough of it, artists and their labels could afford to bypass traditional promotional routes, like pitching to regulated media outlets and producing rock-crossover records, as Def Jam had done in the mid-1980s with mixed results. Priority Records manufactured and distributed *Straight Outta Compton* and Eazy-E's debut studio album *Eazy-Duz-It* widely. But the company invested few resources in marketing the music to radio and television program directors. Like Eazy-E, Turner thought it was a waste of money and manpower when the product he was pushing drew plenty of free publicity (a lesson he had learned well with the success of the California Raisins). Eazy-E was pleased to have a profit motive to encourage his crew to express themselves without limit, to create music they liked without regard for recording industry standards, and to drive the genre forward by elevating the West Coast.[95]

*Straight Outta Compton* stunned rap fans and critics alike. It was an album packed with expletives, which was still a rather extraordinary phenomenon in hip-hop music; its obscene content alone was fodder for music writers, particularly in the wake of the protests following the RIAA's controversial decision to place "parental advisory" stickers on music it deemed indecent. "Explicit lyrics on parade," *Billboard* alerted its readers. The *Independent* noted sardonically that NWA's debut "involves heavy rotation of the word 'motherf—er,' without which the album would be considerably shorter." The *Guardian* compared the group's music to Andrew "Dice" Clay's comedy, in that both dared to "say the unsayable" to test the boundaries of liberalism. Rather than "blunt or transcend the savagery of their milieu," it continued, "they appear to revel in it."[96] Meanwhile, a pop music writer for the *Los Angeles Times* noted that NWA's "X-rated tales about gang violence" had drawn the ire of critics "who feel the records glorify gang behavior." Still, that reviewer's assessment of the album was that "for all its crudeness, [NWA] exhibits a sense of artistic spirit and vision."[97]

Fanning further curiosity—and outrage—was the group's own name, which it did not spell out but left as an acronym for audiences to surmise. The group effectively baited reporters and critics into filling in the forbidden epithet and then finding themselves in a conversation about race. Only in late 1989, after months of awkward press descriptions of the group's moniker, did Ice Cube disclose on Fox Television's *Pump It Up!* that he and his bandmates chose the name "Niggaz Wit Attitudes" because "we wanted to scare a lot of people, start a little commotion." The name alone was a deliberate choice, Eazy-E later told *Spin*, crafted to assert "the 'I don't give a fuck' attitude."[98]

More impactful than anything else the young talents at Ruthless / Priority did, they cast themselves as the black outlaw face of LA and, by doing so, asserted a bold corrective to the standard mythologies of the place. "Whenever the media shows California," Ice Cube told the *Guardian* in 1989, "all they picture is beaches and pretty girls; they never go to our neighborhood."⁹⁹ There had always been tales of Los Angeles, of course, that challenged La-La Land lore; in the 1980s, these included neo-noir and cop films. Crime and poverty, gang wars and drug trafficking, death and despair were all on display in big studio productions like *Repo Man, To Live and Die in L.A., Lethal Weapon,* and *Colors.* Film narratives captivated audiences with fictional interpretations of the seamy underside of America's most fabled promised land. But they did so through a white lens. As Ice Cube argued, even the controversial *Colors,* which employed real Los Angeles gang-affiliated youth as extras, was filmed on gang turf, and included a range of complex and sympathetic black characters, was at its core a film about a pair of white LAPD officers. *Colors* exposed many Americans to LA's gang crisis for the first time, Cube noted, but what they witnessed was mainly "the police point of view" rather than a story that evoked his personal reality. Priority's Bryan Turner took every opportunity to echo this theme, telling the music press that his artists "lived the things they talk about," in sharp contrast to the script and screenplay writers out there. Indeed, in the context of a growing fascination with troubled Los Angeles, and sensational national news reporting on crimes in the region, *Straight Outta Compton* sounded like documentary. "This is the real world of *Colors,*" one critic pronounced.¹⁰⁰

When NWA first appeared on *Yo! MTV Raps* in the spring of 1989, just a few months after both its album and MTV's new hip-hop show had debuted, the group's shock-oriented marketing strategy had only barely paid dividends, even with an album brimming with scandalous content. In the fall of 1988, the National Academy of Songwriters picked Eazy-E, Dr. Dre, and Ruthless manager Jerry Heller, as experts on LA rap, to star as keynote speakers at a "Raptalk" seminar in

Santa Monica. A few significant adds on urban contemporary radio, and Eazy-E's appearance on the Top Pop Album chart, also earned Priority Records a feature in a December 1988 issue of *Billboard*. The trade publication credited the label with "zeroing in on the hardcore side of California hip-hop."[101] It was not much compared to the hype swirling around New York-based acts like Run-DMC and LL Cool J, or around the emerging Afrocentric "New School" artists, including De La Soul, Queen Latifah, and Public Enemy. But it was enough to secure NWA a prized spot as guests on *Yo!*

The MTV show presented rap music videos within the context of human-interest stories, and NWA had the potential to be the most interesting story of them all. *Yo!* host Fab 5 Freddy took MTV's cameras into Compton. As was his usual mode of operation, he refused to sequester his LA guests inside the network's stuffy New York studio and instead traveled west to embed himself in their world. There, both host and subject worked to rouse the viewing audience with images that contradicted popular California clichés. Freddy introduced the NWA segment with a nod to the prevailing narratives of Los Angeles—that it produced Hollywood celebrities, beach bodies, and suburban bliss, but not street rap. Then the members of NWA appeared, draped around the "Welcome to Compton" stone marker and dressed, in spite of the sunny weather, in layers of black Los Angeles Kings and Raiders gear. Eazy-E, the crew's ringleader and Freddy's prime focus, was most prominently outfitted in a white, bulletproof vest. The group escorted *Yo!* through their Compton haunts, suggesting along the way that the bungalows and palm trees were not the signposts of paradise after all. This was a ghetto landscape where gangs roamed, police loomed, and black kids were vulnerable to both.

Part music variety show, part investigative reporting, *Yo! MTV Raps* provided NWA's members with their first significant, nationally televised opportunity to assert themselves as young innovators who mattered as much for the art they produced as for the reality they personified. The video for "Straight Outta Compton" was not yet complete, so they used their time on *Yo!* to improvise a powerful visual narrative and demonstrate that "the hardest stuff is coming out of this beautiful place."[102] The NWA episode of *Yo!* offered glimpses of easygoing black youth culture in LA, including kids horsing around at a swap meet, friends meandering along Venice Beach, and young men cruising around the neighborhood in classic cars. But it also presented bracing allusions to poverty and violence. The appearance bolstered NWA's street credibility, giving them a platform to speak as if on behalf of their LA peers, including those in gangs. The rappers could posture as "ghetto reporters" with more authority than the most embedded of CNN correspondents.[103]

The scenes they and Fab 5 Freddy curated resonated with *Yo!*'s viewers, many of whom, in spite of their interest in hip-hop culture, did not know the group or anything about Compton.[104] Atlanta's Antwan "Big Boi" Patton was barely fourteen when NWA unmasked Los Angeles for MTV's rap fans, but remembered the show well. "It was cold blooded," he said, "it was like, damn, this is their neighborhood! You got introduced to what Compton looks like." In Philadelphia, Ahmir "?uestlove" Thompson's reaction was more visceral: "Bulletproof vests? What the hell!?"[105] Fab 5 Freddy remembered the NWA episode as a potent introduction to an otherwise little-known California group and to their unusually hardcore hip-hop brand. *Yo! MTV Raps* gave the nation its first taste of Los Angeles reality rap, or as the press preferred to call it, "gangsta rap."[106]

One month after MTV introduced America to NWA, however, the network refused to air the group's music video for
"Straight Outta Compton." Claiming that its hardcore depic-
tion of a police gang sweep of black teens "glorified violence,"
MTV executives passed on a short film that, for all intents and
purposes, just reinforced the portrait of "gangsta rap" the
channel had already showcased. More importantly, the cable
outlet that had always seemed willing to rile censors with rock
videos now proved uncomfortable with a dramatization of
the sort of police harassment considered routine in black Los
Angeles. After introducing its national audience to the most
provocative rap group in the genre's history, immersing viewers in NWA's striking West Coast origins, and extolling Los
Angeles rap's "ghetto truths," MTV was refusing to show the
most fundamental truth of them all.

NWA and Priority Records deeply resented MTV's decision for two related reasons. First, the group, especially its
founder Eazy-E, craved commercial success. After years of
scraping by as self-sustaining independent artists and struggling to hit six-digit sales numbers, the Ruthless crew had
dared to dream that MTV would launch them into the mainstream. There were precedents for that hope in, for instance,
the explosive success of Philadelphia's DJ Jazzy Jeff and the
Fresh Prince, Compton's own Tone Loc, and even NWA's labelmate J.J. Fad, who all made it big following MTV's airing
of their music videos.[107] Priority Records' Bryan Turner, a
disciple of the original infomercial empire, was incensed with
MTV for depriving his most promising act of the promotional exposure the channel could supply. He sent out press
releases slamming MTV for censorship and charging the
company with racism, an accusation that MTV easily refuted
with a statement from hip-hop heavyweights at Def Jam,

who defended the network's decision to "play what they think is right for their program."[108]

Second, as Ice Cube made clear in fiery interviews, the group was angered by a sense of disempowerment. In the course of developing their identities as artists, the young Los Angeles rappers had discovered that commercial success could amplify the voices of the disenfranchised. Notoriety could be leveraged to challenge enemies, including those representing the power of law enforcement. Glen "Daddy-O" Bolton of Stetsasonic noted that NWA "talked about issues," which made the Compton rappers heroes of "the underground, because they're saying what people want to hear."[109] But NWA wanted that message to resonate aboveground, too. "Yo! Shit's fucked up," Ice Cube proclaimed. "Somebody's gonna pay attention."[110]

The American public did pay attention, and the fact that MTV did not want it to only sharpened interest. MTV's refusal to play NWA's riveting music video was a decision that drove untold numbers of rap fans to the channel's competitors. *Video Jukebox Network* (aka *The Box*) took particular advantage of the situation when it launched nationwide, in March of 1989, under the leadership of a former MTV executive. Its vow was to "play things you are not going to hear on . . . any of those other channels," including those rap videos "that wouldn't fly anywhere else."[111] That music video fans had access to "Straight Outta Compton," even as MTV blacklisted it, gave NWA a bigger platform. Now they were icons of the era's free speech debates, as well as symbols of LA's urban crisis. In the spring of that year, NWA graced the cover of an *LA Weekly* issue featuring an in-depth article on the MTV controversy. *Melody Maker, Spin, Yo!, Word Up!, The Guardian, New Musical Express, Billboard*, the *Washington*

*Post,* and the *Los Angeles Times,* among others, covered "Compton's Controversial Posse" with fervor. By the summer, NWA's debut album *Straight Outta Compton* was certified gold, an achievement sweetened by a sudden burst in ticket sales for the group's summer concert tour—a venture that Eazy-E arranged hastily that May after plans for the group to perform on Ice-T's tour fell through. In the space of a month, NWA rose from being an opening act to headlining its own sixty-city concert tour.[112]

■   ■   ■

When, back in 1987, Capitol Records Chairman Joe Smith thumbed his nose at Jerry Heller's proposal to sign Eazy-E and NWA, he had asked the wrong question. Smith had challenged Heller's logic in sponsoring a bunch of California kids who rapped about guns, gangsters, and police: "Who's going to listen?" The more astute question would have been, "Who's going to watch?"[113]

In a twist, NWA was able to capitalize on music television promotion, generating sales and a torrent of publicity, by highlighting the fact that MTV would not play its music. NWA recognized the opportunities embedded within the rapidly changing media environment of the Reagan era, when visual consumption of music came to the fore and controversy was currency. The group and its label spotted opportunities and used them strategically to garner the kind of attention that would drive commercial success, to pull the focus of hip-hop to the West Coast, and to expose Americans to a veiled corner of LA society. The members of NWA viewed these goals as compatible and even mutually reinforcing; fame promised them strong sales numbers, a spotlight for West Coast rap, and clout as "truth tellers."

It was a path that made NWA the focal point of hip-hop. It made Los Angeles gangsta rap a target of the FBI. And it primed the public for Rodney King.

CHAPTER **5** · # Without a Gun and a Badge

■ **Though never released as a single** or a music video, "Fuck tha Police" was, by the summer of 1989, the most recognized song in NWA's repertoire. Its profane lyrics were quotable, the chorus an obscene three-word earworm, the conceit an anti-state tongue-lashing. "Fuck tha Police" was theatrical, funky, and unusually explicit, with the track's very title censored on all packaging and promotional materials for the *Straight Outta Compton* album. It was also considered dangerous and inflammatory. According to the Parents Music Resource Center, the national Fraternal Order of Police, and at least one FBI public affairs officer, the song advocated violence.[1] Even in an era of "punk riots," "porn-rock" Senate hearings, and "parental advisory" stickers, "Fuck tha Police" was a grenade of controversy.[2]

Ice Cube called the record his "revenge fantasy." It was a fictional courtroom drama in which each member of NWA took turns prosecuting the Los Angeles Police Department, on trial for abuse of power.[3] With Judge Dr. Dre presiding, Cube, MC Ren, and Eazy-E portrayed ferocious attorneys and star witnesses, detailing in rhyme a litany of crimes including harassment (*"Fuckin' with me 'cause I'm a teenager / With a little bit of gold and a pager"*), excessive force (*"They're scared of a nigga / So they mace me to blind me"*), privacy violations (*"Search a nigga down and grabbin' his nuts"*), and racial profiling (*"Searchin' my car, lookin' for the product / Thinking every nigga is sellin' narcotics"*). Each rapper punctuated his evidence with retaliatory, epithet-filled threats. Ice Cube promised to *"swarm / On any muthafucka in a blue uniform,"* and mused about a *"bloodbath of cops dyin' in LA."* Ren challenged his uniformed nemesis to *"take off the gun"* and stand toe-to-toe with him—*"And we'll go at it, punk, and I'm-a fuck you up!"* Then, he imagined that with the officer disarmed, he would pick up his gun and transform into a modern-day wild-west vigilante, *"takin' out a cop or two."* Eazy-E, the *"gangsta"* with *"flava,"* echoed Ren with his own provocation: *"Without a gun and a badge, what do you got? / A sucker in a uniform waiting to get shot."* At the end of the drama, Judge Dre issued his final verdict to the imagined defendant: *"The jury has found you guilty of being a redneck, white-bread, chicken-shit mutherfucker."*[4]

"'Fuck tha Police' isn't a metaphor for anything," wrote *LA Weekly*'s culture writer Jonathan Gold in May 1989, attentive to the national furor swirling around NWA's album cut. The rappers were as literal as they came, Gold concluded, even when they spun vengeance tales. They were also transparently tormented by the system the *"chicken-shit mutherfucker"* represented. The song that, by the summer, riled the censors and outraged law enforcement was, Gold wrote, "the sort of snarling anti-cop rant left unsaid until the black-and-white is around the corner and safely out of earshot."[5] It was the equivalent of kicking a trash can.

*LA Weekly* had spent a spring day that year interviewing the NWA rappers for their first-ever magazine cover feature.

The paper determined that the once-obscure rap group, who in 1988 played second fiddle to pop-crossover label mates J.J. Fad, had earned the *Weekly*'s treasured spotlight. *Straight Outta Compton* was certified gold; hip-hop's illustrious ambassador Fab 5 Freddy had profiled the group on the nationally broadcast *Yo! MTV Raps;* and the crew had moved from opening for the dance-crossover sensation Salt-N-Pepa to headlining over rap star MC Hammer. Plus, along the way, the music press eagerly underwrote the rappers' claim to being "street reporters." It was a title with growing cachet in the emerging culture of cable news and tabloid television—a genre that included Geraldo Rivera's *American Vice*, the crowdsourced crime series *America's Most Wanted*, and, by that spring, Fox Broadcasting's *Cops*.[6] The young Los Angeles rappers recognized the industry's fascination with their "urban-gangster life," and in a slew of media appearances, they delivered on the buzz. The newly-minted hip-hop stars prepared for their big *LA Weekly* photo shoot by rummaging through a canvas duffel bag stuffed with pistols, shotguns, and rifles. Ice Cube boasted to the magazine, "NWA can't get any harder unless the streets get harder, know what I'm saying?" But the menacing props, just like the "gangsta rap" label affixed to NWA's brand of hip-hop, obscured the deepest message embedded in the group's most controversial song. As Jonathan Gold understood, "Fuck tha Police" was an uncensored expression of powerlessness—a fantasy about scoring a victory when defeat was already a burning reality.[7]

■   ■   ■

Through 1988, national headlines announced that "gang-related" crimes had become as much the hallmark of life in South Los Angeles County as the palm trees that hovered above. There were lurid features about "yuppie havens" under threat, where, in the worst of scenarios, upstanding citizens died in gang crossfire. Leaders in Sacramento warned of LA's rampant "street terrorism" spreading like a cancer to the Inland Empire and as far north as Portland, Oregon. Film and television directors composed backdrops of urban blight and black crime, and white fear contaminated California's vaunted promised land.[8]

With the swirling drama of the late 1980s as leverage, LAPD Chief Daryl Gates was able to amass the political and moral capital he needed to intensify his department's already aggressive anti-gang operations. A popular mandate and the support of the LA County Sheriff's Department allowed the chief to redeploy the six-ton battering ram that had been retired in 1985 after public outcry. He reauthorized his drug task force to coordinate cover-of-night raids in residential communities thought to house narcotics traffickers. And, with the cooperation of the county sheriff, Gates conducted his signature gang sweeps in predominantly black "gangland areas" throughout South Los Angeles. South Central native Maxine Waters, an LA councilwoman at the time, lamented that as her community grappled with real challenges including drug abuse and gun violence, Chief Gates had made it dangerous for black residents to call for help. His bellicosity, she argued, produced a "Catch-22" for her people, who were frustrated with the "abuse" of their trust, their safety, and their children. An African-American legal aide serving Los Angeles citizens caught up in gang sweeps and drug raids was blunt: "Who will protect us from the police?"[9]

National attention to LA's street gang crisis rose throughout 1988 and peaked in 1989. As it did, police action in these local gangland regions broadened and intensified to such a degree that one Los Angeles civil rights activist characterized it as "police gangbanging." Yet, with all the media coverage of juvenile crime, turf wars, and drive-by shootings, there was little room for and little interest in a discussion about the parallel—and historically rooted—dilemma of police violence, which, in Los Angeles, directly affected the day-to-day lives of people already challenged by crime in their communities.

In the midst of escalating tensions in his hometown, Dr. Dre addressed his band's growing reputation as Los Angeles rap outlaws. NWA was "nasty and hardcore," he readily conceded to a *Los Angeles Times* reporter, but that was beside the point. His group's music, and specifically a track like "Fuck tha Police," mattered because it laid bare a basic truth about kids in black communities like Compton: "That's how they feel about the cops."[10] Ice Cube reaffirmed Dre's point, explaining, "You have no voice. Nobody can hear you scream." As music artists with access to the tools of production and promotion, Cube said, NWA aired "all that pain and frustration" with the expectation that someone would listen.[11]

The members of NWA argued that their intent in making such provocative music was to get attention, not only from the world of hip-hop, which had long thumbed its nose at the West Coast, but from a nation that either had no sympathy for them or ignored them altogether. It was the same compulsion felt by many generations of disempowered people who have made art to comment candidly on their underrepresented position in society. Back in the mid-1970s, as the black arts movement began to wane, the NAACP had talked about "the urge to think, act, and feel black" in the public arena without restrictions; NWA's music was a product of that. On the broad spectrum of "black identity," hardcore rap was a point, and thus a contribution to the ever-changing cultural dialogue about black experiences in America. And, as civil rights activists had predicted years before the decade of cable television, portable CD players, and music videos, innovations in the production and consumption of media could animate and, more significantly, amplify those experiences as never before. The "power" of popular culture in the late twentieth century could, black leaders hoped, revive critical discussions about racial inequality that had gone quiet as Americans allowed themselves to believe that the nation's racial problems had been solved in the Sixties.[12] Those imagining the form a new radical black arts movement might take, including those who had embraced the violence and hypermasculinity of blaxploitation films and other controversial creative works of the post–Black Power era, may not have anticipated NWA's "Fuck tha Police" or its impact.

*Straight Outta Compton* was, first, a product of and response to a climate of oppression in South Los Angeles County—an environment in which young men were subject to a brutal and indiscriminate "by all means necessary" police plan to eradicate gang crime—where, as MC Ren said, kids were targeted for what they wore and where they lived.[13] Just as Toddy Tee's "Batterram" had, four years earlier, roared from cars cruising through African-American neighborhoods under siege, "Fuck tha Police" served as an outlet for young people who wanted to vent frustration over their inability—and their community's failure—to check the omnipresent forces governing their lives. "I'm black, male, and young, so what's happening to me is likely to be happening to NWA's audience," Ice Cube said of the track he co-wrote, pinpointing a key reason that his lyrics resonated in his hometown. "I know what it's like," one LA gang member said of the song's core sentiment. "I've been harassed by the police, I've been thrown down on the ground, and I had to hop fences." Alert to his own oppression, he reveled in the spirit of insurrection emanating from NWA's lyrics, and he claimed it for himself: "That was my freedom of speech."[14] For Louis "B-Real" Freese, a Chicano kid from a mixed community just north of Compton, "Fuck tha Police" was as cathartic as it was revelatory. The aspiring rapper, who later penned his own indictment of police abuse as a member of Cypress Hill, appreciated hearing NWA describe the same indignities he endured.[15] When he began film school, South Central native John Singleton considered Rob Reiner's 1986 movie *Stand By Me* incomparable as a work of coming-of-age cinema, but the story represented only white childhood. As he puzzled over how to dramatize the lives of boys in the 'hood, he heard in NWA's music young black artists just like him, "giving voice to everything I had seen growing up."[16]

But by the end of 1989, *Straight Outta Compton* reverberated more widely, with "Fuck tha Police" emerging as the linchpin of its popularity. "That's my shit," Brooklyn rapper Glen "Daddy-O" Bolton said of NWA's "Fuck tha Police." He told *Spin* in early 1989 that even in New York, a city notoriously protective of its exclusive claim to hip-hop, and where attitudes were generally averse to West Coast rap, the record was consumed like a powerful new drug "you never had . . . before." He thought NWA mesmerized kids in New York because "they're visual, they're talented," but more importantly, the group hit big in his city "because they're saying what people want to hear."[17] Another Brooklyn native, Shawn "Jay-Z" Carter, discovered in NWA's music something that, in his view, had been "missing" from even the most militant New York rap. *Criminal Minded,* the 1987 debut from South Bronx-based Boogie Down Productions, and *It Takes a Nation of Millions to Hold Us Back,* the radically political album by Long Island's own Public Enemy, appropriated themes of the inner-city ghetto in ways that spoke to some of Jay-Z's experiences. He heard in their music some acknowledgment of poor, black kids like him who adopted the ways of the "street hustler," did not always abide by the law, and rejected victimization. But in songs like "Straight Outta Compton" and "Fuck tha Police," he found more than a nod in his direction. He heard his own voice.[18] Meanwhile, in a Philadelphia high school orchestra class, Tariq "Black Thought" Trotter passed his headphones to Ahmir "?uestlove" Thompson and invited him to listen to *Straight Outta Compton*. Already a hip-hop enthusiast, the sixteen-year-old ?uestlove was thunderstruck. "There were certain things that artists didn't do," he remembered. "You just didn't say, 'Fuck the police.'" With a sense that he was witnessing something both musically and culturally transformative, he borrowed the cassette. "I ditched chamber orchestra and sat in the furnace room with a cheap-ass GE walkman and listened to that album from start to finish."[19]

In 1988, before NWA recalibrated the rap landscape with *Straight Outta Compton*, hip-hop had already begun to shift in favor of greater regional and artistic diversity. Whereas only a handful of hip-hop acts (Beastie Boys, Run-DMC, LL Cool J, Dana Dane, Fat Boys, and Whodini) managed to break into the *Billboard* Top 100 in 1987, all of them from New York and most tied to production teams at Def Jam or Profile, 1988 marked a watershed moment when the genre broke free from Russell Simmons's mold. That year, the pop charts were studded with hip-hop albums, including commercial triumphs from New York's EPMD, Eric B & Rakim, Biz Markie, Public Enemy, and Boogie Down Productions, dance crossovers from Salt-N-Pepa and Ruthless Records' own J.J. Fad, a first release from Philadelphia's DJ Jazzy Jeff & the Fresh Prince and a rerelease from hardcore Philly

rapper Schoolly D, a Miami bass rap album from South Florida's 2 Live Crew, and Los Angeles rap hits by way of Ice-T's
*Rhyme Pays* and the *Colors* soundtrack, a rap compilation
tied to Dennis Hopper's film. Recognizing the sea change,
large record distributors, including RCA, Columbia, and
Warner Brothers, moved to sign artists from across the rap
spectrum and leapt into partnerships with smaller hip-hop
labels, like Jive and Cold Chillin' Records, providing precisely
the access to industry resources and retail markets that these
small enterprises had long desired. The impact of industry
investment in hip-hop on the genre was especially dramatic
after *Yo! MTV Raps* ensured that rap artists would enjoy the
same visual platform that had fast-tracked the careers of acts
like Duran Duran, Madonna, and Whitney Houston. Within
just two years, the destiny of hip-hop as an evolving, thriving,
commercially viable creative force tipped from uncertain to
manifest.

The same was evident for West Coast rap, as a disproportionate number of California-based hip-hop artists snagged
spots on the charts for both top pop and top black album well
before NWA headed out on its first multicity concert tour
in the summer of 1989. Already by 1988, Too $hort and MC
Hammer, both natives of East Oakland in Northern California, and a roster of Los Angeles rappers, including Crenshaw's
Ice-T, Compton's Tone Loc, King Tee, Eazy-E, NWA, and The
D.O.C. (who came to LA by way of Dallas) had scaled the *Billboard* charts. The center of gravity for hip-hop seemed to be
shifting away from New York's concrete jungles and toward
the land of infinite coastline. Moreover, the new cultural ar-
chetype of the California "gangster" continued to take hold.
Ice-T invoked it in advertising for *Power* by claiming to be the
"world's biggest dope dealer" and when he boasted that the

guns used as props on the album's cover were in fact his. Roger "King Tee" McBride's studio debut *Act a Fool*, for all the pleas for peace in its lyrics, had him on the album cover stepping purposefully from his white Cadillac onto an LA street with a sawed-off shotgun dangling from his right hand. Also wearing Locs sunglasses and "house shoes," he epitomized Compton street style.[20] Public enthusiasm for an LA noir redux—a fresh iteration of the classic noir juxtaposition of urban nightmare and California Dream—was apparent to Ice Cube, and he drew from it in promoting *Straight Outta Compton*. "When most people think of LA, they think of palm trees and beaches and girls in bikinis," he told *Melody Maker* in August 1989, "but there's another side to the city which is kept hidden from view."[21]

"Fuck tha Police" was a breakout hit on an album that benefited from these cultural shifts. Supported by word of mouth, cassettes, and handheld devices like ?uestlove's "cheap-ass GE walkman," it captivated hip-hop fans across the country and fed their growing appetite for West Coast rap and gangster aesthetics. Priority CEO Bryan Turner believed that much of NWA's appeal to consumers in 1989 was in its willingness to push the boundaries of hip-hop's established street canon. Whatever the reasons, within weeks of its release, *Straight Outta Compton* did what few other hip-hop albums, and virtually no non-New York projects, had. It penetrated far-flung consumer markets, broke the top 40 on the *Billboard* 200, and spent nearly fifty weeks on the top black albums chart. Very quickly, the group found itself in an elite class that included music acts like Bobby Brown, Paula Abdul, and New Kids on the Block.

"Fuck tha Police" was like no LA rap hit before it, particularly because it hooked listeners who had never set foot in

South Los Angeles County. It was quite unlike Toddy Tee's "Batterram," that locally cherished early track virtually unknown outside of the battering ram's LA theater of operations, and it surpassed the grassroots success of "The Boyz-N-The Hood." By the time *Straight Outta Compton* debuted, NWA could benefit from the dramatic changes in entertainment media and in hip-hop production that had occurred since that 1987 single hit the streets. But content mattered as much as context. The fundamental message in "Fuck tha Police" did not depend on knowledge of phenomena unique to South Los Angeles. The "Batterram" was site-specific, resonating with those familiar with the LAPD and its bizarre armored weapon. Similarly, "Boyz" played best in markets in the West and the South, where rap fans were well-versed in low-rider car culture. "Fuck tha Police" was, of course, grounded in local grievances. But it also spoke directly to a problem plaguing all of black America.

When talk-show host Arsenio Hall addressed how the track had underscored poor police-community relations in the group's hometown, Dr. Dre corrected him: "Not only Compton. Not only Compton." MC Ren spoke up, too, to say the record he co-wrote was not, by intention, a revolutionary cry, but rather an expression of a common—though privately voiced—feeling about state authority. "In everybody's lifetime, they get harassed by the police for no reason," Ren explained, "and everybody wants to say it, but they can't on the spot 'cause something will happen to them." With fame working as both megaphone and shield, NWA dismissed the risks that normally accompanied such a protest, seizing an opportunity to confront police power as others could not. "We're getting back at them," Ren told Hall's television audience, "for all the years we couldn't do nothing."[22]

∎    ∎    ∎

"We as a country, and we as a police organization, can't stand by and let people feed this to the youth." In the summer of 1989, Dewey Stokes, the national president of the Fraternal Order of Police (essentially a labor union for the nation's law enforcement officers), announced that his organization was drafting a resolution to advise its members to "refuse to work at or provide security for concerts by any group advocating violence against police officers"—in effect, making a coordinated effort to keep NWA from being able to stage concerts. The Fraternal Order of Police also implored private security firms not to provide their services. The national organization, with its 203,000 members, also passed an official resolution to boycott any event or product associated with the rappers "who are out trying to get brother police officers killed."

The Los Angeles rappers, who were riding a wave of album sales and publicity that spring, had just announced their first national headline tour when the attempts to silence them started. Local police departments in cities on the planned tour began receiving messages via an informal "fax campaign" from other officers around the country. Managers of performance venues, too, shared copies of lyrics from *Straight Outta Compton* with their counterparts in other cities, highlighting the most "inflammatory" language in "Fuck tha Police." All these communications served to galvanize law enforcement communities from Philadelphia to Shreveport in opposition to gangsta rap.[23]

In Richmond, Virginia, for instance, enraged patrolmen called for city managers to rescind an event permit for an NWA show booked at the Richmond Coliseum—and asked the public more broadly to boycott the music. The acting mayor of Kansas City declared that the rappers were not welcome in his town. On- and off-duty officers from Toledo refused to provide security for the group's Ohio stop. In Baltimore's Prince George's County, police successfully barred NWA from appearing at a rap festival held at the Capital Centre. In Shreveport, Louisiana, police positioned barricades all around a concert site so it could monitor everyone coming and going on the grounds. The Cincinnati Police Department tripled the number of officers it typically assigned to large concerts at the Riverfront Coliseum, expecting trouble.[24]

Local police officials in Detroit tried a different approach, sending members to stake out the NWA show at the Joe Louis Arena from inside so they could monitor the "bad boys of hip-hop" and their fans who reportedly chanted "Fuck tha Police" at every concert. Of particular interest was whether NWA would respond to the chants and perform its most controversial track, despite having agreed to leave it off the set list. So far, in other cities, NWA had chosen not to perform it. But, perhaps as a statement on Detroit's more aggressive policing, or perhaps as a spontaneous celebration of this final tour show in Detroit, the group used an encore to launch into it. They had not completed the first verse before management at the Joe Louis Arena cut sound and turned up the house lights, ending the show. After tussling with NWA's staff, and later detaining members of the group briefly at their hotel, one Detroit officer told the press, "We just wanted to show the kids that you can't say 'fuck the police' in Detroit."[25]

The real problem for the FOP and for local law enforcement in most of these cities was not that NWA itself would insult them. The bigger threat was in the group's swelling

popularity. Rumors of fans gleefully yelling anti-cop expletives at each concert suggested that NWA had become a conduit for protest. Police abuse was a hot-button local issue in
many of these concert tour stops, in which black residents
had contended with patterns of harassment similar to the
kind described in "Fuck tha Police." In the months before
NWA first arrived in Toledo, Ohio, its police chief, Martin
Felker, had responded to an uptick in crime in the city's Old
West End district by instructing his officers to "pay attention
to groups of black juveniles." He issued orders to stop and
question these youths, implying in his directive that race was
probable cause enough. When an association of African-
American lawyers filed a federal civil rights lawsuit against
Toledo law enforcement, Felker rescinded his order, but the
relationship between the city's small black population and its
mostly white police force remained strained; in the weeks
leading up to NWA's Toledo appearance, a prominent black
clergyman quoted the rappers in a letter to Police Chief
Felker noting that the city's black community was of the mind
that "police think they have the authority to kill a minority."[26]
In another corner of the state, Cincinnati, juvenile courts had
become flooded with teenagers from "inner-city black areas"
as local police acted on the theory that poor, African-American kids were working as cocaine couriers, bolstering Ohio's
sudden "culture of the crack house."[27] The anger in Detroit,
one of America's most racially segregated and violent cities,
had been simmering longer. There, black residents complained
about "racist" police functioning as if they were private security forces serving the white suburbs—whose residents were
"truly terrified," in the words of social commentator Ze'ev
Chafets, by Detroit's "racial composition, and the physical
threat they associate with blacks."[28]

As NWA headed out on its first national tour, these tensions plus a ream of high-profile cases of police misconduct in the East put the growing conflict between individual rights and urban systems of law and order on full display. The result was an amplification of the problems portrayed in Los Angeles rap at the same moment that NWA's promotional push for its controversial debut album was at its apex.

In August, the group was slated to headline a rap showcase at the Capital Centre in Washington, DC, but the late summer timing put the show right in the midst of turmoil surrounding a recent police killing. A couple of months earlier, just east of DC, four white officers in Prince George's County, Maryland, had beaten two Ghanaian brothers, Martin and Gregory Habib, during a traffic stop. The four county cops left Martin with a broken jaw and internal bleeding; Gregory Habib was killed, a result of crushing blows to his chest and abdomen that damaged his heart and lungs.[29] "It's unfortunate and I feel very, very bad about the death of the young man," the county's police chief, Michael Flaherty, told a local reporter, "but as unfortunate as it is, I don't know if there was any misconduct on the part of the officers."[30] The *Washington Post* profiled Chief Flaherty, emphasizing the burdens of his job, particularly in light of an "exploding wave of crime and violence, fueled by an epidemic of crack cocaine," and record-breaking homicide numbers.[31] A county grand jury considering charges against the four patrolmen issued no indictments. State's Attorney Alex Williams, the first black prosecutor to hold the job, cried foul, warning that tensions between the mostly white police force and the mostly black community had been mounting for years, and Gregory Habib's death might be a tipping point. The local press noted that NWA's planned concert appearance had come at a bad time for police, particularly because the rappers refused to sign a contract promising that they would not perform any portion of their song "Fuck tha Police." Under pressure from county officials, Capital Centre promoters dropped NWA from the showcase.[32]

At the same time, in New York, where NWA had no planned concerts but its fan base was swelling, a cascade of alarming reports highlighted the tragic consequences of, as one criminal justice advocate put it, the "racist attitudes permeating the New York Police Department."[33] In Brooklyn, for instance, police dragged a father from his car for protesting a parking violation, knowingly endangering the man's three-week-old baby, who was left alone in the cold by arresting officers who referred to the child as "the little nigger." In a 1987 case, a white resident who attempted to document the bloody beating of a cuffed black teen at a Manhattan subway station was himself handcuffed, injured, detained on specious charges, and kept in custody for two days.[34] In January 1989, outrage grew over an incident in Queens, in which New York police surrounded seventy-one-year-old Ann Hamilton while she sat in her car eating peanuts. Officers smashed in the elderly woman's windshield and dragged her from the vehicle, arresting her for "reckless endangerment," an accusation the department justified by noting that Hamilton had been digging in her glove compartment while parked in what police described as a drug zone. Calls from the woman's family, from African-American religious leaders, and from the local black press to prosecute police for their involvement in a "reign of terror" resulted in an apology from Mayor Ed Koch, but little else. In early 1989, Hamilton's lawyer told *New York Amsterdam News* that police misconduct was a product of the Koch administration and its unwillingness to protect black New Yorkers from civil rights abuses.[35]

In the wake of that incident, news broke that eight black and Latino boys had been arrested for the brutal rape of a white Central Park jogger named Patricia Meili. After Manhattan's District Attorney announced charges against five of the teens, described in the national press as "wilding" (a term derived from a rumor that rapper Tone Loc's hit "Wild Thing" was the inspiration behind the boys' alleged crimes), civil rights advocates and police watch dogs in New York poked holes in the evidence and accused investigators of subjecting the boys to torturous interrogation conditions reminiscent of Russia in "the Josef Stalin era." Meanwhile, prominent New York real-estate mogul Donald Trump paid for a large ad in the New York press—Trump's "High-Priced Graffiti," as one critic referred to it—sounding the alarm about "the complete breakdown of life as we know it" and calling for New York's political leaders to "unshackle [cops] from the constant chant of 'police brutality' which every petty criminal hurls immediately at an officer who has just risked his or her life to save another's." Trump's full-page indictment of "wild criminals . . . of every age" and his explicit call to "bring back the death penalty" was black-and-white proof of the cultural chasm between those who lived with the injustices underpinning legal processes and those who denied any injustice existed at all.[36]

"Advocating violence and assault is wrong," Milt Ahlerich, an FBI public affairs officer, wrote to NWA's label in his August 1989 letter, "and we in the law enforcement community take exception to such action." The "fax campaign" undertaken by an informal network of police officers to alert other departments to the lyrical content in *Straight Outta Compton* had apparently reached Ahlerich's office, and claiming to represent "the FBI's position," he scolded Priority Records for music that was "discouraging and degrading" to police officers at

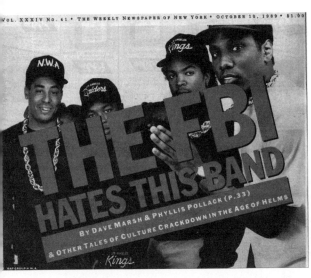

VOL. XXXIV No. 41 • THE WEEKLY NEWSPAPER OF NEW YORK • OCTOBER 10, 1989 • $1.00

Fig 5.1 *Village Voice* cover, October 1989, featuring NWA and in bright red, the title of the issue's lead story: "The FBI Hates This Band." *Village Voice.*

a time when the number of cops killed annually in the line of duty was on the rise. Without explicitly referencing "Fuck tha Police," his letter detailed the government's concerns about "this song and its message," noting "music plays a significant role in society."[37] It was the first time an FBI official had so formally objected to a form of creative expression. Moreover, even though local law enforcement activism in protest of NWA had been ongoing since the group first announced its multi-city tour in May, and although rap music had already seeped into regional clashes over juvenile crime and the policing of black communities, the August FBI missive thrust NWA into the center of a national dialogue about free speech. As a cover of *The Village Voice* declared that October, "The FBI Hates this Band" (Fig. 5.1).[38]

The spectacle made NWA the poster child in a campaign against federal government overreach—a liberty-protecting position that, in the 1980s, seemed more aligned with President

Ronald Reagan and his "government is the problem" ideology than with black youths wanting to call attention to police brutality. "The black kid out there don't give a fuck about who's mayor or who's governor or who's the president," Ice Cube explained. "All that shit don't matter to them. The only piece of government they see is police. The police is the government in the ghetto." By the end of 1989, the group could credibly claim that "Fuck tha Police" was not simply a comment on law enforcement abuses but a grand statement about institutional state power. "It's like fuck Uncle Sam," Ice Cube told *The Source* in 1991. "We just narrowed it down to the police."[39]

FBI admonishment and law-enforcement boycotts were designed to derail NWA's promotional campaign for *Straight Outta Compton* and to prevent the group and its handlers from profiting off what critics defined as "cop killer" music. NWA and Priority Records, however, treated the conflict as a springboard for broad exposure and, ultimately, public sympathy. "That song," and in turn the reaction to it, as Ice Cube remembered, was "the essence of what the group had become."[40] The group's publicists, with eager reception from music journalists, reacted to the Milt Ahlerich letter as an Orwellian attack on free speech, and argued that this pressure from a governmental authority "makes valid everything" described in "Fuck tha Police." When Dr. Dre heard that NWA was now on the FBI's radar, he later recalled, "That's when I knew we had something." Ice Cube agreed: "When the FBI has your name, you know you're doing work. You know you're making a difference."[41] The Los Angeles rappers were no longer metaphorically kicking trashcans but could claim, with an air of pride, that they did have the power to "threaten society," as MC Ren asserted. With its music officially de-

clared dangerous, NWA welcomed in the new decade with a
new identity: as "the rappers the FBI tried to silence, the
group the police messed with."[42]

■    ■    ■

The "Fuck tha Police" track, with its fictional courtroom setting, kept the spotlight trained on NWA long after the group
had moved on from its studio debut and began promoting
new projects, including an EP teaser called *100 Miles and
Runnin'.* Their condemnation of the police in Los Angeles
and their brazen resistance to the FBI's attempt to intimi-
date them continued to drive the group's publicity and kept
them at the forefront of tense national conversations around
policing, racial violence, and the First Amendment. NWA's
popularity continued to rise even as the group created a set
of problems for itself that threatened to undermine its brand.
It had become known for its fearlessness in the face of authority, but news about the group emerging in the summer
of 1991 suggested something more akin to recklessness. For
instance, Denise "Dee" Barnes, host of a television series
called *Pump It Up,* filed a $23 million dollar lawsuit against
Dr. Dre, charging him with assault and battery; with plenty
of witnesses to the beating standing by, Dre quickly settled
for an undisclosed amount. Eazy-E attended a Senate Republican fundraiser where George H. W. Bush was speaking,
bewildering many; "It's pretty nice coming here, you know,"
he told a reporter. "It's cool. I've met some nice people." And
Dre and Eazy-E each made disconcertingly insensitive jokes
about Rodney King not long after he was brutally beaten by
LAPD officers, defying the expectations of anyone who knew
NWA's usual outrage over police abuse.[43] Beyond the off-

brand signals, there were obvious signs that the group was dissolving amid contract disputes, the departure of Ice Cube, and rumors that Dr. Dre would defect next.

Yet NWA had accomplished with *Straight Outta Compton*, and especially "Fuck tha Police," something that would allow its members to transcend the criticism and preserve their images as radical heroes. "In all their irresponsibility," pop writer Jon Pareles wrote in 1989, "NWA's songs illuminate tensions that wouldn't go away if the band were silenced."[44] Pareles was referring then to the music rather than to the men and their controversial behavior in the early 1990s, but his observation applied broadly to what ultimately mattered to rap fans. Within hip-hop, NWA exploded a powder keg, blowing the boundaries of the genre wide open, giving new permission for artists and their labels to explore an unlimited range of topics, including the most politically and culturally divisive ones, without restriction. It mattered less and less to fans whether the purpose was public enlightenment or personal profit—NWA freely admitted again and again that controversy made them rich. Rap audiences were drawn to the sound and pleasure of defiance that LA gangsta rap delivered. When Harvard's Henry Louis Gates, Jr. wrote about NWA in the *New York Times* in the summer of 1990, his article was headlined "Rap: Slick, Violent, Nasty and, Maybe Hopeful." Hardcore rappers like NWA and 2 Live Crew, he pointed out, along with young black filmmakers like Spike Lee and John Singleton and comedians like Eddie Murphy and Keenan Ivory Wayans, were now expressing "things we could only whisper in dark rooms. They're saying we're going to explode all these sacred cows. It's fascinating, and it's upsetting everybody—not just white people but black people. But it's a liberating moment."[45]

That following summer, mired in legal trouble and public-facing dysfunction, NWA released its sophomore album *Efil-4zaggin*. Like *Straight Outta Compton*, it defied the odds of the music industry. The group still lacked the production and promotional resources afforded by major label representation. They continued to rely upon Eazy-E's Ruthless Records for capital and the independent Los Angeles-based Priority Records for marketing and distribution. Scathing early reviews of the record's X-rated content, flagrant disrespect for women, allusions to rape, and glorification of homicide threatened to undermine Priority's promotional push. Indeed, with its objectionable title—Niggaz4Life, spelled backward—and luridly misogynistic tracks like "To Kill a Hooker," "Findum, Fuckum, & Flee," and "One Less Bitch," *Efil4zaggin* proved even more of a challenge for distributors than *Straight Outta Compton* had been. Major record outlets in Canada and Europe refused to stock the album. In the United Kingdom, the government's Obscene Publications Squad seized twenty-four thousand copies of the record and effectively banned sales of the album in the country.[46] In the United States, anti-pornography crusader Jack Thompson led a successful campaign to remove *Efil4zaggin* from all Musicland stores, and many businesses throughout the country chose not to stock it rather than risk criminal prosecution for selling material labeled "obscene" to minors.[47]

Yet *Efil4zaggin* was a commercial triumph. The record debuted on the Billboard Pop Album chart at number two, the highest debut for an album since Michael Jackson's *Bad* and the best chart showing for an independent album in over a decade. Within just two weeks of its release, *Efil4zaggin* reached number one and earned platinum RIAA certification for selling over one million copies.[48] In spite of what record buyers cited as a moral quandary, American distributors stocked up and sold out. Eazy-E marveled at it in a *Rolling Stone* interview: "How can some motherfuckers with a street record get Number One over motherfucking AC/DC, Paula Abdul?" DJ Yella ventured a response: "everybody's buying it just to see what the fuck is going on."[49]

In a rare social critique of an album's content, a *Billboard* writer commented on the implications for NWA's crossover success with *Efil4zaggin:* "Some would say it is clear evidence of the acceptance of rap in the mainstream. Cool. But look at it this way: A lot of kids paying to hear a group of black gangstas call themselves 'niggaz' not once but continuously throughout the album rife with images of violence and personal disrespect—that's gotta be popular in the new racially charged era."[50] NWA, as *Billboard* charged, was producing something far more corrosive than anything the anti-obscenity crusaders of the PMRC could have imagined in the mid-1980s. The debates over the group's promotion of "gangsta chic," misogyny, violence, and conspicuous consumption mattered far less than the fact that Los Angeles gangsta rap appeared to be exacerbating race prejudice. NWA and its affiliates, including Ice Cube, stood accused in the press of feeding Americans a set of toxic ideas about black youth and the inner city. The danger was, as *Billboard's* writer argued, that NWA threatened to further divide the country along racial fault lines. The group, throwing caution to the wind, risked crystalizing the very racial anxiety and bigotry they railed against in their music. All the while, they composed seductive anthems of resistance for those who sympathized with their perspectives on injustice.

As the new decade opened, Compton City councilwoman Pat Moore appealed to her black constituents, many of whom shared precisely the concerns outlined in *Billboard*. Moore

asked her community to acknowledge that even the most vul-
gar rap was an honest response to hard times, and that young
fans—their own children and grandchildren—found precious value in that. Replying to local alarm over the announcement of the 1990 Compton Rapfest, a music showcase
starring NWA, Councilwoman Moore told the *Los Angeles
Sentinel*, "Members of these groups have survived and are
still alive and they have mastered the system better than we
(as parents) have because they are talking about things that
are real to our young people and they have their attention."
To those still outraged by the music's content, she explained
that these black performers "are reaching our young people
and are role models for them."[51] The preeminent hip-hop
journal *The Source* asserted that LA rap mattered not only
because black kids in LA County were engaging with it but
because, more broadly, its artists compelled the nation to
litigate its own flaws: "To discuss NWA is to discuss the
fundamental problems, conflicts, and opportunities of our
society."[52]

NWA's public spat with the country's most powerful law
enforcement agency helped re-center the national conversation about hip-hop, turning the focus to the West. The group's
relentless assertion of its right to free speech, and sophisticated and sometimes unabashed employment of "truth" as a
promotional tool, made it a champion of nonconformity and,
at the same time, a harbinger of mounting crises. NWA's ability to cover so much ground made it the first rap group to
appeal simultaneously to four distinct kinds of listeners: the
traditional, mostly nonwhite hip-hop fans in the proverbial
"urban North"; the grassroots LA rap loyalists; the southern
black rap fans who had been primed to gravitate toward West
Coast rap; and the predominantly white, suburban listeners

who, as cultural commentators were beginning to describe, were filled with burning anger and disillusionment exacerbated by recession and who, until *Straight Outta Compton*, had found punk and heavy metal more compelling than rap.[53] (Buyers for national record chains Camelot and Kemp Mill noticed that, from 1989 through 1991, NWA product sold best in suburban shopping malls and stores typically specializing in heavy metal and rock, a detail that implied white teens were buying but that didn't preclude the possibility that nonwhite rock fans were also crossing over.) Randy Davis, a record buyer for StreetSide stores who was well versed in the history of rock 'n' roll, noted that Los Angeles had made rap "the rebellious music of the '90s."[54] As *The Source* noted about the chart-topping popularity of NWA's sophomore album (which it referred to as *Niggaz4Life*), "For every Black hip-hop fanatic driving through Detroit, Houston, and of course Los Angeles pumping *Niggaz* from their rides, there's a group of baseball-cap wearing white kids listening to *Niggaz* in their room. . . . Everywhere you turn, the youth of America is tuned in to NWA."[55]

Vernon Reid, black frontman for the rock band Living Colour, was uncertain about the ramifications of such cultural influence. "What frightens me about them is that they're really good."[56] He wasn't the only one to feel that way. Within music industry circles, there were others who argued even more forcefully that LA rappers had abused their public platform by promoting an apolitical version of black militancy, even violent anarchy. According to management at A & A Records & Tapes, which pulled copies of *Straight Outta Compton* from all of its chain stores, NWA's music could only be called "blatantly destructive."[57] In the same vein, voices representing earlier waves of hip-hop argued that LA rappers had undermined the narrative of black uplift that had been a mainstay of 1980s b-boy rap and so central to the New York-based "four elements" hip-hop philosophy, a cultural doctrine sacrosanct on the East Coast. Andre "Doctor Dré" Brown, the *Yo! MTV Raps* host and hip-hop trendsetter, expressed concerns about the "idiotic brothers out there" who might find in NWA's music a convenient justification for making trouble. He considered "Fuck tha Police" specifically to be reprehensible. "Instead of worrying so much about what the police are doing," Brown argued in the black press nearly two years after the song was released, "we need to be policing ourselves."[58] Music critic Nelson George, a longtime champion of hip-hop, told the *Los Angeles Times* in 1990 that NWA made "black exploitation records."[59] A music writer at the *Sentinel* labeled gangsta rappers "the ultimate sell-outs."[60]

But a more ominous critique came from inside South Central Los Angeles, where youth counselor and black activist Leon Watkins fretted over the swelling popularity of NWA, predicting that "nothing good" would come of music so contemptuous of social order. He was particularly concerned about the additional burdens Los Angeles gangsta rap might create for the communities in his city already struggling against gang domination. While the *Village Voice* made a pitch for recognizing LA rappers as delivering "an organic expression of south-central LA's half-hidden gang world," Watkins worried that NWA and Ice Cube were normalizing gang violence and urban blight, thereby aggravating the "frustration" already crippling his city and his people.[61] These young men penning lyrics about the real crises Watkins watched metastasize, including socioeconomic isolation and distrust of systems of justice, were "taking advantage" of "a volatile situation," he argued. Watkins conceded that NWA's records alone were not likely to spark an uprising, but he supposed that a crisis of some kind would "[set] things off, and then the music becomes a battle cry."[62]

■   ■   ■

On the night of March 3, 1991, during a police traffic stop along the San Fernando Valley freeway, an African-American motorist, twenty-five-year-old Rodney King, was brutally beaten. In the presence of twenty-one LAPD officers on the scene, at least four patrolmen Tasered, clubbed, and kicked King to such a degree and at such length that the young man thought he had died. (According to King, the officers thought the same; he remembered that in the moments after the hitting stopped, someone threw a sheet over his head.)[63] The beating was not fatal but it did leave King debilitated, with a broken ankle, a broken jaw, a cracked eye socket, a shattered cheekbone, skull fractures, brain damage, partial paralysis, a dozen electrical burns, and internal bleeding. In a news conference, King's attorney said of the injuries, "None of the POWs taken by Saddam Hussein came back beaten this badly."[64] As noted later by black Angelenos, leaders of the local Coalition Against Police Abuse, the NAACP, the ACLU, and police watch activists nationwide, the brutality exhibited that night, though reprehensible, was not remarkable; there were recently documented cases in Los Angeles, New York, and Baltimore, too. King was only the latest victim of law enforcement violence.[65]

But the March 3 traffic stop was an extraordinary event because, unlike other cases, this one was captured on home video. Watching from his apartment balcony above the strip of the busy street where King's arrest turned violent, Lake View Terrace resident George Holliday had grabbed a camcorder and captured nearly ten minutes of the beating. The video that became widely known as the "Holliday tape" was aired nationally and on loop, the gripping images tailor-made for television news. As NBC's nightly news producer Steve Friedman explained, the tape was undoubtedly the only reason King's beating became a network news story at all. "It's a picture medium," he said, noting that "you don't mention" an event without images, no matter how tragic or deadly. "If you have great pictures of flames leaping out, you use it."[66] In the King footage, networks across the country found a fire like none other. It spurred immediate outrage, particularly among those who had never before witnessed or experienced such an egregious display of state barbarism. It also primed the viewing public for more damning details to come about that night and about rampant racial bigotry inside the most powerful police force in the country.[67]

Once the tape became public, over a dozen witnesses came forward to fill in details of what had happened before local resident George Holliday began filming. Many of them disputed the LAPD's official claim that King's erratic and defiant behavior had compelled them to respond so forcefully. One nearby resident who, like Holliday, had been awakened by the sound of police helicopters overhead and voices over a loudspeaker below, told reporters that she saw King trying to cooperate with officers, who nonetheless struck him again and again, even as he lay prone on the ground. "He was face down and he wasn't fighting or anything," Dawn Davis told the *Los Angeles Times*. "I was crying. I was praying for the guy." Other witnesses, who did not want to be identified, said that the officers seemed intent on killing King. "They weren't beating him to subdue him," one remarked, "it was like they were really angry." A local couple, who tried to return to bed after watching paramedics cart King away from the scene, reported that they were left "just numb" realizing that "if it could happen to him, it could happen to anybody."[68]

Then, in the midst of the gripping coverage of the "Rodney King beating," transcripts emerged of LAPD patrol car communications. In them, police joked about "gorillas in the mist" (alluding to a 1988 film by that name), called King a "lizard," indicated he was "dusted" (high on PCP, or, colloquially, "angel dust"), and bragged that his arrest was "a big-time use of force." One seemingly boastful dispatch sent from the car assigned to two of the officers appearing in the Holliday tape read, "I haven't beaten anyone this bad in a long time."[69]

The responses from citizens and local, state, and federal leaders came swiftly. Days after the Holliday tape emerged, some three hundred people marched in front of LAPD headquarters in protest, chanting, giving speeches, and sharing stories of their own experiences with police harassment and racial bigotry.[70] California lawmakers Maxine Waters and Don Edwards made public statements demanding that the Los Angeles District Attorney issue swift indictments of all police officers involved. Following Police Chief Daryl Gates's curt characterization of Rodney King's beating as nothing more than an "aberration," a chorus of public figures, including stalwart conservative George Will, Democratic US Senator Joe Biden, and civil rights activist Jesse Jackson, called for the LAPD chief's resignation. In anticipation of a City Council meeting to address Gates's leadership, the Los Angeles Urban League told local reporters that city officials must make the chief accountable for his officers' being "out of control." Los Angeles Mayor Tom Bradley issued a stern response that no "objective person" could "regard the King beating as an aberration." Taking one of his own agencies to task for misconduct, the mayor announced, "We must face the fact that there appears to be a dangerous trend of racially motivated incidents running through at least some segments of our Police Department." The city's police commissioner, Melanie Lomax, also broke ranks with the chief by choosing to publicly decry the department's treatment of King. It looked, she said, like something "straight out of South Africa and the Deep South."[71] Meanwhile, the Southern California chapter of the ACLU referred to Gates's police force as a "gang" in "blue uniforms," echoing the words of Los Angeles gang members who had, for nearly two decades, drawn the same parallel. ACLU leaders also called on the chief to resign. In many ways, the Rodney King beating was an eerie echo of an incident across the country in 1989, when another black motorist, Gregory Habib, was ruthlessly beaten by four police officers during a traffic stop in Prince George's County, Maryland. The violence had resulted in Habib's death—but efforts of activists to force police officials to take responsibility for the killing proved futile.[72]

At the federal level, the Congressional Black Caucus demanded a recognition by Congress that the catastrophe in Los Angeles was emblematic of a national crisis. Armed with a deep file of cases collected by the ACLU and the NAACP, the CBC took pains to demonstrate in DC that the Rodney King beating was only an anomaly because it was caught on film, and that, in fact, such abuse was epidemic in American policing. Members called for the US Justice Department to broaden the scope of its investigations of police abuse to include all urban law enforcement agencies throughout the country; only such an expansive review could uncover "the systematic nature" of state-sanctioned brutality in the United States. Congressman John Conyers of Michigan beseeched his colleagues, "If we can't protect citizens against the kind of videotaped violence that occurred in LA that night, we're a nation in jeopardy."[73]

At the same time, the Holliday tape gave leaders like Conyers, and the general public, reason to be hopeful. It was widely believed that the existence of videotaped evidence of such a flagrant, even criminal, abuse of authority ensured there would be justice. With irrefutable proof of felony misconduct, there would likely be a jury trial, convictions, and perhaps lengthy sentences; under California law, an individual convicted for inflicting severe bodily injury could serve up to seven years in state prison. More crucially, people thought, there would be a long-overdue reckoning inside law enforcement agencies around racial bias and its ramifications. "Without the tape, the LAPD might have argued anything and been believed by a jury," said a member of the Los Angeles District Attorney's investigatory team in March 1991. "With the tape, it looks like the city might as well just start writing the check to King's lawyers." The consensus among city leaders, legal experts, and the broader public was that gross misconduct would net guilty verdicts in Rodney King's case against the officers and, perhaps, new legislation limiting law enforcement agencies' use of violent force. And there would be no new Watts Rebellion; justice would defuse outrage and mitigate protest in the streets. As one victim of police abuse said, in hopeful anticipation of an institutional transformation after the publicity of King's beating, "We are blessed that this incident happened."[74]

That spring, Compton rapper Eazy-E told a reporter that the Holliday tape vindicated his group and their controversial music. It reaffirmed NWA's claim that news could be reported from the ground, and that the very people who bore witness to injustice and made a record of it were as close to "truth" as were journalists. Though he and bandmate Dr. Dre were quoted in *Spin* as "laughing hysterically" at King's misfortune—after such a beating, Eazy-E guessed that King "don't know his ass from a hole in the ground!"—both also made the case for crediting George Holliday rather than King with any progress it might fuel. "Rodney King didn't help us," Dre emphasized. "The muthafucka that videotaped it helped us."[75] As Eazy-E argued, the American public could no longer dismiss as hyperbole his group's complaints about police abuse or the ways in which Los Angeles rap music reflected real black lives in danger. Once the raw, black-and-white footage of King's beating became a media sensation, captivating television viewers across the country, Eazy-E said, "They understand now."[76]

Ice Cube's reaction was similar: "We finally got y'all . . . on tape."[77] Estranged from NWA for over a year and growing into his new roles as chart-topping solo artist and Hollywood actor, Cube found fresh cause to revisit his old defense of "Fuck tha Police." It was, after all, a song he had co-written and then wielded like the burning symbol of the First Amendment it was, shaming censors for muzzling his group's honest response to a real American crisis. Now, having seen the news about Rodney King's beating and the grizzly images of King's broken body and disfigured face in print and on television, Cube was again in a position to warn his critics against dismissing gangsta rap's tales as mere burlesque.

With a certified platinum solo album and a critically acclaimed EP under his belt, plus Hollywood credibility—and

an NAACP Image Award nomination, thanks to the success
of John Singleton's film *Boyz N the Hood*—Ice Cube prepared
to release his much-anticipated second album, *Death Certificate*. Buoyed by the silver-screen exposure and his durable
reputation as a rap provocateur, he spoke of his second album in the context of an escalating climate of racial bigotry
and anti-black violence in Los Angeles, along with "drugs . . .
the penitentiary and this capitalist system." *Death Certificate*,
he told *The Source*, was as much a response to the beating of
Rodney King as it was to the killing of Latasha Harlins, a fifteen-year-old Compton girl shot to death by a Korean storekeeper over a bottle of orange juice.[78] *Death Certificate*, in
that political context, was a move to double down on themes
he had explored as a member of NWA, and to force a public
reaction.

It worked. After *Death Certificate's* November 1991 release, music distributors, pop critics, civil rights groups, and
religious leaders denounced it as violently racist and xeno-
phobic, citing especially a set of bars in "No Vaseline" interpreted as anti-Semitic and the racial slurs used in the song
"Black Korea," in which Cube as protagonist tells a Korean
merchant to *"pay respect to the black fist / Or we'll burn your
store right down to a crisp."* Still vilified for rapping on "Fuck
tha Police" about *"a bloodbath of cops, dying in LA,"* Ice Cube
found himself newly castigated for indulging in vengeance
fantasies and for conflating black militancy with vigilante
justice.[79] The fact that Cube leaned into the charges further
infuriated those who viewed the LA rapper as a danger to society. He told the *Los Angeles Times*, for instance, that he did
indeed mean his lyrics in "Black Korea" to be taken literally,
because "if things don't get better, we're going to burn their
stores down."[80] In protest, thousands of Korean merchants

across the nation boycotted St. Ides, a beer brand Ice Cube had promoted. The Simon Wiesenthal Center, a Jewish human rights organization, lobbied record chain stores to remove *Death Certificate* from shelves. A writer in the *Village Voice*, the progressive weekly that had put NWA on its cover in 1989 to champion them as heroes in the fight against a "cultural crackdown," referred to Cube as "a straight-up racist, simple and plain"—a flagrant reference to Cube's musical ally Public Enemy and the group's critique of white supremacy in "Fight the Power."[81] And in a wildly unprecedented move, *Billboard* published an editorial charging Ice Cube with "the rankest sort of racism and hatemongering," and argued that his lyrics, which the trade journal characterized as the "unabashed espousal of violence against Koreans, Jews and other whites," blurred the line between art and "advocacy of crime."[82]

Meanwhile, *Death Certificate* smashed sales records, entering the Billboard 200 Top Albums at number two and tying NWA's *Efil4zaggin* as the highest-debuting rap album in the history of the genre.[83] The attention to the record and its content, however, was evocative of *Straight Outta Compton*. During a period of heightened racial tension in Los Angeles, and following the decision by an LA judge to fine Korean storekeeper Soon Ja Du $500 for the murder of Latasha Harlins, Ice Cube's song "Black Korea" created an uproar reminiscent of "Fuck tha Police." While not a single, "Black Korea" became *Death Certificate*'s most notorious cut, and the public outcry it generated provided him a platform to highlight, by any means necessary, the relationship between the exploitation of power and the degradation of black people. Ice Cube reveled in his ballooning public role as one of hip-hop's "most streetwise and politically complex" voices, and used it to argue, yet again, that black lives were systematically discarded in Los Angeles, just as they were nationwide. In interview after interview, he warned that it was a mistake to assume that gangsta rap, which reflected the fantasies, pleasures, travails, and fears of black kids on the block, was devoid of social or political meaning. And to vilify him or his violent lyrics was to miss the point and to willfully ignore the inhumanity in the Du sentencing and the Holliday tape. The demoralization was nothing new, Ice Cube noted, but the repercussions for it might be. As he told *The Source* in late 1991, "Pretty soon, shit's gonna blow up."[84]

Months later, it did.

On April 29, 1992, veteran news correspondent Dan Blackburn drove with his television crew into South Central Los Angeles, through neighborhoods only recently memorialized in Ice Cube's lyrics and John Singleton's film. They were on a mission that night to cover the ugly first hours of a major riot in Los Angeles. As mayhem unfolded, Blackburn and his news crew became, themselves, targets of the violence borne of decades of political and economic neglect and unchecked police abuse. As Blackburn reported, "I was in the Chicago riots. I covered DC when the riots happened after the Martin Luther King assassination. I've never seen anything that comes close to this."[85]

The violent uprising escalated quickly. By the end of the first day, Los Angeles was in a state of emergency. Governor Pete Wilson made preparations to deploy National Guard troops; the California Highway Patrol blocked exits from the Harbor Freeway and the Santa Monica Freeway to prevent motorists from entering zones of protest in Inglewood, South Central, and downtown Los Angeles; the city halted bus service in the area; Los Angeles Unified School District announced its plan to close schools; the Federal Aviation Administration redirected flights approaching LAX; and LA's mayor, Tom Bradley, issued a desperate plea for peace, then signed a curfew order.[86] Two days after Dan Blackburn and CNN began covering the unrest, the riots had taken hold of the whole county, and leaders declared a full-blown national disaster. FBI SWAT team officers, Border Patrol agents, California National Guardsmen, and Los Angeles police officers joined some 4,500 members of the US Army and the Marine Corps, many of them recently deployed in the Persian Gulf War, who descended upon Los Angeles "as if they were responding to an international crisis in Panama or the Middle East." Troops were outfitted in fatigues, flak jackets, and helmets, and armed with M-16 rifles and 9mm pistols. Ready for battle, they rolled through smoke-filled avenues in Humvees, ten-ton trucks, and armored vehicles. One National Guardsman offered a summary of the scene as he took up his position in South Central, the heart of the riot zone. "Welcome to Beirut West."[87]

Through five days and nights, every major television news organization and cable news outlet, most of them employing news choppers, streamed live footage of the so-called Rodney King Riots.[88] It was a national media event like no other in American history, a spectacle of unrest precipitated by two other unprecedented media spectacles that were considered, as CBS-TV reporter Harvey Levin said, impossible to "match . . . from the standpoint of drama." First, there had been the airing of the videotaped police beating of twenty-five-year-old black motorist Rodney King. Then had come the widely reported trial (including live, gavel-to-gavel coverage on Court TV) of the four Los Angeles police officers charged in King's assault.[89]

Yet, on April 29, 1992, following weeks of nationally broadcast trial proceedings, the nearly all-white jury declared the officers not guilty. Los Angeles resident Linda Johnson Phillips was in the Simi Valley courtroom when the verdicts were announced. Outraged, she ran out, and through tears told the gathered reporters, "The color of your skin determines the degree of justice you get."[90] *Boyz N the Hood* director John Singleton, also in Simi for the announcement, expressed frustration but little surprise. As he told the press, "There is still no justice in this country." Across the nation, protesters gathered in front of courthouses and police headquarters, activists planned marches, university students held candlelight vigils, high school students staged walkouts, local communities scheduled gatherings to discuss racial injustice, and police officials and citizens alike registered their shock at how, as Syracuse Mayor Tom Young said, "the legal system failed."[91] In San Francisco, the Brooklyn rap group X-Clan interrupted an afternoon concert on the San Francisco State University campus to share the national breaking news with its audience, then led them in a spontaneous protest march chanting, "Whose streets? Our streets!" and "Fuck tha police!"[92] In the city's downtown shopping districts and in the Mission, San Francisco police in riot gear kept watch over crowds of demonstrators and arrested some caught vandalizing property.[93] From further away, the foreign press assessed the weight of the acquittals. The Munich *Muenchner Merkur,* for instance, asserted that "the whole world" now viewed United States justice as "a disgrace." From Tokyo, the *Asahi* commented more specifically that the verdict demonstrated in dramatic fashion "how weak the rights of the black minority are in front of the white majority (in the United States)."[94] As a black business owner in Inglewood told *Newsweek,*

"That verdict was a message from America."[95] Rose Brown, who had driven from her home in LA to the Simi Valley courthouse to hear the verdicts, told a local reporter she was heartbroken. And then she predicted violence. "You just watch," Brown said. "Something's going to break."[96] John Singleton agreed. "This is a time bomb," he said. "It's going to blow up."[97]

The speed with which the arson, violence, and looting spread throughout Los Angeles that first day after the verdicts were announced stunned even those who had experienced the Watts Rebellion firsthand. "With the Watts riots in 1965 it built and built and on the third day the city went mad," one Los Angeles police commander noted. "This was completely different—the city went wild in just an hour and a half."[98] In San Fernando Valley, at the original site where King had been beaten, a mostly black crowd gathered along the busy thoroughfare, holding signs declaring "Honk Your Horns for Guilty" and chanting, "We want justice!" In South Central, along Normandie Avenue, black Angelenos gathered on sidewalks to vent their anger, placing handmade signs in the street decrying racist cops. Some along the avenue threw rocks and bottles at passing cars. Others shouted their dissent as if to an entire nation at fault. Tonia Smith stood on the strip yelling, "We're tired of being slaves!"[99] Meanwhile, angry citizens flooded phone lines at local newspapers, radio, and television stations. By the evening, twenty-five square blocks of central Los Angeles were aflame. Opportunists of every race, class, and age had gutted chain stores, strip-mall businesses, and mom-and-pop shops in the area. At the intersection of Florence and Normandie, groups of black men dragged white motorists from their cars and beat them. A news helicopter captured one particularly brutal attack of

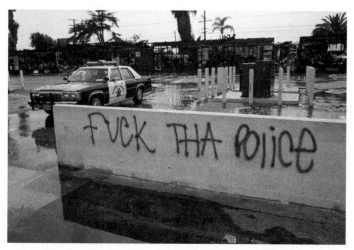

Fig 5.2 Graffiti on a wall in the Los Angeles riot zone referring to NWA's 1989 anthem, spelling and all. Photo by Peter Turnley, 1992 / Corbis Historical / Getty Images.

white gravel-truck driver Reginald Denny, and the bloody scene was broadcast live. In Compton, where a year before the fatal shooting of ninth-grader Latasha Harlins and the virtual exoneration of her killer, Soon Ja Du, had heightened an already-combative relationship between African-American and Korean Angelenos, black protestors trashed Asian-owned businesses while some Korean residents armed themselves in defense. Downtown, the city's symbols of law and order were under siege, with the guardhouse outside LAPD headquarters torched, a fire ablaze inside City Hall, and the glass facade of the Criminal Courts building smashed to bits.[100] And across the riot zone, graffiti declaring, for instance, "BLK PWR," "Latasha Harlins," "This Is For Rodney King," "Look What You Created," and "Fuck Tha Police" testified to the layers of extreme tension fueling insurrection (Fig. 5.2).[101]

"I'm not saying I told you so," Ice-T told the *Los Angeles Sentinel* early that May, before the smoke of the uprising had even cleared, "but rappers have been reporting from the front for years."[102] Tupac Shakur, then an emerging Bay Area rapper and aspiring actor following in the footsteps of Ice Cube, echoed Ice-T. "We've been reporting this," Shakur said of West Coast rappers, with a nod to Los Angeles. "We've warned, 'If you don't clean up, there's going to be . . . mass destruction." Luther Campbell, frontman for Miami's oft-censored group 2 Live Crew, blamed the nation's self-proclaimed moral guardians for covering their ears. For years, he noted, rappers had been "screaming out what the problem is," while authorities were effectively muzzling them, "screaming back, 'Don't say what you're saying.'"[103]

But more than any other rap celebrity, Ice Cube proclaimed to have prophesied the 1992 uprising. "Anything you wanted to know about the riots was in the records before the riots." Indeed, he could plausibly claim the longest and most varied track record as an artist offering tracings of the problems brewing in Los Angeles, which by April 1992 included his work with NWA and three solo recording projects. Beyond the music, there was his breakout performance as a young Crip named Doughboy in the film *Boyz N the Hood*, which had illustrated the fateful impact of daily indignities, big and small, on the lives of black boys in South Central. For half a decade, Ice Cube noted, he had "given so many warnings on what's gonna happen if we don't get these things straight."[104] In the immediate aftermath of the 1992 LA uprising, he had cautioned the nation against dismissing the rioters as it had dismissed gangsta rap artists, considering them mere nihilists. And he warned moral crusaders and law-and-order politicians against summing up youth rebellion in the streets as mere delinquency. "The whole country can be shut down," he asserted. "America needs to know that these kids are willing to shut the country down for liberation."[105]

Because Los Angeles rappers, in particular, were so vocal in demonstrating "the feeling" undergirding the 1992 insurrection, some charged that the artists themselves were to blame for the disaster and all of its economic and political fallout—an indictment that many wore as a badge of honor.[106] NWA's MC Ren championed those who participated in the uprising, framing them as insurgents using extreme measures to demonstrate that it is not "all right to destroy black males." Channeling the black militants and revolutionaries of his parents' generation, Ren refused to decry the violence, seeing it as a tool for challenging the assumptions of an entire system of oppression. "Everybody looks at black people different now," he stressed. "Black people are no joke."[107]

Then, as the post-riot reconstruction began, some rappers took the spirit of the spring rebellion into the recording booth. The *Get The Fist Movement,* a collaboration bringing together a roster of emerging gangsta rappers, including Compton's King Tee, MC Eiht of Compton's Most Wanted, South Gate's Cypress Hill, and Ice Cube's protégés Da Lench Mob, recorded music that framed upheaval, even bloodshed, as empowerment. The movement's self-titled single "Get the Fist" stood in stark contrast to pre-Riot increase-the-peace rap anthems like "Self-Destruction" and "We're All in the Same Gang," which were aimed at addressing problems of black-on-black crime rather than police-state oppression.[108] Every verse of "Get the Fist" was an account of rebellion, told from the perspective of a righteous rebel with no regrets. "*Get a taste of the heat / While I burn down the streets,*" King Tee began, referencing "*what they did to Rodney,*" and warning those *"skeezin' on my race / I'm black and I'm proud to be lootin' in your face."* MC Eiht challenged the champions of respectability politics, who aimed to blame young men like him for black plight—*"I guess it's time for brothers to turn the page"*—and provoked his listeners in the tradition of NWA by toying with the fantasy of outlaw vigilantism—*"Let out some rage and bang a Caucasian."*[109]

Ice-T also tapped into dark fears about the potential implications of black rebellion. In the 1980s, the pioneering LA rapper had touted his very real gang affiliations, but when it seemed his commercial exposure was at risk he adhered to the old adage that it paid to soften the hard edges of his music and his image. But NWA, and then Ice Cube, had demonstrated beyond a shadow of a doubt that uncompromising rap records sold, and some of them crossed over, turning fringe artists into national stars. On his album, *Home Invasion,* recorded in the wake of the uprising and released months later, Ice-T took something that the press had referred to as rap's "cultural invasion" and hurled it back at white America: *"I'm takin' your kids' brains / You ain't gettin' 'em back."*[110] The *Washington Post* asked him to clarify, and he obliged, emphasizing the fundamental connection between rap music and the Los Angeles riots. The public, particularly "white kids," could not look away, which meant "black rage" finally had a mainstream audience.[111]

Through the first two years of the 1990s, the prognosis for gangsta rap and its "hardcore rap" kin remained nearly as dire as it had been in the mid-1980s. From the perspective of the prophets of the music industry, all the sensationalized attention paid to, for instance, Ice Cube's militancy, Public Enemy's black nationalism, the controversy surrounding 2 Live Crew's sexual vulgarity and the Geto Boys' grisly themes, and, of course, NWA's confrontation with the FBI, may have generated a spike in sales and some measure of celebrity. But the popularity was unsustainable. In late 1990, *Variety* predicted that, from that point forward, "video will drive hip-hop toward the pop mainstream" leaving "more hardcore rap acts" without a clear course forward. The future of hardcore rap, the trade journal asserted, was radio blackouts, a diminishing fan base, and exclusion from the commercial mainstream.[112] The implication was that gangsta rap was dying, and for sure this time.

But the 1992 Los Angeles riots proved to be a catalyst for the commercialization of the very genre of rap that had been pigeonholed as too dangerous and too divisive to thrive. The riots made palpable the complicated, and sometimes destructive, human responses to oppression that LA rap had narrated for years already. Put another way, the twenty-four-hour streaming news coverage of rebellion in Los Angeles functioned, for gangsta rap, better than any music video in drawing widespread attention to the music and making a case for its cultural relevance. Thus, *Variety* was only half right.

■    ■    ■

Two of the bestselling, highest acclaimed, industry-shaping rap records in the history of the genre were released in the months following the 1992 Los Angeles riots. Both studio albums—Ice Cube's *The Predator* and Dr. Dre's solo debut, *The Chronic*—were from former members of LA's trailblazing gangsta rap group, NWA.[113]

In *The Predator*, Ice Cube explicitly engaged with issues of black economic marginalization, mass incarceration, abuses of power, and white supremacy, as he had in his first three solo projects and in the music he made with NWA. Again, he role-played as the outlaw vigilante, taunting his song's villains, including the Ku Klux Klan, racist political leaders, white juries, and the police—*"Nappy head, nappy chest, nappy chin / Never seen with a happy grin"*— all the while pondering his fate—*"Will they do me like Malcolm?"*[114] Interludes included segments of news reports from the 1960s, excerpts from television interviews with Louis Farrakhan, and clips of a Malcolm X speech. In the album's liner notes, Ice Cube invoked W. E. B. Du Bois's notion of African-American double consciousness. But in his lyrics, he drew the history of black protest forward, examining the Rodney King beating and the Simi Valley trial in "We Had to Tear This Motherfucka Up" and "Who Got the Camera?" to explain mass insurrection—*"To get some respect we had to tear this mothafucka up."* He also detailed his violent fantasies about King's abusers, including the officers at fault—*"Born wicked, Laurence Powell, foul / Cut his fuckin throat and I smile"*—and the justice system that pardoned them—*"Somebody knows the address of the jury / Pay a little visit, 'Who is it?' (Oh, it's Ice Cube)/ 'Can I talk to the Grand Wizard,' then, BOOM!"* As the nation scrambled to draw meaning from the seemingly implausible verdict in the Rodney King trial and the anarchy that followed, *The Predator* furnished Ice Cube's reply— *"April 29th was Power to the People / And we might just see a sequel."*[115]

*The Predator* was Ice Cube's most commercially successful album to date. It debuted at number one on the *Billboard* 200 Top Albums chart, and it was certified platinum within two months of its release. It was a controversial record, one bolstered by the sensational coverage of the riots in the months leading up to its release, but *The Predator* was also a thoroughly listenable record. Although the lyrical content earned it a Parental Advisory sticker—the mark of Cain in terms of radio play—its singles had commercial appeal with the speaker-thumping production of respected LA DJs Pooh and Muggs. Featuring a tapestry of recognizable soul and funk samples, including melodies mined from Wilson Pickett's "Mustang Sally," The Ohio Players' "Funky Worm," and the Isley Brothers' "Footsteps in the Dark," clean versions of "Wicked," "Check Yo Self," and "It Was A Good Day" became favorites at urban contemporary and crossover outlets.[116]

Like *The Predator*, much of Dr. Dre's debut solo project, *The Chronic*, was recorded before, during, and after the Los Angeles riots unfolded. "I don't know what kind of album *The Chronic* would have been without the riots," said Kurupt, a Los Angeles–based artist and guest on the album. "It was coming from the middle of it all, saying this is what happened."[117] A Compton native born the same year as Rodney King, Dr. Dre used his music to respond to the fact that his city was on fire. In "The Day the Niggaz Took Over," he paired verses describing the arson, shooting, and looting with excerpts from interviews with black Angelenos in South Central reacting to the acquittals of the LAPD officers charged with the near-fatal assault of Rodney King. "If you ain't down for the Africans here in the United States," one man proclaimed in a sampled audio clip, "Devil, you need to step your punk ass to the side and let us brothers and us Africans step in and start putting some foot in that ass!" *The Chronic*, however, diverged sharply from the tone of Ice Cube's project. The title alone, a slang term for high-potency marijuana, signaled a contrasting perspective on a set of similar topics. While *The Predator* forced the audience to relive the events and, in doing so, to confront the forces of oppression as tirelessly as Ice

Cube did himself, *The Chronic* provided a way for its audience to memorialize and then move on from the uprising. Dr. Dre's soul and funk samples, including selections from Parliament, the Ohio Players, Solomon Burke, Leon Haywood, Isaac Hayes, The Kay-Gees, Willie Hutch, and Bill Withers, paired with live instrumentation and the booming bass lines he had become known for as a producer. And the laid-back lyrical delivery of Dr. Dre and each of his guest MCs—particularly his young protégé Snoop Dogg—invited listeners to reflect, rage, and, willfully, escape.

*The Chronic* was a certified hit album that outperformed even *The Predator,* an industry triumph in its own right. *The Chronic* sold more than twice as many copies as Ice Cube's *The Predator* in its first months of release, and within just one year, *The Chronic* had been certified three times Platinum by the RIAA. *The Chronic* spent ninety-three weeks on the *Billboard 200 Top Albums* chart, peaking at number three, and it topped the *Billboard R&B/Hip-Hop Albums.* Its three singles, "Nuthin But A 'G' Thang," "Dre Day," and "Let Me Ride," were each ranked in the top ten on the *Billboard* singles charts. And across the spectrum of the recording industry it was critically acclaimed for its production. Plus, the commercial success of the album helped launch the careers of an all-star line-up of West Coast MCs and vocalists, including Snoop Dogg, Warren G, Kurupt, That Nigga Daz, Nate Dogg, and eventually Tupac Shakur. Rapper and producer Kanye West explained years later that *The Chronic,* through the 1990s and the first decade of the twenty-first century, was the benchmark for commercially viable black music. Artists, engineers, producers, and labels looked to Dre's music for inspiration. Asked by a *Rolling Stone* journalist whether hip-hop artists had gained reverence for Dre after he delivered *The*

*Chronic,* West replied, "It's like asking a Christian if he believes Christ died for his sins."[118] Brooklyn MC Talib Kweli, recalling the hip-hop landscape after December 1992, said Dr. Dre "smothered the game." If the curious gaze of rap audiences had first been drawn westward by early gangsta rap, along with the news emanating from Los Angeles, the Rodney King incident, and the 1992 Uprising, *The Chronic* provided them with a more lasting impression. It recast hip-hop in the mold of LA rap. Even in New York, a city with a long history of ignoring the West Coast scene, *The Chronic* was a revelation. As Kweli remembered, "That was it, that's what everybody was listening to."[119] LA rapper Kurupt, who described *The Chronic* as "a blueprint and a map through the emotions" of Los Angeles in 1992, summed up the response to the music: "Not only did the streets feel it, Americans felt it."[120] As *Billboard* put it, *The Chronic* made rap "mainstream."[121]

■   ■   ■

The first generation of LA gangsta rappers, with NWA as its vanguard, presented in their music and their promotional pitches evidence that sixties rebellion, organized black militancy, grassroots civil rights organizing, police-watch advocacy, respectability politics, electoral wins, and the growth of the black middle class had failed to make their young lives matter. Their art was a counterpoint to the zeitgeist of the 1980s—a decade that saw an awkward marriage in mass politics of small-government doctrine and law-and-order champions, a broad rejection of race and racism as meaningful frameworks for thinking about injustice, and the rise in calls for censorship to fend off social degradation. But LA rappers did more than rile their critics by muddying truth and fiction, reflecting viscerally on hardship, indulging in vice, complaining of abuse while condoning it, tying militancy to millionaire dreams, and thumbing their noses at every faction—the hip-hop establishment, included—that viewed them as a threat to black advancement.

LA gangsta rap represented an insurrection, and a social threat, because its artists improvised ways to ensure a broad, expansive audience for all of it. NWA was not "the most dangerous group" because its members pointed to the unraveling of American society. It was the most dangerous group because its members reshaped the commercial music scene in their image. They popularized their own rebellion, and in doing so, made young black perspectives on American society the industry's driving force.

CONCLUSION · LA County Blues

■ **In 2016, Kendrick Lamar,** a young Compton rapper born in 1987 and influenced by the Los Angeles gangsta rap that grew up with him, was invited to perform at the Fifty-Eighth Annual Grammy Awards. He chose music from his album *To Pimp a Butterfly*. This, Lamar's third studio production, was nominated that year for Best Rap Album and Album of the Year. *To Pimp a Butterfly* was also significant because it included "Alright," a song that itself had earned four Grammy nominations and became an anthem of the #BlackLivesMatter movement. Activists embraced the record's chorus of *"We gon' be alright!"* as a message of black fortitude, and it became a chant of resistance against law-enforcement abuses. Lamar's planned stage set was to include "Alright" as well as a rendition of "The Blacker the Berry," a lyrical indictment of white America that featured the lines *"You hate me don't you? / You hate my people / Your plan is to terminate my culture."* During an election year and against a backdrop of swelling black protest, emboldened white nationalists, widely publicized cases of racially motivated police killings, and the end of the country's first black presidency, Lamar's Grammy performance promised to be "very controversial."[1]

Kendrick Lamar took the stage in shackles. Cuffed and chained, his hands were linked to four other black men, all of them outfitted in the blue uniforms of the California state prison system, an iteration of what Ice Cube called the "county blues" in NWA's 1988 single "Gangsta Gangsta." The men limped from the shadows into a spotlight and down a corridor of barred cells that held others dressed like them. Accompanying the jingle of chains were somber saxophones playing a stripped-down form of ensemble jazz, a style derivative of the blues. The horns went silent as Lamar took his position at the microphone, lifting his chains over the stand. He began suddenly, in sync with two thunderous, staccato beats. Drum cracks like gunshots were paired with flashes of light. The men behind Lamar threw their hands up, displaying cuffs, then lowered their arms and stepped out of line as a saxophonist behind bars riffed in minor key outbursts. Lamar rapped from "The Blacker the Berry": "*I'm guarding my feelings, I know that you feel it / You sabotage my community, making a killing.*" The line that followed—"*You made me a killer, emancipation of a real hitter*"—ended with the prisoners freeing themselves and Lamar proclaiming "*Trap our bodies, but can't lock our mind,*" an echo of a lyric in Jay-Z's 1996 song "Can I Live."

In sparks and smoke, the prison vanished. Lamar and the others, glowing blue under black lights, joined a group of African dancers who gave life to the charged lyrics of Jamaican dancehall artist Assassin. Guided by African dancers and drums, the group progressed toward a massive bonfire where Lamar launched into "Alright." In front of a wall of fire, calling to mind the blazes of the 1992 Los Angeles riots and 2015 police protests in Baltimore, the dancers performed. Then, the wailing blues saxophone led Lamar away from the flames and back to a darker, bluer stage. Alone, in front of the microphone, the spotlight strobed over his face like the lights of an LAPD patrol car. Lamar rapped his final, forceful lyric—"*Conversation for the entire nation / This is bigger than us*"—and a glowing image of Africa appeared, emblazoned with one word in Old English gangland font: Compton.

That Kendrick Lamar's 2016 set was roundly praised as the most important performance of the night and, perhaps, in the entire history of the televised award show is rather stunning, considering that the Recording Academy had failed to acknowledge rap as a genre until 1989. Even then, it had relegated its solitary hip-hop award, Best Rap Performance, to an untelevised portion of the show. In later years, as hip-hop began to dominate the American music landscape, the Academy expanded its Rap category and included those awards in the prime-time ceremony. Rap artists also began earning nominations in the general music categories, signifying that the recording industry's overlords had at last knighted America's newest and blackest music genre as culturally relevant. Yet, after nearly thirty years, a disproportionate number of nominations went to white rap artists. Rap had won just three general category awards, one of which Kendrick Lamar lost to the white hip-hop duo Macklemore & Ryan Lewis (a group that beat Lamar in three other rap categories that same year). In other words, year after year, the Grammy Awards either snubbed the music or undervalued its black voices, or both.

By inviting Lamar to perform in 2016, the Academy may have been attempting to right that wrong. Or perhaps something else was behind the decision. As Los Angeles filmmaker John Singleton put it, the show's producer "knows that excluding a genre of music made up largely of black people is a bad look, so he brings them into the fold, gives them a stage, offers them a set of rap-specific trophies to share among themselves, and watches the ratings rise."[2] Whether or not the Academy was exploiting Lamar by offering him a spot on the show, however, was beside the point. Lamar leveraged the cultural moment to remind everyone that his rap—the rap that topped the charts, captivated a young generation of activists, and grew from the ganglands of LA County—was as candid as the blues, as American as mass incarceration, and as unapologetically black as Africa and Compton. It was not pop. It was not universal. It was not colorless. And, as camera shots of a sea of tight jaws and wide eyes in the audience illustrated, it was not intended to soothe white viewers tuning in.

Lamar, who was born into Police Chief Daryl Gates's Los Angeles, reared in the path of the battering ram, and molded by the legacies of the LA riots, delivered a performance on that Grammy stage that was a symphony of reflections on being black in the promised land. And he did so before a nation that continued to champion the arrival of a post-racial America as it simultaneously scoffed at black humanity—the very same political and cultural contradiction that had defined the 1980s, the decade of his birth. Before an audience of millions, Lamar evoked a lineage of Los Angeles rappers who, in Michael Eric Dyson's words, "do not find conventional methods of addressing personal and social calamity useful." He honored a core tenet of meaningful contemporary art, that, as author and rap fan Ta-Nehisi Coates explained, "had no responsibility to be hopeful or optimistic or make anyone feel better about the world" but instead presented "the world in all its brutality and beauty, not in hopes of changing it but in the mean and selfish desire to not be enrolled in its lie, to not be coopted by the television dreams, to not ignore all the great crimes around us." The *Washington Post* would later explain of Lamar's Pulitzer Prize–winning music that he was a rapper who delivered "the sound of a broken nation struggling to understand itself."[3]

In 2012, just a few years before Kendrick Lamar became a household name, before the Compton rapper was lauded for making "the most significant music of our time," the *Los Angeles Times* had lamented the sorry state of rap music. That year, the newspaper marked the twentieth anniversary of the Los Angeles riots with a series of essays, including a piece about LA rap. It had also been twenty years since the release of Ice Cube's *The Predator* and Dr. Dre's *The Chronic*, the critically acclaimed records that emerged from the riot-torn landscape. The essayist argued that, since that moment in the 1990s when national turmoil produced such cultural dynamism, rap had lost its way, to the point that now, in the twenty-first century, the genre was unrecognizably trite. Worse, it was benign, "coopted by the mainstream." Rappers, once so "conscious," were now shameless boosters of caricature and consumption. In contrast to that vaunted, old-school "Golden Era," hip-hop's new school abandoned "the subject of social ills in favor of bragging about bling." Now, rap was pop, and that was bad.[4]

The essay articulated what has become in this new century the standard narrative about rap's historical trajectory, and more specifically, about the contrast between the genesis era of hip-hop and each successive wave thereafter. Within this framework, NWA is sometimes credited, rightfully, for fashioning success from below: their seed money was their own; they built a recording label from scratch; they paid to have their records pressed; and they proved how effective promotion can be when you do it yourself and on your own terms. The members of NWA were independent artists who curated their own sound, their own image, and their own fame. Even when embedded industry entities came into the picture— Jerry Heller was a veteran insider, Priority's Bryan Turner descended from the K-Tel dynasty, and Jimmy Iovine was Interscope's engineer-cum-mogul—the young men refused to relinquish control, as a matter of course.

As NWA began plotting its own path into the commercial mainstream, the conventional wisdom was that their hardcore street sound wouldn't survive the journey. To "cross over"—a term that, in the world of hip-hop, had become synonymous with selling out thanks to EPMD's scathing 1992 track "Crossover"—rappers had to soften the *"hardcore (rough, rugged, and raw)"* in the music. They had to tone it down and ham it up for the suburban masses.[5] In 1990, when hip-hop started to lean more toward the pop market, as the explosive popularity of Vanilla Ice and MC Hammer seemed to indicate, *Variety* predicted that rap as a candid, blunt, "sometimes-graphic," and resolutely black form of expression would fade away.[6] Def Jam's Rick Rubin, the producer who helped mold Run-DMC's stripped-down b-boy edge, told *Spin* in 1991 that rap "is dying," and laid the blame squarely on the crass pursuit of profit. "I think MTV and the big music companies are responsible," he concluded.[7] When the trade press pondered whether rap would become "pop for the '90s," the tone was ominous.[8] The implication was that maybe the industry skeptics of the 1980s who had predicted a short shelf life for hip-hop were right after all. Hip-hop was doomed to oblivion because artists wanted, as Erick Sermon of EPMD rapped, *"to go platinum and clock mad green."*[9]

"I wanna be a billionaire," Ren told *Spin* in the same issue that featured Rick Rubin mourning rap's death.[10] Dr. Dre was similarly blunt with his commitment to the bottom line, noting that NWA's "only responsibility is to make records, make money, and eat."[11] Even when he split from the group to partner with black nationalist rappers Public Enemy for a solo project, Ice Cube spoke unapologetically of rap as his golden goose, even channeling the character Bud Fox from Oliver Stone's 1987 film *Wall Street.* "I want an apartment complex, muthafuckin' shopping centers," Cube told *Rolling Stone.* "I want all kind of shit . . . Hire a muthafucka to have my headache."[12] These young men—who had spent most of the 1980s scraping by as small-label artists, performing in backyards and small clubs, hawking promo vinyl out of car trunks, and wooing radio programmers—reveled in the fact that their tireless work hustling for attention was at last paying off. At the end of the decade, they had the opportunity to seize the sort of wealth and celebrity they could see celebrated everywhere in Reagan's America.

The members of NWA, and Ice Cube after he went solo in 1990, actively pursued commercial success but rejected the music industry's blueprint for crossing over, including the model established by Run-DMC, hip-hop's first platinum-selling rap artists. NWA broke free from the New York mold that critics identified with battle rhymes and moral messaging, and instead, as one reviewer noted, espoused "every antisocial action from murder to gang-rape" and effectively transformed hip-hop's signature "rap braggadocio" into "death threats."[13] Their music riled the censors, but it was cinematic, taking artistic cues from television, film, and cable news; *Straight Outta Compton, Efil4zaggin, AmeriKKKa's Most Wanted,* and *Death Certificate* were collages of ghetto narratives as tantalizing as scenes from *Miami Vice* and as hair-raising as the drama that unfolded in *Scarface*. Plus, as both artists and public figures, Eazy-E, Ren, Dr. Dre, and Ice Cube each deliberately blurred the boundaries between truth and fiction, as did producers of the era's new tabloid talk shows and "reality" cop dramas; when they mixed journalistic exposé with flagrant spectacle, the public tuned in.

Ice Cube, MC Ren, and The D.O.C. (who co-wrote music for NWA, Eazy-E, and, later, Dr. Dre) penned lyrics filled with colloquialisms, local slang, and detailed references to South LA subcultures unfamiliar to outsiders; they crafted storylines that pivoted around the kids they knew, the cityscapes they traversed, and the impressions they had of black life in LA. Their music, though influenced by the original New York hardcore scene, sidestepped classic East Coast hip-hop themes and instead chose neighborhood-specific allusions to lowriders, gangbangers, bungalows, and palm trees. The rappers' renderings of black Los Angeles contradicted white mythologies of the sunny California Dream. In these ways, LA rap generated voyeuristic interest—white and black—in the genre's "reporting" on gangsters, dope fiends, and police brutality in the shadows. MTV News anchor Kurt Loder put his finger on how NWA managed to seduce a broad audience when he asked Ice Cube in a 1989 television interview to explain, "How come there's such a hard rap sound in California? The hardest stuff is coming out of this beautiful place."[14]

Significantly, NWA also made creative choices, again and again, with the expressed goal of provoking the public. At a time when the government held hearings on explicit lyrics, the rappers let obscenities fly in the studio and on stage. In a political climate in which aspiring leaders in both major parties touted law-and-order positions, and both national and statewide elections pivoted on voter concerns about crime, NWA associated itself with gang culture and brandished guns in public appearances.[15] Even the logo of a vilified football franchise was put to use: Ice Cube said the group wore Los Angeles Raiders gear because the team's bad-boy image defied the "fun and sun" brand of the city, while representing "an LA that was unseen to the rest of the world."[16] At a moment when media coverage of the nation's explosive crack epidemic muffled the voices speaking against police brutality, these young men broadcast their own fury about racial profiling—that *"every motherfucker with a color is most wanted,"* and that cops operated on the belief that *"they have the authority to kill a minority."*[17] In the process, they recalibrated the national conversation about urban policing, using avenues of popular entertainment to make the public uncomfortable about abuses long ignored. When *Washington Post* music writer Chris Richards defined rap music in 2018 as "an implicit conversation about the conjoined legacies of slavery, segregation, police brutality and other hideous injustices that our society doesn't care to solve," he encapsulated the legacy of Los Angeles gangsta rap and honored the fearlessness—even recklessness, considering the context—of its original practitioners.[18]

NWA, Ice Cube, Dr. Dre, and their fellow 1990s Los Angeles artists including King Tee, The D.O.C., Snoop Dogg, DJ Quik, Cypress Hill, MC Eiht, Daz Dillinger, and Kurupt, were gangsta rappers who made music in the tradition of the blues, in two ways. First, their music, like the blues, used raw candor, allegory, and fantasy to express deeply personal, and sometimes distressing, ideas about American society. Theirs was art steeped in the ethos of self-reliance, egotism, and insubordination—the creative responses to hardened systems of oppression. In the era of the blues, those systems had been marked by the threat of white violence and, three generations later, they still were.[19] Second, LA gangsta rappers, like blues singers, directly engaged with people on the fringes even as they knowingly provoked, and elicited animus from, those with the power. Folks who embraced each genre experienced the music as a form of affirmation, even as critics viewed songs as lewd, profane, and replete with caricatures. Like blues artists in their time, gangsta rappers were lambasted as smut peddlers by some and exalted as truth tellers by others, the assumption being that peddling smut was incompatible with revealing truth.

In the late 1980s and early 1990s, Los Angeles rappers took the candid but calculated spirit of the blues, with all of its audacity, and secured for it a mass audience. It is an important part of their story that they were on an urgent quest for recognition—from the hip-hop community, from the music industry, and from a nation that rendered their communities invisible.[20] But it is also important to note that this goal was yoked to an unapologetic pursuit of material success. "We're not making records for the fun of it," Eazy-E said in 1989, "we're in it to make money." For both fortune and fame, the men of NWA tapped their musical talents and their insights into the hidden realities of urban disinvestment, racial isolation, unemployment, and militarized policing—and found ways for their product to exploit a shifting, spectacle-hungry media environment.

The original members of NWA were not the first hip-hop artists to defy the illusion of a post-racial America. But they were the first rappers who crossed over *because* they asserted themselves as the personification of that defiance. Their success was propelled by the fact that audiences were both horrified and mesmerized. Seen from this perspective, LA gangsta rap stands as both the preface to the 1992 Los Angeles riots and its epilogue. The music was, as Ice Cube explained in 1991, a forewarning that "shit's gonna blow up."[21] And in the aftermath of the riots, through the prism of the nation's most destructive urban uprising in its history, hip-hop was transformed into an incomparable cultural and commercial force, made up of the very elements a *Los Angeles Times* essayist, twenty years later, would blast as rap's ruin.

The lasting legacy of Los Angeles gangsta rap is not a hip-hop genre "co-opted by the mainstream" but rather a twenty-first century pop culture landscape co-opted by hip-hop.[22] Commercial success did not doom hip-hop into oblivion. It afforded access, as Compton's Kendrick Lamar knew in 2016, to a mass audience that could be at once entertained, unnerved, and inspired.

# NOTES

## Preface

1    Bilge Ebiri, "Gape at William Friedkin's Near-Masterpiece 'To Live and Die in L.A.,'" *Village Voice*, June 14, 2017.

2    Tupac Shakur, actually a Bay Area rapper, became associated with LA through his work for Suge Knight's Death Row Records and the role he played in a brutal feud between New York rappers and Knight's Los Angeles set. Incidentally, Tupac also had a single entitled "To Live & Die in LA," which was released posthumously under an alias: Makaveli [2Pac], "To Live & Die in LA," single (Death Row Records, 1996), vinyl, 12".

## Introduction: They Don't Even Know

1    Cecilia Rasmussen, "Klan's Tentacles Once Extended to Southland," *Los Angeles Times*, May 30, 1999; "Ku Klux Klan!" *Los Angeles Times*, January 24, 1921, II4; "Police Ban on Klan at Beach," *Los Angeles Times*, April 27, 1922, I2; "Pair, Passing Ku Klux Klan Handbills, in Accident; Plane Falls to Earth Near Pomona Country Club," *Los Angeles Times*, June 22, 1924, 3; "Ku Klux Klan Officers Ask Reinstatement on Force at Pasadena," *Los Angeles Times*, June 16, 1925, 11.

2    Johnny Otis, *Upside Your Head! Rhythm and Blues on Central Avenue* (Middletown, CT: Wesleyan University Press, 1993), 21.

3    Morrow Mayo, *Los Angeles* (New York, A. A. Knopf, 1933), 42.

4    US Census Bureau, "Statistics of the Population of the United States at the Tenth Census: 1880" (Washington, DC: Department of the Interior, Census Office, 1880), 51; US Census Bureau, "Number and Distribution of Inhabitants, Fifteenth Census of the United States: 1930" (Washington, DC: Department of the Interior, Census Office, 1930), 252.

5    W. E. B. Du Bois, "Editorial," *The Crisis* 6, no. 3 (July 1913), 131.

6    "The Lynching Protest," *The Crisis* 3, no. 3 (January 1912), 105; "Colored California," *The Crisis* 6, no. 4 (August 1913), 193.

7    *Liberator,* September 1901, 1; *Liberator,* April 21, 1911, 6; *Liberator,* January 31, 1913, 1; Lawrence B. De Graaf, Kevin Mulroy, and Quintard Taylor, eds., *Seeking El Dorado: African Americans in California* (Seattle: University of Washington Press, 2001), 133–135.

8    "Colored California," 193–194.

9    Horace Tapscott, interviewed by Steven Louis Isoardi, May 1, 1993, Central Avenue Sounds Oral History Project, Tape I, Side Two, Oral History Collection, UCLA Library; Douglas Flamming, *Bound for Freedom: Black Los Angeles in Jim Crow America* (Berkeley: University of California Press, 2005); US Census Bureau, "Number and Distribution of Inhabitants, Fifteenth Census, 1930."

10   Art Pepper and Laurie Pepper, *Straight Life: The Story of Art Pepper* (New York: De Capo Press, 1994), 42–43; Clora Bryant, Buddy Collette, William Green, et al., eds., *Central Avenue Sounds: Jazz in Los Angeles* (Berkeley: University of California Press, 1998), 35, 143, 197, 309, 351.

11   "Colored California," 193–194.

12   Josh Sides, *LA City Limits: African American Los Angeles from the Great Depression to the Present* (Berkeley: University of California Press, 2003), 15.

13   Although the bulk of scholarship focused on pre–World War II black migration centers on the North and the Northeast, a few California historians have explored the experiences of African Americans in early Los Angeles. Several provide examinations of the "black promised land" idea as a product of opportunity, diversity, and sprawl. These include, most notably, De Graaf, Mulroy, and Taylor, *Seeking El Dorado*; Flamming, *Bound for Freedom*; and Sides, *LA City Limits*.

14   A great deal has been written about California as the "arsenal of democracy" during World War II, including a wealth of scholarship exploring the era's dramatic economic changes. Although focused on the Bay Area, Marilynn Johnson, *The Second Gold Rush: Oakland and the East Bay in World War II* (Berkeley: University of California Press, 1996) outlines the impact of war industry and mass migration on the state as a whole. For examina-

tions of California's immigrant groups and black migrants in wartime, see Roger W. Lotchin, ed., *The Way We Really Were: The Golden State in the Second Great War* (Urbana: University of Illinois Press, 2000), De Graaf, Mulroy, and Taylor, *Seeking El Dorado*; and Sides, *LA City Limits*.

15   US Census Bureau, "African American Population in California and Its Major Cities, 1940–60," cited in De Graaf et al., *Seeking El Dorado*, 33; 1940 US Census data cited in Lotchin, *The Way We Really Were*, 189–190.

16   *Liberator*, September 1901, 1; Bryant et al., *Central Avenue Sounds*, 46.

17   California Office of the Attorney General, *Police Training Bulletin: A Guide to Race Relations for Police Officers* (Sacramento: Department of Justice, State of California, 1946).

18   For reflections on housing covenants in South Los Angeles County and black responses to them, see Jackie Kelso, interviewed by Steven Louis Isoardi, May 15, 1990, Central Avenue Sounds Oral History Project, Tape VIII, Side Two, Oral History Collection, UCLA Library; booster descriptions of Compton quoted in Josh Sides, "Straight into Compton: American Dreams, Urban Nightmares, and the Metamorphosis of a Black Suburb," *American Quarterly* 56, no. 3 (September 2004): 583–605.

19   Bryant et al., *Central Avenue Sounds*, 24.

20   *In Quest of Full Citizenship: George Beavers*, Ranford B. Hopkins, interviewer George Beavers, "In Quest of Full Citizenship," transcript of interviews by Ranford B. Hopkins, April–July 1982, Tape I, Side One, April 29, 1982, Oral History Program, University of California, Los Angeles, Special Collections, UCLA Library.

21   Gerald Horne, *Fire This Time: The Watts Uprising and the 1960s* (Charlottesville: University Press of Virginia, 1995), 3; [California] Governor's Commission on the Los Angeles Riots, "Violence in the City—An End or a Beginning? A Report," December 2, 1965, 1–2.

22   *The National Broadcasting Company presents Meet the Press*, TV episode, produced by Lawrence E. Spivak, August, 29, 1965, National Broadcasting Company, Inc.

23   California Governor's Commission on the Los Angeles Riots, 3–9, 27–36, 77.

24   *Newsweek*, August 30, 1965, cover.

25   Otis, *Upside Your Head*, 21–23.

26   "Dootsie: Ideal Watts Entrepreneur," *Los Angeles Sentinel*, March 6, 1969, F5.

27  "Dootsie: Ideal Watts Entrepreneur"; Doc Young, "Community Center Becomes Vital Cog," *Los Angeles Sentinel*, August 15, 1963, B3.

28  Doc Young, "'Mexican Pie' Dootsie's Slice: Mexican Land Trust," *Los Angeles Sentinel*, May 22, 1975, A3; Doc Young, "Anatomy of a Robbery," *Los Angeles Sentinel*, October 22, 1970, A6; Doc Young, "Center for Sale," *Los Angeles Sentinel*, November 28, 1974, A7.

## 1. The Batterram

1  Jerry Heller and Gil Reavill, *Ruthless: A Memoir* (New York: Simon Spotlight Entertainment, 2006), 57–58.

2  For more on KDAY's rich history, its music programming, and its uneven relationship with black listeners in the 1960s and 1970s, see "Radio-TV Programming: Wolfman Jack to KDAY; Sets New Syndie Network," *Billboard* 84, no. 17 (April 22, 1972), 14; "Music News: Alan Freed Joins KDAY as R&B Jock," *Billboard* 72, no. 20 (May 16, 1960), 16; "KDAY Shoots at Negro Market," *Billboard Music Week* 74, no. 21 (May 26, 1962), 32; "KDAY Drops R&B Format," *Billboard* 78, no. 31 (July 30, 1966), 8, 12; Sean Ross, "Radio: KDAY LA's Glory Days," *Billboard* 103, no. 15 (April 13, 1991), 12–13.

3  Ross, "KDAY LA's Glory Days," 12.

4  Brian Cross, ed., *It's Not about a Salary: Rap, Race, and Resistance in Los Angeles* (New York: Verso, 1994), 154.

5  Von Jones, "Rapping with Radio Rappers," *Los Angeles Sentinel*, May 2, 1985, A1.

6  Toddy Tee, "Batterram," single (original self-produced cassette-tape format, 1985; Evejim Records, 1985), vinyl, 12".

7  Daryl F. Gates, *Chief: My Life in the LAPD* (New York: Bantam Books, 1992), 338.

8  United States Senate, Subcommittee on Juvenile Justice of the Committee on the Judiciary, Gang Violence and Control: Ninety-eighth Congress, First Session on Gang Violence and Control in the Los Angeles and San Francisco Areas With a View to What Might Be Done by the Federal Government, February 9, 1983 (Washington, DC: United States Government Printing Office, 1983), 3, 10.

9  "1984 Summer Olympics," *Official Website of the Los Angeles Police Department*, http://www.lapdonline.org/history_of_the_lapd/content_basic _view/1130.

10   David Freed, "Policing Gangs: Case of Contrasting Styles Strides Made by Sheriff's Dept. Cast a Pall on Methods Used by the L.A. Police Dept.," *Los Angeles Times*, January 19, 1986, 1; Gates, *Chief,* 334–345.

11   "L.A. Declares War on Gangs," *Globe and Mail* (Canada), November 22, 1984; Jack Katz, "If Police Call It Gang Crime That Doesn't Make It True," *Los Angeles Times*, September 28, 1989; Gates, *Chief,* 334–345.

12   "Los Angeles Police: Not So Angelic," *Economist*, June 18, 1983, 26.

13   "Mayor's Statement for Press Conference on Gang Violence," 1984, Box 4213, Folder 31, Mayor Tom Bradley Administration Papers 1920–1993, UCLA Special Collections, Charles E. Young Research Library, University of California, Los Angeles; Jesse Katz, "Tracking the Genesis of the Crack Trade; Series: The Cocaine Trail," *Los Angeles Times*, October 20, 1996.

14   "Mayor's Statement for Press Conference on Gang Violence."

15   Gates, *Chief,* 319.

16   Toddy Tee, "Batterram."

17   Patricia Klein, "Police Ram Opens Door to Debate," *Los Angeles Times*, June 4, 1985, 1, 14–15.

18   Toddy Tee, "Batterram."

19   Gates, *Chief,* 320–321.

20   Patricia Klein and Stephanie Chavez, "Pacoima Leaders Protest Police Use of Motorized Ram," *Los Angeles Times*, February 9, 1985.

21   Gates, *Chief,* 320–321; Greg Braxton, "Second 'Rock House' Raid in Pacoima Nets Drugs," *Los Angeles Times*, March 6, 1985, VA6.

22   Braxton, "Second 'Rock House' Raid"; Patricia Klein, "Couple Ask L.A. for $60-Million Damages in Battering-Ram Case," *Los Angeles Times*, April 5, 1985.

23   Klein and Chavez, "Pacoima Leaders Protest Police Use of Motorized Ram."

24   [California] Governor's Commission on the Los Angeles Riots, "Violence in the City—An End or a Beginning? A Report," December 2, 1965; Kerner Commission, *Report of the National Advisory Commission on Civil Disorders* (Washington: United States Government Printing Office, 1968); Roy Wilkins, "Police Review Board Idea Is Very Well Worth Trying," *Los Angeles Times*, February 21, 1966, A5; *Muhammad Speaks*, May 1962, cited in "K of C against Police Review Board Here," *Los Angeles Times*, August 28, 1980. See also

Gerald Horne, *Fire This Time: The Watts Uprising and the 1960s* (Charlottesville: University Press of Virginia, 1995); and Joshua Bloom and Waldo E. Martin, Jr., *Black against Empire: The History and Politics of the Black Panther Party* (Berkeley: University of California Press, 2014).

25   Jocelyn Stewart, "Michael Zinzun, 57; Ex-Black Panther Challenged Southland Police Agencies," *Los Angeles Times*, July 12, 2006; Coalition Against Police Abuse, "C.A.P.A. Proposal to Liberty Hill, Exhibits," 1976, Folder 6, Box 3, CAPA Papers, Liberty Hill Foundation Collection, Southern California Library.

26   "Police 'Picketed' Today," *Los Angeles Sentinel*, May 6, 1976, A3; Coalition Against Police Abuse, "Statement of Purpose," n.d., Box 10, Folder 19, CAPA Papers, Liberty Hill Foundation Collection, Southern California Library.

27   Nick Brown, "Police Abuse Attacked," *Los Angeles Sentinel*, May 18, 1978, A1.

28   Coalition Against Police Abuse, "Statement of Purpose."

29   H. Vincent Price, "Community Backs Cop Abuse Seminar," *Los Angeles Sentinel*, December 9, 1976, A1.

30   H. Vincent Price, "Church *Marches On 77th Precinct; Church Rally Slated at Police Station,*" *Los Angeles Sentinel*, March 3, 1977, A1; H. Vincent Price, "Sheriff Picket 'Spirited,'" *Los Angeles Sentinel*, June 30, 1977; "LAPD Hit with Major Lawsuit; Suit Seeks Names," *Los Angeles Sentinel*, July 28, 1977, A1.

31   Nick Brown, "LAPD to Answer Spying Charges," *Los Angeles Sentinel*, July 6, 1978, A3.

32   Gates, *Chief,* 200–201; Peggy Rowe Estrada, "Don't Weaken City Charter to Get at LAPD," Opinion, *Los Angeles Times*, January 23, 1992.

33   Gates, *Chief,* 174; Martín Sánchez Jankowski, *Islands in the Street* (Berkeley: University of California Press, 1991), 255.

34   Emphasis in original document; Los Angeles Police Department, "Training Bulletin Volume X, Issue 11, Use of Force Part II," May 1978, Box 10, Folder 3, CAPA Papers, Liberty Hill Foundation Collection, Southern California Library.

35   John Mitchell and Doug Shuit, "Eulia Love: Anatomy of a Fatal Shooting," *Los Angeles Times*, April 16, 1979.

36   Mitchell and Shuit, "Eulia Love"; Claire Spiegel, "Bullets Also Shattered Lives of 3 Daughters," *Los Angeles Times*, October 4, 1979.

37　Gates, *Chief,* 222; Doug Shuit, "Gates Pins Police Shootings on Crime," *Los Angeles Times,* April 27, 1979.

38　Gates, *Chief,* 224.

39　Spiegel, "Bullets Also Shattered Lives"; Mitchell and Shuit, "Eulia Love."

40　Claire Spiegel, "Probe of Love Shooting—a Question of Credibility," *Los Angeles Times,* May 8, 1979; "Controversy Brews in Shooting of L.A. Woman," *Jet,* February 1, 1979, 30–31.

41　Spiegel, "Bullets Also Shattered Lives."

42　Mitchell and Shuit, "Eulia Love."

43　"Controversy Brews in Shooting of L.A. Woman."

44　"Controversy Brews in Shooting of L.A. Woman"; L. C. Fortenberry, "Love Death Draws Concern," *Los Angeles Sentinel,* January 18, 1979, A1.

45　Sandy Banks, "New Cynicism: Watts: Many Churches but How Helpful," *Los Angeles Times,* August 19, 1980; Fortenberry, "Love Death Draws Concern."

46　James G. Bellows, *The Last Editor: How I Saved* The New York Times, *the* Washington Post, *and the* Los Angeles Times *from Dullness and Complacency* (Kansas City, MO: Andrews McMeel, 2002), 235.

47　Bill Farr, "3 L.A. Policemen Charged in Shooting at Gas Station," *Los Angeles Times,* March 22, 1980.

48　"All Should Be Concerned," editorial, *Los Angeles Times,* August 18, 1980, C8.

49　Michael Seiler, "Nickerson Gardens—a View from a Black-and-White," *Los Angeles Times,* October 8, 1979; Jerry Belcher and Tim Waters, "Police Critical of TV Newsman's Report," *Los Angeles Times,* November 16, 1979.

50　Fortenberry, "Love Death Draws Concern."

51　"Justice: L.A. Style," editorial, *Los Angeles Sentinel,* April 26, 1979, A1.

52　Jerry Belcher and Myrna Oliver, "Police Protecting Witness Shoot 15-Year-Old Boy," *Los Angeles Times,* April 27, 1979.

53　Ed Davis, "Cop Shooting in Valley Feeds Fire: Youth Near Death," *Los Angeles Sentinel,* May 3, 1979, A1.

54　Cassandra Smith, "Should Civilians Be Allowed to Police the Police? Part II of a Series," *Los Angeles Sentinel,* September 13, 1979, A8.

55　Yusuf Jah and Sister Shah-Keyah, *Uprising: Crips and Bloods Tell the Story of America's Youth in the Crossfire* (New York: Scribner, 1995), 159–160.

56  Jah and Shah-Keyah, *Uprising,* 121, 132, 135.

57  Brian Hiatt, "NWA: American Gangstas," *Rolling Stone,* August 27, 2015.

58  The *Los Angeles Times* conducted two separate polls of police approval in Los Angeles, one among African Americans and another of the city's entire population. Participants were defined as "black," "white," or "Hispanic." Whites, who were most likely to approve of the department, expressed greater uncertainty about police misconduct than they had in 1977. It is also notable that the evidence of rising disapproval offered by the *Times* refuted an LAPD survey that showed a staggering 97 percent of residents approved of police conduct and services. Chief Gates ultimately conceded that the discrepancies could be attributed to the manner in which the poll was administered: participants were selected from a pool of those who had called the police department for help; George Skelton, "Public Taking Dimmer View of L.A. Police," *Los Angeles Times,* May 15, 1979.

59  Doug Shuit, "L.A. Deputy Chief Hits Love Slaying," *Los Angeles Times,* April 27, 1979.

60  Skelton, "Public Taking Dimmer View."

61  "Medals of Valor Given to Seven L.A. Policemen," *Los Angeles Times,* May 10, 1979.

62  "Medals of Valor Given"; "Love Whitewash Incites Outrage: Police Killing Upheld," *Los Angeles Sentinel,* April 19, 1979, A1.

63  In 1950, a coalition of over a dozen organizations formed the Permanent Coordination Committee on Police and Minority Groups to lobby New York City's mayor to deal with growing "police misconduct in their relations with Puerto Ricans and Negros specifically." In response, the New York Police Department installed a civilian review board within its department. Citizen complaints were investigated and judged by board members—often police deputies—selected by the NYPD. In 1965, when Mayor John Lindsay attempted to pressure the department to appoint citizens to the board, the Patrolman's Benevolent Association managed to collect enough signatures to place a measure on the 1966 ballot barring civilian appointments. The measure passed by a wide margin. For more on this, see Vincent J. Cannato, *The Ungovernable City: John Lindsay and His Struggle to Save New York* (New York: Basic Books, 2001), 155–188.

64  "Los Angeles: The Love Affair," *Economist,* June 14, 1980.

65  David Johnston and Joel Sappell, "Police Spying Data Was Channeled to Top Brass," *Los Angeles Times,* October 11, 1982.

66   Robert Lindsey, "Los Angeles Police Find Image of Efficiency Fades," *New York Times,* June 16, 1980; Johnston and Sappell, "Police Spying Data Was Channeled to Top Brass."

67   Gates, *Chief,* 208; Shuit, "Gates Pins Police Shootings on Crime."

68   "March on Crime," editorial, *Los Angeles Sentinel,* March 1, 1984, A6.

69   "Crime Prevention Week Asks Citizens to Behave," *Los Angeles Times,* February 17, 1952, B1; see also Edward J. Escobar, "Bloody Christmas and the Irony of Police Professionalism: The Los Angeles Police Department, Mexican Americans, and Police Reform in the 1950s," *Pacific Historical Review* 72, no. 2 (May 2003): 171–199.

70   "Wholesome Recreation Curbs Delinquency Says Hahn," *Los Angeles Sentinel,* May 24, 1951, B1; "Fairness Promised Minorities by Chief," *Los Angeles Times,* July 2, 1949, 1; "New Chief," *Los Angeles Sentinel,* August 10, 1950, A8.

71   Brad Pye, "Teenagers, Police Clash in Compton: Incident Stories Conflict," *Los Angeles Sentinel,* October 26, 1961, A1; Stanley G. Robertson, "L.A. Confidential: The 'Real Villains' in the Park," *Los Angeles Sentinel,* September 13, 1962, A7; "Negroes Hostile, Police Are Victims," *Los Angeles Sentinel,* April 30, 1964, A1. For more on the escalating conflict between black youth and the police leading up to the Watts Rebellion, see Horne, *Fire This Time*; and Josh Sides, *LA City Limits: African American Los Angeles from the Great Depression to the Present* (Berkeley: University of California Press, 2003).

72   L. M. Meriwether, "Citizens, Police in Head-On Clash: Incidents Alarm Public," *Los Angeles Sentinel,* April 16, 1964, A1.

73   Listing of Physical Attacks on RTD Buses, Report Submitted by SCRTD Manager of Employee Relations John S. Wilkens to Earl Clark, General Chairman of United Transportation Union, March 3, 1975, in "Unprovoked Attacks"; and Earl Clark, General Chairman of United Transportation Union to Peter F. Schabarum, Los Angeles Board of Supervisors, March 3, 1975; both in Box 2091, Folder 9, Mayor Tom Bradley Administration Papers 1920–1993, UCLA Special Collections, Charles E. Young Research Library, University of California, Los Angeles.

74   Cynthia Hamilton, "The Making of an American Bantustan," *LA Weekly,* December 30, 1988–January 5, 1989, 32; letter from Manager of Operation George W. Heinle of SCRTD to Mr. Earl Clark, General Chairman of United Transportation Union, April 13, 1976, in "Unprovoked Attacks," Box 2091, Folder 9, Mayor Tom Bradley Administration Papers

1920–1993, UCLA Special Collections, Charles E. Young Research Library, University of California, Los Angeles.

75  Von Jones, "The Life and Times of a Gang Leader," *Los Angeles Sentinel,* February 21, 1985, A1; United States Senate, Gang Violence and Control, 3.

76  "CRASH Knows 'Who' of Westside Gangs," *Pico Post—Century City,* August 7, 1980; Bob Baker, "County May Act on Rising Gang Violence," *Los Angeles Times,* October 13, 1980; Assembly Bill No. 788, Chapter 1030, Section 1, "Gang Violence Suppression," filed with Secretary of State, September 30, 1981, Box 130, Folder 7, Mayor Tom Bradley Administration Papers 1920–1993, UCLA Special Collections, Charles E. Young Research Library, University of California, Los Angeles.

77  Steven R. Cureton, "Something Wicked This Way Comes: A Historical Account of Black Gangsterism Offers Wisdom and Warning for African American Leadership," *Journal of Black Studies* 40, no. 2 (November 2009), 351–352.

78  Jah and Shah-Keyah, *Uprising,* 259.

79  Saleem Ibrahim, "'Freeze' Means: Stop All Action," *Los Angeles Sentinel,* November 27, 1980, A5.

80  Ibrahim, "Freeze."

81  "Change or Perish," editorial, *Los Angeles Sentinel,* November 28, 1974, A6.

82  "March on Crime."

83  "A Fighting Chance," editorial, *Los Angeles Sentinel,* August 23, 1984, A6; "Compton Battles Crimes," *Los Angeles Sentinel,* December 6, 1984, A1.

84  "A Critical Situation; Police Deployment in South Central LA," *Los Angeles Sentinel,* editorial, June 7, 1984, A6.

85  Dan Divito, Affidavit Statement, April 16, 1978; and Robert W. Barnwell, Statement to CAPA on "Events of September 30, 1977," October 2, 1977, both in Box 10, Folder 3, CAPA Papers, Liberty Hill Foundation Collection, Southern California Library; Los Angeles Police Department, "Training Bulletin"; "L.A. Panel Orders Inquiry on Police Chief's Remarks," *Christian Science Monitor,* May 14, 1982, 2.

86  "Coast Police Chief Accused of Racism," *New York Times,* May 13, 1982; see also "Gangbusters," in Mike Davis, *City of Quartz: Excavating the Future in Los Angeles* (London: Verso, 1990).

87  "Los Angeles Police End Use of Choke Hold That Stops Air," *New York Times,* May 8, 1982, A20; "Urban League in Los Angeles Asks Police Chief

Suspension," *New York Times*, May 12, 1982, A24; "Coast Police Chief Repri-
manded for Remark," *New York Times*, June 2, 1982, A18; Daryl F. Gates,
"Memorandum No. 6: Moratorium on the Use of Upper Body Control
Holds," Office of the Chief of Police, June 18, 1982, Box 10, Folder 2, CAPA
Papers, Liberty Hill Foundation Collection, Southern California Library.

88   Jocelyn Y. Stewart, "Michael Zinzun, 57; Ex-Black Panther Challenged
Southland Police Agencies," *Los Angeles Times*, July 12, 2006.

89   Klein and Chavez, "Pacoima Leaders Protest Police Use of Motorized Ram."

90   "LAPD's Battering Ram Draws Suit," *Los Angeles Sentinel*, February 28,
1985, A8.

91   "A Change of Pace," editorial, *Los Angeles Sentinel*, February 21, 1985,
A6; Chief Daryl F. Gates, Letter to the Editor, *Los Angeles Sentinel*, August 1, 1985, A6.

92   Klein and Chavez, "Pacoima Leaders Protest Police Use of Motorized
Ram"; Betty Pleasant and Michael Taylor, "Police May Have Wrecked
Wrong House; Armored Attack Decried," *Los Angeles Sentinel*, February 14,
1985, A1.

93   Betty Pleasant, "Ram Smashes City's Largest Rock House," *Los Angeles
Sentinel*, May 2, 1985, A1.

94   Patricia Klein, "LAPD's Battering Ram Sitting Idle: Critics Say It's the
Pressure; Police Claim It's Not Needed," *Los Angeles Times*, February 10,
1986, A8D.

95   "Mayor's Statement for Press Conference on Gang Violence," 1984, Box
4213, Folder 31, Mayor Tom Bradley Administration Papers 1920–1993,
UCLA Special Collections, Charles E. Young Research Library, University of
California, Los Angeles; James Rice, Letter to the Editor, *Los Angeles Sentinel*, August 1, 1985, A6.

96   Cross, *It's Not about a Salary*, 146.

97   Mixmaster Spade, interview by The Poetess, "Mixmaster Spade,"
March 17, 2003, in *Davey D's Hip Hop Political Palace*, http://
politicalpalace.yuku.com/topic/10286/Mixmaster-Spade-is-on-Life
-Support-He-s-NOT-Dead#.WKdD0MPytE4.

98   Cross, *It's Not about a Salary*, 146.

99   UTFO "Hanging Out / Roxanne, Roxanne," single (Select Records, 1984),
vinyl, 12"; for examples of "Weird Al" Yankovic's parodied pop hits, see *Weird*

*Al Yankovic*, album (Rock 'n' Roll, 1983), vinyl, LP; *In 3-D*, album (Rock 'n' Roll, 1984), vinyl, LP; *Dare to Be Stupid* (Rock 'n' Roll, 1985), vinyl, LP.

100  Whodini, "Freaks Come Out at Night," single (Jive, 1984), vinyl, 12"; Rappin' Duke, "Rappin' Duke," single (JWP Records, 1985), vinyl, 12"; Toddy Tee, "Batterram," single (original self-produced cassette-tape format, 1985; Evejim Records, 1985), vinyl, 12".

101  Sacha Jenkins, ed., *Ego Trip's Book of Rap Lists* (New York: Macmillan, 1999), 108.

102  "The L.A. Riots: 20 Years Later; Rhythm of the Street," *Los Angeles Times*, May 2, 2012, A1; Robin D. G. Kelley, "Straight from the Underground," *The Nation*, June 8, 1992, 793.

103  Johnny Mann, "Interview: MC Eiht," *Elemental Magazine*, issue 63, 2004, available at http://halftimeonline.net/mc-eiht/.

104  Eric Bailey, "The Gangs of Long Beach: Signs Are Obvious; Graffiti, Poverty, Drugs, Turf Wars, Murders," *Los Angeles Times*, December 1, 1985; Jonah Weiner, "The Lion Smokes Tonight," *Rolling Stone*, May 23, 2013.

105  Klein, "LAPD's Battering Ram Sitting Idle"; Toddy Tee, "Batterram."

106  Jah and Shah-Keyah, *Uprising*, 121.

## 2. Hardcore LA

1      Frank Owen, "Run DMC: Homeboys' Home Truths," *Melody Maker* 62, no. 21 (May 23, 1987), 24–25; Jess Cagle, "All Hell Breaks Loose at a Run-DMC 'Raising Hell' Rap Concert in California," *People*, September 1, 1986; Sacha Jenkins, ed., *Ego Trip's Book of Rap Lists* (New York: MacMillan, 1999), 108; Bill Adler, *Tougher Than Leather: The Rise of Run-DMC* (Los Angeles: Consafos Press, 1987), 5.

2      "Violence Silences Rap Group," *Los Angeles Times*, August 19, 1986.

3      Brian Cross, ed., *It's Not about a Salary: Rap, Race, and Resistance in Los Angeles* (New York: Verso, 1993), 156–157; Daryl Kelley, "Council Asks How Riot Hit, How It Can Avoid Replay," *Los Angeles Times*, August 21, 1986; Chris Morris, "Venue Reads Riot Act Following Melee," *Billboard* 98, no. 35 (August 30, 1986): 7, 77.

4      Morris, "Venue Reads Riot Act"; Adler, *Tougher Than Leather*, 4.

5      Morris, "Venue Reads Riot Act"; "42 Are Hurt as Gang Fighting Breaks Up California Concert," *New York Times*, August 19, 1986.

6    George Ramos, "30 Injured at Long Beach Concert; L.A. Show Off," *Los Angeles Times,* August 18, 1986; George Ramos, "40 Hurt at Long Beach Concert; Palladium Drops 'Rap' Group," *Los Angeles Times,* August 19, 1986.

7    Morris, "Venue Reads Riot Act."

8    George Ramos, "'Rap' Musicians' Concert Is Canceled at Palladium after Long Beach Fights," *Los Angeles Times,* August 19, 1986; Eric Hubler, "Rap Repercussions?," *Washington Post,* August 19, 1986; Ed Kiersh, "Run D.M.C. Is Beating the Rap," *Rolling Stone,* December 4, 1986.

9    Owen, "Run DMC: Homeboys' Home Truths"; "Violence Silences Rap Group"; *The Warriors,* motion picture, directed by Walter Hill (1979; Paramount Pictures, 2001), DVD; Patrick Goldstein, "Can Rap Survive Gang War?" *Los Angeles Times,* August 24, 1986; Adler, *Tougher Than Leather,* 5–6.

10   *And You Don't Stop: 30 Years of Hip Hop,* mini-series documentary, directed by Richard Lowe and Dana Heinz Perry (2004; Bring the Noise LLC), TV broadcast.

11   Steve Hosley, "On the Record: Sugarhill Gang," *Sepia,* May 1980, 14; Jerry Heller and Gil Reavill, *Ruthless: A Memoir* (New York: Simon Spotlight, 2006), 35; Glenn Collins, "Rap Music, Brash and Swaggering, Enters Mainstream," *New York Times,* August 29, 1988; Greg Tate, "They're Gonna Smash Their Brains In," *Village Voice,* April 9, 1985, 61; Andrew Mason, "Blondie Rose to Stardom Out of New York City's Burgeoning Downtown Scene of Punk Rock and New Wave," *Wax Poetics* 60 (November 2014), accessed via www.waxpoetics.com.

12   Owen, "Run DMC: Homeboys' Home Truths."

13   Annette Stark, "There's a Riot Going On," *Spin* 2, no. 9 (December 1986): 68–74.

14   Peter H. King, "Punk Rockers Put on Notice by Santa Ana," *Los Angeles Times,* Orange County edition, Section 2, January 9, 1982, 1, 8; Cary Darling, "41 Arrested at L.A. 'Punk Riot,'" *Billboard* 95, no. 8. (February 26, 1983): 30, 35; Dan Nakaso, "Punk Rock May Cost Theater Owner His License," *Los Angeles Times,* South Bay section, January 20, 1983, 1.

15   Mike Boehm, "Kids of the Black Hole: The 1970s Were Waning When Orange County's Punk Rock Scene Roared Its Dark, Hostile Message," *Los Angeles Times,* July 23, 1989; Darling, "41 Arrested at L.A. 'Punk Riot'"; Peter H. King, "Punk Rockers Put on Notice by Santa Ana: Punk Rock: Santa Ana Is Wary," *Los Angeles Times,* January 9, 1982.

16   Patrick Goldstein, "Is Heavy Metal a Loaded Gun Aimed at Its Fans?" *Los Angeles Times,* January 26, 1986; "Record Labeling" Senate Hearing before the Committee on Commerce, Science, and Transportation, United States Senate, First Session on Content of Music and the Lyrics of Records, Sept. 19, 1985 (Washington, DC: US Government Printing Office, 1985), 10–17; Dennis McLellan, "Spikes and Studs: Tipping the Scales against Heavy Metal, Punk," *Los Angeles Times,* Orange County edition, View section, February 21, 1985, 1, 20–22.

17   Bob Schwartz, "1 Dead, 3 Hurt in Violence at Rock Concerts," *Los Angeles Times,* June 16, 1986, 3.

18   Goldstein, "Can Rap Survive Gang War?"; "Brawl Erupts at Rap Film in New York," *Washington Post,* December 29, 1985, A10.

19   "Security to Be Beefed Up for RUN-DMC Concert Sat," *Atlanta Daily World,* August 21, 1986.

20   Adler, *Tougher Than Leather,* 4, 21, 169.

21   Goldstein, "Can Rap Survive Gang War?"; *USA Today,* quoted in Adler, *Tougher Than Leather,* 176.

22   Owen, "Run DMC: Homeboys' Home Truths."

23   "40 Injured at 'Rap' Concert as Gangs Go on Rampage," *Sun Sentinel,* August 19, 1986; Owen, "Run DMC: Homeboys' Home Truths"; Cagle, "All Hell Breaks Loose"; Kelley, "Council Asks How Riot Hit"; Goldstein, "Can Rap Survive Gang War?"; Adler, *Tougher Than Leather,* 4–6.

24   *Breakin' 'n' Enterin',* documentary, directed by Topper Carew (1983; Rainbow TV Works).

25   Jesse Thorn, "Ice-T Revisits His O. G. Roots in the Documentary *Something from Nothing: The Art of Rap,*" *A.V. Club,* July 5, 2012, http://www .avclub.com/article/ice-t-revists-his-og-roots-in-the-documentary-isom-81987, accessed April 9, 2017.

26   Prior to the late 1980s, "graffiti" in Los Angeles was synonymous with "tagging" one's name, initials, crew moniker, or gang insignia. The "aerosol art" or "spray-can art" commonly associated with the colorful, cartoonish murals painted on New York City subway trains (and later on canvases for art galleries downtown), was virtually absent from LA cityscapes, save for the interiors of venues like The Radio that aimed for a New York aesthetic. For more on tagging in 1970s and 1980s Los Angeles and the late introduction of large-scale subway-style graffiti to the region, see "El Chingaso" in Ulysses L. Zemanova, *The Ulysses Guide to the Los Angeles River,* vol. 1:

*Biology and Art* (Grimmelbein Kitamura Editions, 2009), np; *Bombing L.A.,* documentary, directed by Gary Glaser (1991; Glaser Productions), VHS.

27   Chris "The Glove" Taylor, interview by Stefan Schuetze, *West Coast Pioneers* (website, now defunct), July 2004, accessible at https://soundcloud .com/sabinedegaetani/interview-chris-the-glove.

28   Cross, *It's Not about a Salary,* 174.

29   Richard Cromelin, "Street Art at Lingerie; L.A. Takes the Rap from N.Y. Movement," *Los Angeles Times,* February 7, 1983, F1; Flea, "Brendan Mullen," *Los Angeles Times,* October 14, 2009.

30   Al Martinez, "Hip-Hoppin' with Afrika and Ice T," *Los Angeles Times,* July 18, 1985.

31   *Breakin' 'n' Enterin'.*

32   "Interview with Ice-T," *Behind the Beat,* television series (originally aired in 1988; BBC TV Pebble Mill).

33   Jim Fricke and Charlie Ahearn, eds., *Yes, Yes, Y'all: The Experience Music Project Oral History of Hip-Hop's First Decade* (Cambridge, MA: Da Capo Press, 2002), 309.

34   *Breakin',* motion picture, directed by Joel Silberg (1984; MGM); *Breakin' 2: Electric Boogaloo,* motion picture, directed by Sam Firstenberg (1984; MGM).

35   Rodger Clayton, interview by Stefan Schuetze, *West Coast Pioneers* (website, now defunct), September 2006.

36   Cross, *It's Not about a Salary,* 174; "Interview with Ice-T," *Behind the Beat*; Henry "Hen Gee" Garcia, interview by Stefan Schuetze, *West Coast Pioneers* (website, now defunct), June 2006.

37   Don Snowden and Connie Johnson, "In Search of the Black Beat," *Los Angeles Times,* May 8, 1983, U59, 84–86.

38   Snowden and Johnson, "In Search of the Black Beat."

39   Clayton's Uncle Jamm's Army was first christened as "Unique Dreams Entertainment." Later he and his partners renamed the group Uncle Jam's Army, with one "m," as an homage to Funkadelic's 1979 album *Uncle Jam Wants You.* Clayton later added the additional "m" as his business grew and as he sought to better distinguish his crew from George Clinton's; DJ Zen [Jeff Chang] and Mike Nardone, "Saturday Nite Fresh: An Interview with Uncle Jamm's Army," *Rap Pages,* December 1994, 36–38, 70–74.

40    DJ Zen and Nardone, "Saturday Nite Fresh."

41    In May 1984, Uncle Jamm's Army promoted a benefit concert for Jesse Jackson, which featured Lakeside, Cheryl Lynn, and Shalamar, as well as performances from UJA. Later that year, the DJ outfit hosted the "1984 Music Festival," which was sponsored by Coca-Cola and featured New York rapper Melle Mel, Gladys Night and the Pips, Cameo, Nona Hendryx, Lakeside, and Midnight Star. "Display Ad 380," *Los Angeles Times*, May 13, 1984, L71; "Today's Highlights," *Los Angeles Times*, August 18, 1984, E2.

42    Cross, *It's Not about a Salary*, 155.

43    Tracy Jones, "Uncle Jamm's Army Was the West Coast's Real-Life Answer to *The Get Down*," *LA Weekly*, September 7, 2016.

44    Snoop Dogg with Davin Seay, *Tha Doggfather: The Times, Trials, and Hardcore Truths of Snoop Dogg* (New York: William Morrow, 1999), 35.

45    Gregory "G-Bone" Everett in "The Power of Hip-Hop: Lyrics, Accountability, and Behavior," *ProfessU*, https://www.youtube.com/watch?v=vNYVvIJIBmw.

46    Cross, *It's Not about a Salary*, 146; Toddy Tee, "Batterram," single (original self-produced cassette-tape format, 1985; Evejim Records, 1985), vinyl, 12".

47    Snowden and Johnson, "In Search of the Black Beat."

48    Cross, *It's Not about a Salary* 159.

49    Cross, *It's Not about a Salary*, 121.

50    Jones, "Uncle Jamm's Army."

51    Cross, *It's Not about a Salary*, 155; Rodger Clayton interview, *West Coast Pioneers;* Don Snowden, "Mobile Disco 'Army' Dances to a Different Beat," *Los Angeles Times*, October 30, 1983, U66–67.

52    Rodger Clayton, the founder of Uncle Jamm's Army, referred to himself and his fellow DJs as "programmers," a term that, for him, illustrated the fellowship (and rivalry) between the mobile DJ and the radio jock. Greg Mack, Statement on Death of Rodger Clayton, quoted in Dan Charnas, "Hip-Hop Pioneer Rodger 'Uncle Jamm' Clayton Dies," *The Urban Daily*, October 11, 2010; Snowden, "Mobile Disco 'Army' Dances to a Different Beat," U66; Rodger Clayton interview, *West Coast Pioneers*; Jones, "Uncle Jamm's Army."

53    Dan Charnas, "Hip-Hop Pioneer Rodger 'Uncle Jamm' Clayton Dies," *Urban Daily*, October 11, 2010.

54    Jerry L. Barrow, "Andre Young Is Still Buzzing," *Vibe*, September 1, 2010.

55    Snowden, "Mobile Disco 'Army' Dances to a Different Beat"; Red Bull Music Academy, "Nightclubbing: Uncle Jamm's Army," *Red Bull Music Academy Daily*, October 31, 2017.

56    Diane E. Herz, "Worker Displacement in a Period of Rapid Job Expansion: 1983–1987," *Monthly Labor Review* 113 (May 1990), 21, 31, as cited in John Ehrman, *The Eighties: America in the Age of Reagan* (New Haven: Yale University Press, 2005).

57    For more on the impact of economic decline on African Americans during the Carter and Reagan administrations, see Ehrman, *Eighties*.

58    Snowden, "Mobile Disco 'Army' Dances to a Different Beat," 66.

59    Donnell Alexander, "Do Rappers Dream of Electro-Beats?" *Los Angeles City Beat*, July 28, 2005.

60    Alexander, "Do Rappers Dream of Electro-Beats?"

61    Yusef Jah and Sister Shah-Keyah, *Uprising: Crips and Bloods Tell the Story of America's Youth in the Crossfire* (New York: Scribner, 1995), 259.

62    Snowden, "Mobile Disco 'Army' Dances to a Different Beat."

63    Chris "The Glove" Taylor interview, *West Coast Pioneers*.

64    Henry "Hen Gee" Garcia interview, *West Coast Pioneers*.

65    Sam Sweet, "The Roller Rink Origins of N.W.A.," *New York Times Magazine*, August 13, 2005; also in Sam Sweet, *All Night Menu* vol. 2 (December 2014).

66    Cross, *It's Not about a Salary*, 291.

67    Snowden, "Mobile Disco 'Army' Dances to a Different Beat."

68    Sweet, "The Roller Rink Origins of N.W.A."

69    Egyptian Lover, interview by Chad Kiser, *DUBCNN*, August 2008, http://www.dubcnn.com/interviews/egyptianlover; Lil Rockin G and Madmixer RMG (Knights of the Turntables), interview by Stefan Schuetze, *West Coast Pioneers* (website, now defunct), June 2005; Alexander, "Do Rappers Dream of Electro-Beats?"

70    Egyptian Lover, interview by *West Coast Pioneers*, January 2006, transcript posted at http://www.peoplesrepublicofcork.com/forums/showthread.php?t=105248.

71    Mixmaster Spade, interview by The Poetess, March 17, 2003, transcript posted on *Davey D's Hip Hop Political Palace*, http://politicalpalace

.yuku.com/topic/10286/Mixmaster-Spade-is-on-Life-Support-He-s-NOT-Dead#.WKdDOMPytE4.

72   Ice Cube, interview by Terry Gross, "Hip-Hop Renaissance Man," *Fresh Air,* National Public Radio, January 10, 2005; Robert Hilburn, "The Rap Is—Justice: Ice Cube Finally Talks about the Uprising That He Says Had to Happen," *Los Angeles Times,* May 31, 1992.

73   Ice-T and Douglas Century, *Ice: A Memoir of Gangster Life and Redemption—From South Central to Hollywood* (New York: Random House, 2011), 22; Cross, *It's Not about a Salary,* 181–182; Brian Coleman, ed., *Check the Technique: Liner Notes for Hip-Hop Junkies* (New York: Random House, 2005), 233.

74   Patrick Goldstein, "Pop Eye: Life Is a Rap-sody to California Impresario," *Los Angeles Times,* July 27, 1986.

75   Alexander, "Do Rappers Dream of Electro-Beats?"

76   Jones, "Uncle Jamm's Army."

77   Cross, *It's Not about a Salary,* 155; Ben Westhoff, "KDAY, the Gangsta Rap Oldies Station, Breaks New Ground by Playing Music from the Bad Old Days," *LA Weekly,* August 2, 2012.

78   Toddy Tee, "Batterram"; Patricia Klein, "A Ram at Rest: These Are Quiet Times for LAPD's 'Battering' Vehicle," *Los Angeles Times,* February 10, 1986; Cross, *It's Not about a Salary,* 146.

79   Fricke and Ahearn, *Yes, Yes, Y'all,* 329.

80   John Leland, "It's Like This," *Village Voice,* June 17, 1986, 67, 70; Tate, "They're Gonna Smash Their Brains In."

81   Adler, *Tougher Than Leather,* 57.

82   For more on the influence of early hip-hop groups on the late 1970s and early 1980s Manhattan club scene, see Tim Lawrence, *Life and Death on the New York Dance Floor, 1980–1983* (Durham, NC: Duke University Press, 2016); and Bill Brewster and Frank Broughton, *Last Night a DJ Saved My Life: The History of the Disc Jockey* (New York: Grove Press, 2000); Fricke and Ahearn, *Yes, Yes, Y'all,* 328.

83   Leland, "It's Like This."

84   Leland, "It's Like This."

85   Owen, "Run DMC: Homeboys' Home Truths."

86   Jay-Z, *Decoded* (New York: Spiegel and Grau, 2010), 9–10.

87   The D.O.C., interview by Charlie Braxton, *Murder Dog,* murderdog
.com, 2003.

88   Run-DMC, "It's Like That," and "Sucker M.C.'s (Krush-Groove 1)," *Run-
DMC* (Profile Records, 1984), vinyl, LP; Run-DMC, "It's Tricky," "My Adidas,"
and "Proud To Be Black," *Raising Hell* (Profile Records, 1986), vinyl, LP.

89   "Sucker M.C.'s (Krush-Groove 1)"; "It's Tricky"; "My Adidas."

90   Adler, *Tougher Than Leather,* 82–83; "My Guy, George," *The Jeffersons,*
TV series, directed by Oz Scott (originally aired March 4, 1984; Universal
City: Universal Studios, 1984); Connie Johnson, "Rap Goes Mainstream at
Universal Amphitheatre," *Los Angeles Times,* August 2, 1986.

91   Fricke and Ahearn, *Yes, Yes, Y'all,* 328.

92   Fricke and Ahearn, *Yes, Yes, Y'all,* 329.

93   Fricke and Ahearn, *Yes, Yes, Y'all,* 329.

94   Owen, "Run DMC: Homeboys' Home Truths."

95   Rob Tannenbaum and Craig Marks, eds., *I Want My MTV: The
Uncensored Story of the Music Video Revolution* (New York: Penguin,
2012), 241; Jacob Hoye, ed., *MTV: Uncensored* (New York: Pocket Books,
2001), 70.

96   Hoye, *MTV: Uncensored,* 70.

97   Owen, "Run DMC: Homeboys' Home Truths."

98   Artists United Against Apartheid, *Sun City* (EMI Manhattan Records,
1985), vinyl, LP. The anti-apartheid compilation record included, along
with Bambaataa and Run-DMC, Peter Gabriel, Ringo Starr, Miles Davis,
Keith Richard, Gil Scott-Heron, and Melle Mel, among others.

99   Cromelin, "Street Art at Lingerie"; McKenna, "Taking the Rap in L.A.,"
*Village Voice,* March 7, 1983, G1, 3.

100   Adler, *Tougher Than Leather,* 137, 153.

101   Keith Murphy, "Full Clip: DMC Breaks Down Run-DMC's Catalogue
and Solo Work Feat. Fat Boys, Beastie Boys, Biggie, and Pete Rock," *Vibe,*
February 4, 2011; Kelley, "Council Asks How Riot Hit."

102   "Record Labeling" Senate Hearing, 11.

103   Adler, *Tougher Than Leather,* 172.

104   Morris, "Venue Reads Riot Act."

105   Goldstein, "Can Rap Survive Gang War?"

106 Owen, "Run DMC: Homeboys' Home Truths."

107 Victor Valle, "Some Anxiety Clouds Rap Concert Tonight," *Los Angeles Times,* December 31, 1987.

108 Goldstein, "Can Rap Survive Gang War?"

109 "42 Are Hurt as Gang Fighting Breaks Up California Concert"; Ramos, "'Rap' Musicians' Concert Is Canceled"; Goldstein, "Can Rap Survive Gang War?"

110 Goldstein, "Can Rap Survive Gang War?"

111 "Security to Be Beefed Up for RUN-DMC Concert Sat," *Atlanta Daily World,* August 21, 1986; "Run-DMC Member Shot; Suspect Sought," *Los Angeles Sentinel,* November 26, 1987.

112 Ramos, "30 Injured at Long Beach Concert"; Morris, "Venue Reads Riot Act."

113 Morris, "Venue Reads Riot Act"; Ramos, "'Rap' Musicians' Concert Is Canceled."

114 Morris, "Venue Reads Riot Act."

115 Bob Baker, "Rap Group Hot Item in Street Scene Safety Talks," *Los Angeles Times,* Metro Section, September 16, 1986, 1; Robert Hilburn, "Run-DMC Says Street Scene Festival Ban Is a Bum Rap," *Los Angeles Times,* Calendar Section, September 20, 1986, 7.

116 Edward J. Boyer, "Celebrities Use Airwaves to Take on Street Violence," *Los Angeles Times,* October 10, 1986; Bob Baker, "He Walks the Mean Side of the Street to Help a Few," *Los Angeles Times,* July 27, 1987.

117 Boyer, "Celebrities Use Airwaves."

118 Sean Ross, "KDAY L.A.'s Glory Days," *Billboard Magazine,* April 13, 1991, 12–13.

119 Robert Hilburn, "Rap: Striking Tales of Black Frustration and Pride Shake the Pop Mainstream," *Los Angeles Times,* April 2, 1989, 7, 80–81, 87.

120 Hilburn, "Rap: Striking Tales"; Boyer, "Celebrities Use Airwaves"; "The News in Brief: The Region," *Los Angeles Times,* October 9, 1986, 2.

121 Boyer, "Celebrities Use Airwaves."

122 Boyer, "Celebrities Use Airwaves."

123 Scott Harris, "'We Agree to Stop Killing Each Other': Gang Peace Treaties Being Negotiated," *Los Angeles Times,* November 5, 1986.

124  "Rappers Deny Link to Killing," *Los Angeles Sentinel*, June 30, 1988.

125  Valle, "Some Anxiety Clouds Rap Concert Tonight"; Robert Hilburn, "Groups' Violence-Plagued Image Dogs Concerts in Northwest: Run-DMC and Beasties Subdued?" *Los Angeles Times*, June 17, 1987.

126  Stephen Holden, "The Pop Life: Two Rap Groups Plan Extensive Summer Tour," *New York Times*, May 20, 1987; Valle, "Some Anxiety Clouds Rap Concert Tonight."

127  "Beastie Boys and Run-DMC Discuss the 'Together Forever' Tour," *CBS News Nightwatch*, TV news program (originally aired August 1987; New York: CBS News Production).

128  "Beastie Boys and Run-DMC Discuss the 'Together Forever' Tour"; Lyor Cohen, "On Tour: Dispatch from the Front Lines," commentary, *Billboard* 99, no. 37 (September 12, 1987), 9.

129  Charisse Jones, "A Dirge of Discouragement; Mother of Youth Who Wrote Gang Peace Treaty Can't Afford Funeral," *Los Angeles Times*, March 14, 1989; Charisse Jones, "'Do-Man's' Legacy: Rites Finally Held for Ex-Gang Member Who Wrote Peace Treaty," *Los Angeles Times*, March 18, 1989; Paul Feldman, "'Murder by Strangers': From Gang Gunfire to Freeway Shootings, L.A. County's 1987 Homicides Often Linked by Their Random Nature," *Los Angeles Times*, December 30, 1987, R6; Ralph Bailey, Jr., "Drive-By Wars Claim 8 Lives in 48 Hours," *Los Angeles Sentinel*, December 3, 1987.

130  Valle, "Some Anxiety Clouds Rap Concert Tonight."

131  Cross, *It's Not about a Salary*, 156.

132  Cohen, "On Tour."

133  C.I.A., "Jus 4 the Cash $," track 2 on *The C.I.A.: Cru In Action* (Kru-Cut Records, 1987), vinyl, EP.

### 3. The Boys in the Hood Are Always Hard

1    Linda Moleski, "Grass Route," *Billboard* 98, no. 49 (December 6, 1986), 61.

2    Dave Dexter, Jr., "LA Grows to the Sound of Music for 200 Years," *Billboard* 92, no. 46 (November 15, 1980): 4–6, 8, 12; Sam Sutherland and Roman Kozak, "Report Pressing Outlook Solid," *Billboard* 93, no. 32 (August 15, 1981): 1, 11, 88.

3    "Cadet Records, Inc," advertisement, *Billboard*, November 10, 1973, 33; "Cadet Hit by L.A. Raiders," *Billboard*, September 12, 1981, 86; John

Sippel, "Seized LPs Are VeeJay Beatle Copies," *Billboard*, September 19, 1981, 4, 77; Howard S. Alperin, "Letters to the Editor," *Billboard*, October 3, 1981, 16; "RIAA Probe Fingers Cadet," *Billboard*, October 16, 1982, 92.

4    Dexter, "LA Grows to the Sound of Music"; "Presser Plays Many Roles," *Billboard* 97, no. 11 (March 16, 1985): 77.

5    Egyptian Lover, interview by Stefan Schuetze, *West Coast Pioneers*, January 2006; Ural Garrett, "Egyptian Lover Reminisces over Early West Coast Hip Hop," *Hip Hop DX*, March 24, 2016, http://hiphopdx.com/interviews/id.2877/title.egyptian-lover-reminisces-over-early-west-coast-hip-hop#; *Breakin' 'N' Enterin',* documentary, directed by Topper Carew (1983; Rainbow T.V. Works), online video.

6    Uncle Jamm's Army, "Dial-A-Freak / Yes, Yes, Yes," single (Freak Beat Records, 1983), vinyl, 12"; Egyptian Lover, "Egypt, Egypt," single (Freak Beat Records, 1984), vinyl, 12"; Garrett, "Egyptian Lover Reminisces."

7    Cary Darling, "L.A.: The Second Deffest City of Hip-Hop," *Los Angeles Times*, Calendar section, February 7, 1988, 62, 70.

8    "Presser Plays Many Roles."

9    Darling, "L.A.: The Second Deffest City of Hip-Hop."

10    Darling, "L.A.: The Second Deffest City of Hip-Hop."

11    Egyptian Lover, interviewed by Chad Kiser, August 2008, *DUBCNN*, http://www.dubcnn.com/interviews/egyptianlover/.

12    Darling, "L.A.: The Second Deffest City of Hip-Hop"; Linda Moleski, "Indie Grass Route," *Billboard* 99, no. 15 (April 11, 1987): 65; Moleski, "Grass Route," 63.

13    For more on the history of race, class, and housing in Compton, see Josh Sides, "Straight into Compton: American Dreams, Urban Nightmares, and the Metamorphosis of a Black Suburb," *American Quarterly* 56, no. 3 (September 2004): 583–605; Alex Spillius, "The Short, Shocking Life of Eric Wright," *Guardian*, January 27, 1996.

14    Sandy Banks, "School Denies Problem after Attack: Shooting Site Called Back to Normal," *Los Angeles Times*, September 14, 1983, SD3; Chico C. Norwood, "Gunfire Mars School Opening," *Los Angeles Sentinel*, September 15, 1983, A1; Emily E. Straus, *Death of a Suburban Dream: Race and Schools in Compton, California* (Philadelphia: University of Pennsylvania Press, 2014), 129–130.

15    *Yo! MTV Raps* Eazy-E interview, featured in *NWA: The World's Most Dangerous Group,* directed by Mark Ford (2008; VH1 Rock Docs, 2008), TV broadcast.

16    Jimmy Summers, "Screen Fare Takes Back Seat to Swap Meet at Calif. Ozoner," *Boxoffice* 116, no. 9 (March 3, 1980): M12, M14.

17    Mikey Hirano Culross, "A Long, Legendary Reach," *Rafu Shimpo* [Los Angeles Japanese Daily News] September 26, 2014, http://www.rafu.com /2014/09/a-long-legendary-reach/.

18    Terry McDermott, "Parental Advisory: Explicit Lyrics," *Los Angeles Times,* April 14, 2002.

19    Culross, "A Long, Legendary Reach"; McDermott, "Parental Advisory: Explicit Lyrics."

20    Jerry L. Barrow, "Andre Young Is Still Buzzing," *Vibe,* September 1, 2010.

21    Spillius, "The Short, Shocking Life of Eric Wright"; Martin Cizmar, "MC Ren: What Happened after N.W.A. and the Posse," *Phoenix New Times,* March 18, 2010; Rob Kenner, "Interview: Ice Cube Talks about the Making of Eazy-E's 'Eazy-Duz-It,'" *Complex,* September 13, 2013, http://www .complex.com/music/2013/09/ice-cube-interview-easy-e.

22    Kenner, "Interview: Ice Cube Talks."

23    Brian Cross, ed., *It's Not about a Salary: Rap, Race, and Resistance in Los Angeles* (New York: Verso, 1994), 143.

24    Dennis Hunt, "Dr. Dre Joins an Illustrious Pack in the Last Year," *Los Angeles Times,* October 22, 1989, 76.

25    Ronin Ro, "Shock Treatment," *The Source,* February 1994, 46.

26    Ronin Ro, "Dr. Dre: Moving Target," *The Source,* November 1992, 40–42; Keith Murphy, "Full Clip: Ice Cube Breaks Down His Entire Catalog," *Vibe,* October 8, 2010, http://www.vibe.com/article/full-clip-ice-cube-breaks-down-his-entire-catalogue.

27    Robert Hilburn, "Notorious Ice Cube: Still the 'Most Wanted,'" *Los Angeles Times,* May 27, 1990.

28    Ro, "Dr. Dre: Moving Target," 41.

29    Stereo Crew, "She's a Skag," single (Epic Records, 1986), vinyl, 12".

30    Mark Coleman, "Beastie Boys: Licensed to Ill," review, *Rolling Stone,* November 15, 1986.

31   Murphy, "Full Clip"; The C.I.A., *Cru' In Action*, single (Kru-Cut Records, 1987), vinyl, EP.

32   Jerry Heller, with Gil Reavill, *Ruthless: A Memoir* (New York: Simon Spotlight Entertainment, 2006), 67–68. For samples of Ice Cube's earlier recorded rhymes, see C.I.A., *Cru' In Action*.

33   Kenner, "Interview: Ice Cube Talks."

34   Kenner, "Interview: Ice Cube Talks."

35   Darryl "Lyrrad" Davis, interview by Stefan Schuetze, *West Coast Pioneers*, April 2006; Eazy-E, "The Boyz-N-The Hood / L.A. Is the Place," single (Ruthless/Macola, 1987), vinyl, 12" promo.

36   Eazy-E, "The Boyz-N-The Hood / L.A. Is the Place."

37   Ice-T and Douglas Century, *Ice: A Memoir of Gangster Life and Redemption—From South Central to Hollywood* (New York: Random House, 2011), 92.

38   Not to be confused with A Tribe Called Quest's "8 Million Stories," in which Phife Dawg described his no good very bad day. Tribe's track, recorded for the group's 1993 album *Midnight Marauders*, echoes Kurtis Blow's "The Breaks" more than it does his other song of the same name. Kurtis Blow, "8 Million Stories," single (Polygram Records/Mercury, 1984), vinyl, 12".

39   Divine Sounds, "What People Do for Money," single (Specific Records, 1984), vinyl, 12"; Run-DMC, "It's Like That / Sucker M.C.'s," single (Profile Records, 1983), vinyl, 12".

40   Nelson George, Sally Banes, Susan Flinker, and Patty Romanowski, *Fresh, Hip Hop Don't Stop* (New York: Random House, 1985), 7; Nelson George's quote is reprinted in the album liner notes of LL Cool J, *Radio*, album (Def Jam/Columbia, 1985), vinyl, LP.

41   LL Cool J, "I Can Give You More" / "I Can't Live without My Radio," single (Def Jam Recordings, 1985), vinyl, 12".

42   Boogie Down Productions, "My 9mm Goes Bang," single (B-Boy Records, 1986), vinyl, 12"; Public Enemy, "You're Gonna Get Yours / Rebel without a Pause / Miuzi Weighs a Ton," single (Def Jam Recordings, 1987), vinyl, 12"; D.J. Polo and Kool G. Rap, "It's a Demo / I'm Fly," single (Cold Chillin', 1986), vinyl, 12"; Eric B. featuring Rakim, "Eric B. Is President / My Melody," single (4th & Broadway, 1986), vinyl, 12".

43   Jay-Z, *Decoded* (New York: Spiegel and Grau, 2010), 10; Lisa Robinson, "Jay Z on His Rags-to-Riches Story, Wooing Beyoncé, and How Blue Ivy Is His Biggest Fan," *Vanity Fair*, November 2013, 156.

44   Too Short, "Girl (Cocaine)" / "Shortrapp," single (75 Girls Records and Tapes, 1985), vinyl, 12"; Too Short, *Don't Stop Rappin'*, album (75 Girls Records and Tapes, 1987), cassette, LP; Too Short, *Players*, album (75 Girls Records and Tapes, 1987), cassette, LP. Too $hort added the "$" to his name in 1988, with the release of the *Life Is . . . Too $hort* record.

45   Schoolly D, "Gangster Boogie / Maniac," single (Cut Masters Records, 1984), vinyl, 12"; Schoolly D, "C.I.A . . . (Crime In Action) / Cold Blooded Blitz," single (Schoolly-D Records, 1985), vinyl, 12"; Schoolly D, "P.S.K.—What Does It Mean? / Gucci Time," single (Schoolly-D Records, 1985), vinyl, 12".

46   Brian Coleman, ed., *Rakim Told Me: Hip-Hop Wax Facts, Straight from the Original Artists* (Somerville, MA: Wax Facts Press, 2005), 174; Craig Lee, "A Tongue-lashing from Schoolly D," *Los Angeles Times*, Calendar section, June 5, 1987, 14.

47   Ice-T, *Ice*, 90, 92.

48   Cross, *It's Not about a Salary*, 181–182.

49   Cross, *It's Not about a Salary*, 183. Ice-T's records before 1986 exemplify this, including "The Coldest Rap" / "Cold Wind-Madness," single (Saturn Records, 1983), vinyl, 12"; and "Killers" / "Body Rock," single, (Electro, 1985), vinyl, 12".

50   Cross, *It's Not about a Salary*, 184; Ice-T, "Dog'n The Wax (Ya Don't Quit - Part II" / "6 in the Mornin'," single (Techno Hop Records, 1986), vinyl, 12".

51   This seems to have been an effective tactic, based on music critic Craig Lee's assertion in the *Los Angeles Times*: "If parents have bad dreams about the Beastie Boys or Run-DMC, Schoolly D is a full-blown nightmare." Lee, "A Tongue-lashing from Schoolly D."

52   Toddy Tee, "Batterram," single (original self-produced cassette-tape format, 1985; Evejim Records, 1985), vinyl, 12"; Eazy-E, "The Boyz-N-The Hood / L.A. Is The Place."

53   Kenner, "Interview: Ice Cube Talks."

54   Eazy-E, "The Boyz-N-The Hood / L.A. Is The Place."

55   Spillius, "The Short, Shocking Life of Eric Wright"; McDermott, "Parental Advisory: Explicit Lyrics."

56   Heller and Reavill, *Ruthless*, 121; McDermott, "Parental Advisory: Explicit Lyrics."

57   McDermott, "Parental Advisory: Explicit Lyrics."

58    Heller and Reavill, *Ruthless*, 63, 121; McDermott, "Parental Advisory: Explicit Lyrics"; Dennis Hunt, "The Rap Reality: Truth and Money; Compton's N.W.A. Catches Fire with Stark Portraits of Ghetto Life," *Los Angeles Times*, April 2, 1989.

59    See Chapter 3.

60    Victor Valle, "Some Anxiety Clouds Rap Concert Tonight," *Los Angeles Times*, December 31, 1987; "42 Are Hurt as Gang Fighting Breaks Up California Concert," *New York Times*, August 19, 1986; George Ramos, "'Rap Musicians' Concert Is Canceled at Palladium after Long Beach Fights," *Los Angeles Times*, August 19, 1986; Goldstein, "Can Rap Survive Gang War?"; see also Chapter 3.

61    Darling, "L.A.: The Second Deffest City of Hip-Hop."

62    Jay-Z, *Decoded*, 10, 16; Darling, "L.A.: The Second Deffest City of Hip-Hop."

63    Patrick Goldstein, "Pop Eye: Indie Promo Cutbacks Hurting Young Groups," *Los Angeles Times*, April 6, 1986, R78.

64    Ralph Bailey, Jr., "Drive-By Wars Claim 8 Lives in 48 Hours," *Los Angeles Sentinel*, December 3, 1987; "Summit Meeting on Gangs," *Los Angeles Times*, February 12, 1988; Robert Reinhold, "In the Middle of L.A.'s Gang Wars," *New York Times*, May 22, 1988; Jim Goins, "Compton Awarded Anti-Gang Grant," *Compton Bulletin*, April 29, 1987, Mayor Tom Bradley Administration papers 1920-1993, UCLA Special Collections, Charles E. Young Research Library, University of California, Los Angeles.

65    Christian L. Wright, "Kicking the Ballistics," *Spin*, September 1, 1989, 12–13.

66    Elaine Lafferty and Margaret B. Carlson, "The Price of Life in Los Angeles," *Time*, February 22, 1988.

67    Robert Reinhold, "Gang Violence Shocks Los Angeles," *New York Times*, February 8, 1988; Lafferty and Carlson, "The Price of Life in Los Angeles"; Ivor Davis, "Gangs Invade Yuppie Haven: Violence in Los Angeles," *Times* (London), February 8, 1988; Stanley Robertson, "L.A. Confidential: Won't Find Solutions in 'Ugliness,'" *Los Angeles Sentinel*, February 11, 1988, A6; John M. Glionna, "A Murder That Woke Up L.A.," *Los Angeles Times*, January 30, 1998; Ann Wiener, "Woman Fatally Hit by Gang Gunfire in Westwood," *Los Angeles Times*, February 1, 1988; "Los Angeles Drug Gangs Spread Out Over the West," Chris Reed, *Guardian*, February 20, 1988.

68    "Police Chiefs Hold Summit on Gangs," *Los Angeles Sentinel*, February 11, 1988, A1; Glionna, "A Murder That Woke Up L.A."

69    Wright, "Kicking the Ballistics."

70    "Hahn Seeks 'Summit' to End Gang Wars," *Los Angeles Sentinel*, January 28, 1988, A10; "Police Chiefs Hold Summit on Gangs."

71    Robertson, "L.A. Confidential: Won't Find Solutions in 'Ugliness.'"

72    F. Finley McRae, "Citizens Demand LAPD Deployment," *Los Angeles Sentinel*, February 18, 1988, A1.

73    Daryl F. Gates and Diane K. Shah, *Chief: My Life in the L.A.P.D.* (New York: Bantam Books, 1992), 339; Stanley G. Robertson, "L.A. Confidential: Hit 'Em Again, Harder, Harder," *Los Angeles Sentinel*, March 24, 1988, A6.

74    "Citing Recent Violence by Gangs, Los Angeles to Add 150 Officers," *New York Times*, February 11, 1988; Reinhold, "Gang Violence Shocks Los Angeles."

75    Reinhold, "Gang Violence Shocks Los Angeles."

76    Legislative Counsel's Digest, Senate Bill No. 1555 (1987–1988 Regular Session) Statutes 1988, Chapter 1256, signed by Governor, September 23, 1988; J. Franklin Sigal, "Out of Step: When the California Street Terrorism Enforcement and Prevention Act Stumbles into Penal Code Limits," *Golden Gate University Law Review* 38, no. 1 (January 2007): 1–32; Mike Davis, *City of Quartz: Excavating the Future of Los Angeles* (New York: Verso, 1990), 281–282.

77    Robert Reinhold, "Police Deployed to Curb Gangs in Los Angeles," *New York Times*, April 9, 1988; Lafferty and Carlson, "The Price of Life in Los Angeles"; Jay Mathews, "More Than 600 Arrested in Anti-Gang Sweep by Los Angeles Police," *Washington Post*, April 10, 1988, A3.

78    "'The Ram' Returns to Duty," *Los Angeles Sentinel*, March 17, 1988, A1; Elena I. Popp to David Lynn, Attorney at Law for Police Misconduct Lawyer Referral Service, Los Angeles, "Re: Oakwood/Venice situation," May 26, 1988, Box 6, Folder 2, CAPA Papers, Liberty Hill Foundation Collection, Southern California Library.

79    Ralph Bailey, Jr., "City Declares War on Gangs: Sweeps Stop Gang Killings," *Los Angeles Sentinel*, March 10, 1988, A1.

80    Bob Baker, "'The Hammer' Is Nailing Gangs, LAPD Reports," *Los Angeles Times*, March 13, 1988; "How California Is Fighting Gangs," *Western City*, April 1989, 19.

81    John Johnson, "Night of the 'Hammer': Retaking the Streets of South L.A.," *Los Angeles Times*, July 3, 1989; Wesley D. McBride and Robert K. Jackson, "In L.A. County, a High-Tech Assist in the War on Drugs," *The Police Chief*, vol. 56 (June 1989); Baker, "'The Hammer' Is Nailing Gangs."

82    Mark Thompson, "Los Angeles Seeks Ultimate Weapon in Gang War,"
*Wall Street Journal,* March 30, 1988, 1.

83    "Reagan and Bush Place New Stress on the Drug Issue," *New York
Times,* May 19, 1988, A1.

84    Lynell George and David Dante Troutt, "Guns No Butter," *LA Weekly,*
January 1989, reprinted in *No Crystal Stair: African-Americans in the City
of Angels* (New York: Verso, 1992), 27; Baker, "'The Hammer' Is Nailing
Gangs."

85    George and Troutt, "Guns No Butter."

86    Stan James, "'Reformed' Rebel Dennis Hopper Reveals His . . . True
Colors," *The Advertiser,* July 21, 1988; Reinhold, "Police Deployed to Curb
Gangs in Los Angeles"; Michael Reese, "War on the Mean Streets," *News-
week,* April 18, 1988, 73A.

87    Laurie Deans, "LA Clips: Brouhaha Fading as Colors Opens," *Globe
and Mail* (Canada), April 8, 1988; Michael White, "Film of Los Angeles
Gang Warfare Stirs Up a Feud," *Guardian,* April 12, 1988.

88    "Streets of Blood," *Courier-Mail* (Brisbane), April 30, 1988; Bill Kelley,
"'Colors,' Controversy and Hopper," *Sun Sentinel,* April 17, 1988.

89    *Colors,* directed by Dennis Hopper (1988; Orion Pictures, 2001), DVD;
Kelley, "'Colors,' Controversy and Hopper"; "Gang Movie 'Colors' Will Trigger Violence," *Los Angeles Sentinel,* March 31, 1988, A1.

90    The title sequence of the film offers this information: "The combined
anti-gang force numbers 250 men and women. In the greater Los Angeles
area there are over 600 street gangs with almost 70,000 members. Last
year [1987] there were 387 gang-related killings." Police officials serving as
technical assistants corroborated these statistics. *Colors.*

91    Kelley, "'Colors,' Controversy and Hopper."

92    Sheena Lester, "'Colors': Controversial Film Met with Protest," *Los Angeles Sentinel,* April 14, 1988, A3; Ice-T, *Ice: A Memoir,* 107–108.

93    Ben Cheshire, "Film Stirs Fear of Gang Warfare; Banned," *Sun Herald*
(Sydney), April 10, 1988, 33.

94    "Gang Movie 'Colors' Will Trigger Violence."

95    Reinhold, "Police Deployed to Curb Gangs in Los Angeles."

96    John Voland, "Weekend Box Office: 'Colors' Gives Orion a Big Boost,"
*Los Angeles Times,* May 3, 1988; Sheena Lester, "'Colors' Gets Dismal Re-

views from Public," *Los Angeles Sentinel*; Courtland Milloy, "Profits Top Responsibility in Hollywood," editorial, *Washington Post*, April 19, 1988; *Colors*, Box Office Mojo, http://boxofficemojo.com/movies/?id=colors.htm.

97   Ice-T, *Ice: A Memoir*, 109.

98   Janet Maslin, "Police vs. Street Gangs in Hopper's 'Colors,'" *New York Times*, April 15, 1988.

99   Ice-T, *Ice: A Memoir*, 108–109; Lester, "'Colors' Gets Dismal Reviews from Public."

100  Maslin, "Police vs. Street Gangs in Hopper's 'Colors,'"; "Hopper Is Back in Favor," *Courier-Mail* (Brisbane), August 13, 1988.

101  UK release *Colors* movie poster, image, Metro-Goldwyn-Mayer Studios, 1988, http://www.movieposter.com/poster/MPW-19329/Colors.html; *Colors* movie poster, image, Metro-Goldwyn-Mayer Studios, 1988, http://www.imdb.com/media/rm3990062336/tt0094894.

102  "Niggers With Attitude," *Melody Maker*, August 5, 1989, 42–43.

103  Gates, *Chief*, 339; Ice-T, *Ice: A Memoir*, 111; Thompson, "Los Angeles Seeks Ultimate Weapon in Gang War."

104  *Youth and Violence: The Current Crisis*, Hearing Before the Select Committee on Children, Youth, and Families, House of Representatives, One Hundredth Congress, Second Session (Washington, DC: US Government Printing Office, March 9, 1988), 19–20, 25–28, 38, 65–67, 83, 87; "The Drug Gangs," *Newsweek*, March 28, 1988, 20–27.

105  McDermott, "Parental Advisory: Explicit Lyrics."

106  Eazy-E, "The Boyz-N-The Hood / L.A. Is The Place."

107  Hunt, "The Rap Reality," 80, 87.

108  "Niggers With Attitude," 42–43.

109  David Mills, "Guns and Poses; Rap Music Violence: Glorifying Gangsterism or Reflecting Reality?" *Washington Times*, August 17, 1989, E1.

110  Hunt, "Dr. Dre Joins an Illustrious Pack."

111  Brian Coleman, *Check the Technique: Liner Notes for Hip-Hop Junkies* (New York: Random House, 2002), 124–125.

112  Hunt, "The Rap Reality," 80, 87.

113  Mills, "Guns and Poses," E1.

114  Ro, "Dr. Dre: Moving Target," 42.

115   McDermott, "Parental Advisory: Explicit Lyrics."

116   John Leland, "Rap as Public Forum on Matters of Life and Death," *New York Times*, March 12, 1989.

117   Darling, "L.A.: The Second Deffest City of Hip-Hop."


### 4. Somebody's Gonna Pay Attention

1   "Niggers With Attitude," *Melody Maker*, August 5, 1989, 42–43; Jonathan Gold, "N.W.A.: A Hard Act to Follow," *LA Weekly*, May 4, 1989.

2   Elizabeth Hayes, "Link between Gang Violence and Films?" *Los Angeles Times*, March 25, 1988.

3   John L. Mitchell, "The Raid That Still Haunts L.A.," *Los Angeles Times*, March 14, 2001; Pamela Klein, "By All Means Necessary," *LA Weekly*, December 30, 1988, to January 5, 1989, 43–44, 46; "Looking into a Police Raid," *Los Angeles Times*, August 10, 1988, C6.

4   "Niggers With Attitude."

5   Ted Rohrlick, "A Courthouse Called 'Fort Compton' Lives on the Cutting Edge of Justice," *Los Angeles Times*, February 1, 1988.

6   N.W.A., "Straight Outta Compton," directed by Rupert Wainwright (May 1989; Los Angeles: Ruthless Records), music video.

7   Deborah Russell, "Fragile Going Strong with Hammer and 'Gang' Vids," *Billboard* 102, no. 23 (June 9, 1990), 59–60.

8   Gold, "N.W.A.: A Hard Act to Follow"; Jessica Bendinger, John Leland, Christian Wright, "The Cold Rock Stuff," *Spin* 5, no. 4 (July 1, 1989), 2; Richard Harrington, "On the Beat: The Rap Jive from MTV," *Washington Post*, May 24, 1989, D7.

9   "Niggers With Attitude."

10   "Niggers With Attitude."

11   "The Drug Gangs," *Newsweek*, March 28, 1988, 20–27.

12   John Leland, "Do the Right Thing," *Spin*, September 1, 1989, 68–70, 72, 74, 100.

13   Eazy E, "The Boyz-N-The Hood / L.A. Is The Place," single (Ruthless Records, 1987), vinyl, 12"; examples of early New York street rap include Kool Moe Dee, *How Ya Like Me Now*, album (Jive, 1987), vinyl, LP; Boogie

Down Productions, *Criminal Minded,* album (B-Boy Records, 1987), vinyl, LP; Public Enemy, *Yo! Bum Rush The Show,* album (Def Jam Recordings, 1987), vinyl, LP; Run-DMC, *Run-DMC,* album (Profile Records, 1984), vinyl, LP; Run-DMC, *Raising Hell,* album (Profile, 1986), vinyl, LP.

14   Jerry Heller, *Ruthless: A Memoir* (New York: Simon Spotlight Entertainment, 2006), 109.

15   Heller, *Ruthless,* 110–113; Keith Murphy, "Public Enemies," *Vibe* 16, no. 8 (August 2008): 94.

16   Jim Fricke and Charlie Ahearn, eds., *Yes, Yes, Y'all: The Experience Music Project Oral History of Hip-Hop's First Decade* (Cambridge, MA: Da Capo Press, 2002), 328, 329.

17   Run-DMC's debut single "You Be Illin'" did appear on *Billboard*'s "Hot 100 Singles Spotlight" in the fall of 1986. But a careful scan of industry reports about chart movement and programming additions shows that this was an anomaly, especially in that year; "Hot 100 Singles Spotlight," *Billboard* 98, no. 46 (November 15, 1986): 91.

18   Debi Fee, "The Rap against Rap at Black Radio: Professional Suicide or Cultural Smokescreen," *Billboard* 100, no. 52 (December 24, 1988): R8, R21.

19   Patrick Goldstein, "Indie Promo Cutbacks Hurting Young Groups," *Los Angeles Times,* April 6, 1986, R78; Michael Goldberg, "Grand Juries Investigate Mob Ties to Record Biz," *Rolling Stone,* May 8, 1986; William K. Knoedelseder, Jr., "Growing Force of Investigators Probes Mob Ties to Record Industry," *Los Angeles Times,* October 19, 1986; Tom Brokaw and Brian Ross, "The New Payola," *NBC Evening News,* February 24, 1986; "Ross Plans New Payola Probe," *Radio & Records,* June 26, 1987; "Payola: The Record-Label Connection," *Rolling Stone,* April 21, 1988.

20   Irv Lichtman and Sam Sutherland, "Capitol, MCA Drop Indies; RIAA Subpoenaed," *Billboard* 98, no. 10 (March 8, 1986), 1; Irv Lichtman, "More Key Labels Sever Indie Ties," *Billboard* 98, no. 11 (March 15, 1986), 1; Richard Harrington, "CBS Records Takes on Rolling Stone," *Washington Post,* April 15, 1986; "Black Indie Promotion Dismissal Protest Set," *Black Radio Exclusive* 11, no. 8 (March 21, 1986), 6.

21   John Leland, "Droppin' Science," *Spin,* August 1, 1989, 48–52; for trends in black radio programming, see "Regional Adds" in issues of *Black Radio Exclusive,* particularly from 1985 through 1989.

22   "Inside Urban Radio," *Gavin Report,* issue 1703 (April 22, 1988), 55; "Urban Contemporary Adds," *Gavin Report,* issue 1705 (May 6, 1988);

"R&R National Airplay: Contemporary Hit Radio," *Radio & Records*, issue 740 (June 3, 1988); "National Airplay: Contemporary Hit *Radio*," *Radio & Records*, issue 734 (April 22, 1988); "National Airplay: Contemporary Hit Radio," *Radio & Records*, issue 726 (February 26, 1988): 102; "CHR Adds & Hots," *Radio & Records*, issue 735 (April 29, 1988): 82–85; "D.J. Jazzy Jeff & The Fresh Prince," *Radio & Records*, issue 737 (May 13, 1988): 28; "Hot 100 Singles Spotlight," *Billboard* 100, no. 24 (June 11, 1988): 84.

23    "Colors Ad," *Black Radio Exclusive* 13, no. 18 (May 20, 1988): 40; *Coming to America* ad, cover, *Black Radio Exclusive* 13, no. 24 (July 8, 1988); "Coming to America Feature," *Black Radio Exclusive* 13, no. 24 (July 8, 1988): 10; Duff Marlowe, "Rap Report," *Black Radio Exclusive* (August 5, 1988): 14.

24    Bob Pool, "Station's Neighbors Rap Its Wrap-Around Sound," *Los Angeles Times*, November 4, 1989.

25    Ben Westhoff, "KDAY, the Gangsta Rap Oldies Station Breaks New Ground by Playing Music from the Bad Old Days," *LA Weekly*, August 2, 2012.

26    Alex Henderson, "Rap's Cutting Edge Seeks Next New Creative Frontiers to Stay Sharp—and Successful," *Billboard* 100, no. 52 (December 24, 1988): R6, R16, R20.

27    "Billboard Advertising Supplement: K-Tel," *Billboard* 109, no. 10 (March 8, 1997): K10; SuCarroll Pursell, *Technology in Postwar America: A History* (New York: Columbia University Press, 2012), 100. For more on the Veg-O-Matic and the evolution of the so-called infomercial, see Malcolm Gladwell, "Obsessives, Pioneers, and Other Varieties of Minor Genius," in *What the Dog Saw and Other Adventures* (New York: Little, Brown, 2009).

28    Bartley Kives, "Straight Outta West K," *Winnipeg Free Press*, September 8, 2015; "K-TEL Records," *Billboard* 85, no. 44 (November 3, 1973): UK9.

29    Craig Rosen, "After 10 Years, Priority Proves It's More Than Rap," *Billboard* 107, no. 23 (June 10, 1995): 18; Elliot Wilson, "Ten Years of Priority Records," *Vibe* 3, no. 8 (August 1995): 34.

30    Rosen, "After 10 Years, Priority Proves," 18.

31    Interestingly, though, the dialogue around these anthropomorphic purple fruits, who had exaggerated black facial features and performed for white characters, never addressed minstrelsy; Dave DiMartino, "California Raisins Harvest Success for Priority Label," *Billboard* 100, no. 2 (January 9, 1988): 4, 84; Stanley Mieses, "Raisins," *Spin* 3, no. 9 (February 1, 1988): 74.

32   DiMartino, "California Raisins Harvest Success," 4.

33   Heller, *Ruthless*, 113.

34   "The Drug Gangs"; Bob Baker, "Cold Killers and Fearful Innocents," *Los Angeles Times*, June 26, 1988.

35   "The Drug Gangs."

36   Kives, "Straight Outta West K"; Robert Hilburn, "Making Music the Priority," *Los Angeles Times*, January 6, 1999.

37   Henderson, "Active Indies: Rap's Cutting Edge," R16.

38   Neil Strauss, "The Secret Power in Big Rap: Bryan Turner Makes Rap Records but Escapes the Criticism," *New York Times*, September 3, 1998.

39   Patrick Goldstein, "This Record Exec Takes the Rap—Gladly," *Los Angeles Times*, September 14, 1986.

40   Rob Tannenbaum and Craig Marks, eds., *I Want My MTV: The Uncensored Story of the Music Video Revolution* (New York: Plume, 2012), xxxviii–xiv; for a cultural history of dance television in the disco era, see also Alice Echols, *Hot Stuff: Disco and the Remaking of American Culture* (New York: W. W. Norton, 2011).

41   Tannenbaum and Marks, *I Want My MTV*, 6, 21.

42   Tannenbaum and Marks, *I Want My MTV*, 15.

43   Patrick Goldstein, "Uncertain Notes Hit at Video Music Parley," *Los Angeles Times*, November 16, 1981, G1.

44   Tannenbaum and Marks, *I Want My MTV*, 5, 26.

45   Tannenbaum and Marks, *I Want My MTV*, 22, 60–84, 70; Pekka Gronow, "The Record Industry: The Growth of a Mass Medium," *Popular Music* 3 (January 1983): 53–75.

46   Dennis Hunt, "How Goes the Music Revolution?" *Los Angeles Times*, September 3, 1989, 55.

47   Tannenbaum and Marks, *I Want My MTV*, 207.

48   For the most thorough demonstration of the visual elements so critical to the first five years of hip-hop, see Martha Cooper's incredible collection of photographs and reflections in *Hip Hop Files: Photographs, 1979–1984* (Cologne, Germany: From Here to Fame Publishing, 2004); and Fricke and Ahearn, *Yes, Yes, Y'all*; John Leland, "It's Like That," *Village Voice*, June 17, 1986, 67, 70; Greg Tate, "They're Gonna Smash Their Brains In," *Village*

*Voice*, April 9, 1985, 61. Jonathan Gold, "N.W.A.: A Hard Act to Follow," *Spin*, May 5, 1989.

49   Tannenbaum and Marks, *I Want My MTV*, 60–84.

50   Sugarhill Gang, "Rapper's Delight," music video (Rhino Home Video, 1998; original 1982), VHS; Grandmaster Flash and the Furious Five, "The Message," music video (Rhino Home Video, 1998; original, 1982), VHS; Afrika Bambaataa & Soul Sonic Force, "Planet Rock," music video (BBC TV, 1984; original on Intersong Music / Tommy Boy Records, 1982), VHS.

51   Leland, "Droppin Science."

52   Tannenbaum and Marks, *I Want My MTV*, 244.

53   Nelson George, *The Hippest Trip in America: Soul Train and the Evolution of Culture and Style* (New York: William Morrow, 2014), 138.

54   David Fear, "Dance Dance Revolution: Nelson George on 'Soul Train,'" *Rolling Stone*, April 24, 2014.

55   "Debbie Harry and Funky 4 + 1 More," *Saturday Night Live*, season 6, episode 10, aired February 14, 1981 (NBC Studios); Andrew Mason, "Sound Image: Blondie," *Wax Poetics*, issue 60 (November 21, 2014); *Soul Train*, season 10, episode 336, L.T.D./Seventh Wonder/Kurtis Blow, originally aired September 27, 1980.

56   Tannenbaum and Marks, *I Want My MTV*, 39.

57   Laura Foti, "Taste & Fairness on Video," *Billboard*, December 11, 1982, 10; Nelson George, "Slick Rick Says MTV Is Sick," *Billboard*, February 19, 1983, 53; Tannenbaum and Marks, *I Want My MTV*, 139; see also George, *The Hippest Trip in America*.

58   Cary Darling, "R&B Denied?" *Billboard* 93, no. 47 (November 28, 1981): 4, 62.

59   Laura Foti, "Sylvester Dances into MTV View," *Billboard* 95, no. 15 (April 15, 1983): 82–83; Tannenbaum and Marks, *I Want My MTV*, 139.

60   MTV News, clip and transcript of David Bowie interview cited in "David Bowie Accusing MTV of Racism in '83: Read the Interview Transcript," *Los Angeles Times*, January 12, 2016.

61   Douglas Frohman, "Spotlight on Music Video: Spotlight Talks with MTV," *Back Stage* 25, no. 20 (May 18, 1984): 38B; Jim Bessman, "Majors Look to Youth Movement to Spread Gains, Challenge Platinum," *Billboard* 97, no. 24 (June 15, 1985): BM3; Nelson George, "At Last Black Acts Making MTV Inroads," *Billboard* 101, no. 14 (April 8, 1989): 20.

62   Fred Rothenberg, "NBC Hops on Video Music Bandwagon," *Globe and Mail* (Toronto), July 30, 1983.

63   Nancy Hass, "Music Video Beat," *Back Stage* 25, no. 23 (June 8, 1984): 52–53, 56; Marc Kirke, "'Night Flight' Takes Off," *American Film* 7, no. 10 (September 1, 1982): 26–27.

64   Hass, "Music Video Beat"; "Video Music: Raiding the Ranks of Daytime," *Billboard* 98, no. 15 (April 12, 1986): 61; Chris McGowan, "Music Video on TV: From Youth to Middle Age in Seven Years," *Billboard* 100, no. 46 (November 12, 1988): V1, V5.

65   Rothenberg, "NBC Hops on Video Music Bandwagon"; Richard Lacayo, "The Rock Competition Steps Up a Beat," *New York Times*, August 7, 1983, A23.

66   Steven Dupler, "Jukebox Format Making Waves in Miami," *Billboard* 98, no. 10 (March 8, 1986): 44–45.

67   "Friday Night Videos," *Variety* 312, no. 1 (August 3, 1983): 48.

68   Rothenberg, "NBC Hops on Video Music Bandwagon"; Eric Zorn, "Tempo: NBC Quicksteps into the Music-Video Craze with 'Friday Night Videos,'" *Chicago Tribune*, May 19, 1983, E12.

69   Laura Foti, "NBC Takes a Chance on Rock," *Billboard* 95, no. 26 (July 2, 1983): 34; Rothenberg, "NBC Hops on Video Music Bandwagon"; Kev, "Friday Night Videos," 48.

70   Ken Terry, "ABC-TV's Gotham Outlet Debuts Black-Oriented Video Program; Not Paying for Use of Clips," *Variety*, July 27, 1983; Hass, "Music Video Beat"; Fred Goodman, "'Hot Tracks' Vidclips Now on 80 Stations," *Billboard* 96, no. 19 (May 12, 1984): 66; "Uggams to Host Finals of Break Dance Contest," *New York Amsterdam News*, December 17, 1983, 21; "New York Hot Tracks on Location at Apollo," *New York Amsterdam News*, August 2, 1986, 21; Jay Blotcher, "Airplay's Up and Everyone's High or at Least That's What They Say," *Back Stage* 25, no. 40 (September 28, 1984): 8B; [advertisement] "New York Hot Tracks," *Broadcasting* 106, no. 5 (January 30, 1984): 57.

71   John Dempsey, "More Indie TV Stations Use Vidclips as Staple; MTV Exclusivity Hurts," *Variety* 318, no. 9 (March 27, 1985): 88.

72   Jack McNonough, "California Music Channel Scores," *Billboard* 95, no. 20 (May 14, 1983): 56.

73   Kip Kirby, "Clip Shows Compared to Radio," *Billboard*, October 6, 1984, 6, 70.

74    Jon Pareles, "Music Videos Try a New Tack: Their Novelty Worn Thin, Music Videos Try New Tricks," *New York Times,* April 13, 1986, H1.

75    Pareles, "Music Videos Try a New Tack"; McGowan, "Music Video on TV."

76    Susan Orlean, "Profiles: Living Large," *New Yorker,* June 17, 1991; Jon Caramanica, "Peter Dougherty, Who Brought Rap to MTV, Dies at 59," *New York Times,* October 27, 2015.

77    Tannenbaum and Marks, *I Want My MTV,* 379–382.

78    Leland, "Droppin Science."

79    McGowan, "Music Video on TV."

80    Goldstein, "This Record Exec Takes the Rap—Gladly."

81    Goodman, "'Hot Tracks' Vidclips."

82    "BRE Flicks," *Black Radio Exclusive,* 10, no. 2 (February 5, 1985) photo, 5.

83    Jacob Hoye, ed., *MTV: Uncensored* (New York: Pocket Books, 2001), 96–98.

84    David Samuels, "Yo! MTV Unwrapped," *Spin* 7, no. 6 (September 1, 1991): 44–45; "Chuck D: Rap Addresses Life," *Los Angeles Sentinel,* August 3, 1989, A2; Ted Turner, "My Beef with Big Media," *Washington Monthly* 36, no. 7 (July 1, 2004): 30–37.

85    Caramanica, "Pete Dougherty"; Paul Grein, "Rappers Welcome MTV's Enthusiasm," *Los Angeles Times,* June 18, 1989, 365.

86    George, "At Last Black Acts Making MTV Inroads," 20.

87    Samuels, "Yo! MTV Unwrapped"; Jessica Bendinger, "Public Enemy," *Spin* 3, no. 8 (January, 1 1988): 65–66.

88    Samuels, "Yo! MTV Unwrapped."

89    Grein, "Rappers Welcome MTV's Enthusiasm."

90    Tannenbaum and Marks, *I Want My MTV,* 244.

91    Orlean, "Profiles: Living Large."

92    Orlean, "Profiles: Living Large." For an in-depth, contemporaneous profile of Fred "Fab 5 Freddy" Brathwaite, his participation in the East Village art scene that flowered in the early 1980s, and his role as an ambassador of cultural fusion, see Steven Hager, *Art after Midnight: The East Village Scene* (New York: St. Martin's Press, 1986).

93    Samuels, "Yo! MTV Unwrapped."

94 David Nathan, "L.A.'s Priority Puts West Coast Rap on the Map," *Billboard*, March 18, 1989, 27–28.

95 Nathan, "L.A.'s Priority"; Strauss, "The Secret Power in Big Rap"; Brian Cross, ed., *It's Not about a Salary: Rap, Race, and Resistance in Los Angeles* (New York: Verso, 1993), 36–37.

96 Mark Cooper, "NWA: 'Our Raps Are Documentary. We Don't Take Sides,'" *Guardian*, October 1, 1989.

97 "Album Reviews: Black," *Billboard* 101, no. 8 (February 25, 1989): 70; Andy Gill, "Taking a Rap on the Knuckles," *Independent*, September 8, 1989; Robert Hilburn, "Ice Cube Keeps Cool, Chills Clash," *Los Angeles Times*, March 24, 1989, P4.

98 "Ice Cube / N.W.A. / D.O.C.," *Pump It Up*, TV series, directed by Spencer Thornton (originally aired in 1989; Fox Television Productions, 1989), http://www.youtube.com/watch?v=FFh4BW_V59M; Mark Blackwell, "Niggaz4Dinner," *Spin*, September 1991, 55; Nathan; "Niggers With Attitude"; Henderson, "Active Indies: Rap's Cutting Edge."

99 Cooper, "NWA: 'Our Raps Are Documentary.'"

100 Jane Garcia, "Live: NWA / Eazy-E / Ice-T / King Tee / The DOC," *New Musical Express*, April 15, 1989, 49.

101 "'Raptalk' Slated for Public," *Los Angeles Sentinel*, September 1, 1988; "'Raptalk' Seminar Set," *Los Angeles Times*, September 5, 1988, E10; Henderson, "Active Indies: Rap's Cutting Edge"; "UC Adds and Hots," *Radio & Records* 765 (November 25, 1988): 53; "Urban: National Airplay," *Radio & Records* 767 (December 9, 1988): 56; "Top Pop Albums," *Billboard* 100, no. 50 (December 10, 1988): 76; "Top Pop Albums," *Billboard* 100, no. 51 (December 17, 1988): 79; "Urban: National Airplay: Significant Action," *Radio & Records* 769 (December 23, 1988): 56.

102 *Yo! MTV Raps*, Episode 29, TV series, directors Ted Demme and Moses Edinborough (originally aired April 8, 1989; MTV Networks, 1989); *NWA: The World's Most Dangerous Group*, directed by Mark Ford (2008; VH1 Rock Docs, 2008), TV broadcast.

103 Alan Light, "Beating Up the Charts," *Rolling Stone*, August 8, 1991, 65; "Ice Cube/N.W.A./D.O.C.," *Pump It Up*; Dennis Hunt, "The Rap Reality: Truth and Money," *Los Angeles Times*, April 2, 1989, 80.

104 "Demographics," City of Compton, comptoncity.org, http://www.comptoncity.org/visitors/demographics.asp, accessed June 1, 2018; Michele

Fuetsch, "Latino Aspirations on Rise in Compton: Demographics: Latinos Stream into the Area," *Los Angeles Times*, May 7, 1990.

105  "VH1 Rock Docs: Yo! The Story of Yo! MTV Raps," documentary, directed by Mimi Adams, (VH1 Productions, 2012), TV.

106  Preezy Brown, "The Amazing Oral History of 'Yo! MTV Raps,'" *Vibe*, June 1, 2018.

107  Gold, "N.W.A.: A Hard Act to Follow."

108  Kevin Zimmerman, "Independent Labels Want Their MTV," *Variety*, May 23, 1990.

109  Leland, "Droppin Science"; Peter Watrous, "Rappers Keep Their Music's Content Fresh," *New York Times*, January 10, 1988, 290.

110  Steve Hochman, "NWA Keeping Attitude Alive," *Musician* no. 149 (March 1, 1991): 58–61.

111  Susan King, "Pick a Video: Cable's New Jukebox Network," *Los Angeles Times*, June 13, 1990.

112  Gold, "N.W.A.: A Hard Act to Follow."

113  Heller, *Ruthless*, 110–111.

### 5. Without a Gun and a Badge

1  Richard Harrington, "The FBI as Music Critic; Letter on Rap Record Seen as Intimidation," *Washington Post*, October 4, 1989; Steve Hochman, "Compton Rappers versus the Letter of the Law," *Los Angeles Times*, October 5, 1989, Calendar section, 1, 6; Tipper Gore, "Hate, Rape, and Rap," *Washington Post*, January 8, 1990; Robert Hilburn, "Notorious Ice Cube: Still the 'Most Wanted,'" *Los Angeles Times*, May 27, 1990, F65; David Mills, "Guns and Poses; Rap Music Violence: Glorifying Gangsterism or Reflecting Reality?" *Washington Times*, August 17, 1989, E1.

2  N.W.A., "Fuck tha Police," *Straight Outta Compton*, album (Ruthless/Priority, 1988), vinyl, LP, cassette, and CD; Peter H. King, "Punk Rockers Put on Notice by Santa Ana: Punk Rock: Santa Ana Is Wary," *Los Angeles Times*, January 9, 1982; Dan Nakaso, "Skin Slashed, Furniture and Windows Smashed: Punk Rock May Cost Theater Owner His License," *Los Angeles Times*, January 20, 1983; Cary Darling, "41 Arrested at L.A. 'Punk Riot,'" *Billboard* 95, no. 8. (February 26, 1983): 30, 35; Patrick Goldstein, "Is Heavy Metal a Loaded Gun Aimed at Its Fans?" *Los Angeles Times*, January 26, 1986; "Record Labeling" Senate Hearing before the Committee on

Commerce, Science, and Transportation, United States Senate, First Session on Content of Music and the Lyrics of Records, Sept. 19, 1985 (US Government Printing Office, Washington, 1985). See also Chapter 3.

3    Mills, "Guns and Poses."

4    N.W.A., "Fuck tha Police."

5    Jonathan Gold, "N.W.A.: A Hard Act to Follow," *LA Weekly*, May 5, 1989; Mike Sager, "Cube," *Rolling Stone*, issue 588 (October 4, 1990): 78.

6    *Miami Vice*, created by Anthony Yerkovich (NBC, 1984–1990), TV series; *America's Most Wanted*, created by Michael Linder and Stephen Chao (Fox Broadcasting, 1988–2011), TV series; *Cops*, created by John Langley and Malcolm Barbour (Fox Broadcasting, 1989–2013), TV series.

7    Gold, "N.W.A.: A Hard Act to Follow"; Sager, "Cube."

8    Robert Reinhold, "In the Middle of L.A.'s Gang Wars," *New York Times*, May 22, 1988; Elaine Lafferty and Margaret B. Carlson, "The Price of Life in Los Angeles," *Time*, February 22, 1988; Ivor Davis, "Gangs Invade Yuppie Haven: Violence in Los Angeles," *Times* (London), February 8, 1988; Ann Wiener, "Woman Fatally Hit by Gang Gunfire in Westwood," *Los Angeles Times*, February 1, 1988; "Los Angeles Drug Gangs Spread Out over the West," Chris Reed, *Guardian*, February 20, 1988; "Citing Recent Violence by Gangs, Los Angeles to Add 150 Officers," *New York Times*, February 11, 1988; Laurie Deans, "LA Clips: Brouhaha Fading as Colors Opens," *Globe and Mail* (Canada), April 8, 1988; Michael White, "Film of Los Angeles Gang Warfare Stirs Up a Feud," *Guardian*, April 12, 1988. See also Chapter 4.

9    Pamela Klein, "By All Means Necessary," *LA Weekly*, December 30, 1988, to January 5, 1989, 43–44.

10    Jon Pareles, "Outlaw Rock: More Skirmishes on the Censorship Front," *New York Times*, December 10, 1989; Dennis Hunt, "Dr. Dre Joins an Illustrious Pack in the Last Year," *Los Angeles Times*, October 22, 1989, 76.

11    *NWA: The World's Most Dangerous Group*, directed by Mark Ford (2008; VH1 Rock Docs, 2008), TV broadcast.

12    H. Curtis Wiggins, "Media Power and the Black American," *Crisis* 82, no. 6 (June–July 1975): 210.

13    Klein, "By All Means Necessary"; *The Arsenio Hall Show*, Season 3, Episode 15, created by Arsenio Hall and Marla Kell Brown (Paramount Domestic Television, Sept 28, 1990), TV episode.

14   *Tha Westside,* directed by Todd Williams (2002; Niche Entertainment, 2002), DVD.

15   Brian Coleman, *Check the Technique: Liner Notes for Hip-Hop Junkies* (New York: Random House, 2007), 127; *Cypress Hill,* "Pigs," Cypress Hill, album (Ruffhouse Records, 1991), vinyl, LP.

16   Sam Kashner, "Hollywood in the Hood," *Vanity Fair* (September 2016), 222.

17   John Leland, "Droppin Science," *Spin,* August 1, 1989, 48–52.

18   Jay-Z, *Decoded* (New York: Spiegel and Grau, 2010), 10, 16.

19   Ahmir "?uestlove" Thompson, "N.W.A.," *Rolling Stone,* issue 972 (April 21, 2005): 90.

20   John Leland, "Rap as Public Forum on Matters of Life and Death," *New York Times,* March 12, 1989, Section 2, 29; "Stone Cold Pimpin': From L.A. Hustler to Worldwide Rap Star, Ice-T Gets the Power," *Vibe,* August 2008, 95; King Tee, "The Coolest," *Act a Fool,* album (Capitol Records, 1988), CD.

21   Push, "Niggers With Attitude: Street Hassle," *Melody Maker,* August 5, 1989, 42–43.

22   *The Arsenio Hall Show,* Season 3, Episode 15.

23   Chuck Philips, "Beating the Rap of Concert Violence," *Los Angeles Times,* February 10, 1991; Hochman, "Compton Rappers versus the Letter of the Law"; Mills, "Guns and Poses"; Harrington, "The FBI as Music Critic"; Pareles, "Outlaw Rock"; David Mills, "N.W.A. Flees Stage after Song Lyrics Incite Concert Police," *Washington Times,* August 17, 1989.

24   Harrington, "The FBI as Music Critic"; Carol Motsinger and Cameron Knight, "Ice Cube Recalls Tense '89 Stop in Cincy," *Cincinnati Enquirer,* June 6, 2016.

25   Hochman, "Compton Rappers versus the Letter of the Law"; Mills, "Guns and Poses"; Harrington, "The FBI as Music Critic"; Pareles, "Outlaw Rock"; David Mills, "N.W.A. Flees Stage after Song Lyrics Incite Concert Police," *Washington Times,* August 17, 1989; Dave Marsh and Phyllis Pollack, "Wanted for Attitude," *Village Voice* 34, no. 41 (October 10, 1989): 33–34.

26   Chester Higgins, "Harassment Suit Filed in Toledo," *New York Amsterdam News,* August 27, 1988, 5; "Toledo Police Chief Rescinds His Order to Question Blacks," *New York Times,* August 16, 1988, A25; Marsh and Pollack, "Wanted for Attitude."

27   John Kifner, "As Crack Moves Inland, Ohio City Fights Back," *New York Times*, August 29, 1989, 1, 9.

28   Stephen Franklin, "Murders Torment Detroit," *Chicago Tribune*, January 13, 1987; Ze'ev Chafets, "The Tragedy of Detroit," *New York Times*, July 29, 1990, 326.

29   Norris P. West, "Man Beaten by PG Police Gets $1.9 Million Award," *Baltimore Sun*, March 18, 1993.

30   Debbie M. Price, "Blows Cited in Death of P.G. Suspect," *Washington Post*, May 25, 1989.

31   Debbie M. Price, "P.G. Police Chief Caught in the Eye of the Storm," *Washington Post*, September 25, 1989; John Feinstein and Eugene L. Meyer, "1976 Slayings by P.G. Police Squad Probed," *Washington Post*, February 11, 1979.

32   Price, "P.G. Police Chief"; Matt Neufeld, "Lyrics Get Rap Group Cut from Cap Centre," *Washington Times*, August 22, 1989.

33   Charles Baillou, "Why White Cops Kill Black People," *New York Amsterdam News*, December 3, 1988, 3.

34   Peter Noel, "Prof Files $15M Police Brutality Suit," *New York Amsterdam News*, June 3, 1987, 1.

35   Harold Jamison, "Assault on Woman Draws Pastor's Anger," *New York Amsterdam News*, January 14, 1989, 3.

36   Thomas Collins, "Donald Trump's High-Priced Graffiti," *Newsday*, May 3, 1989, 67; for an example of Donald Trump's celebrity, see the May 1, 1984, issue of *GQ* magazine, which features Trump as its poster boy for millionaire risk-takers and a feature story entitled, "Donald Trump Gets What He Wants."

37   Milt Ahlerich, letter to Priority Records, August 1, 1989, published as figure in Steve Hochman, "Compton Rappers versus the Letter of the Law, *Los Angeles Times*, August 5, 1989; Marsh and Pollack, "Wanted for Attitude."

38   "The FBI Hates this Band, and Other Tales of Cultural Crackdown in the Age of Helms," *Village Voice* 34, no. 41 (October 10, 1989), cover.

39   Ras Baraka, "Endangered Species: Ice Cube," *The Source* no. 24 (September 1991): 34.

40   K Murphy, "Full Clip: Ice Cube Breaks Down His Entire Catalog," *Vice*, October 8, 2010.

41   *NWA: The World's Most Dangerous Group.*

42   Steve Hochman, "NWA Keeping Attitude Alive," *Musician*, no. 149 (March 1, 1991): 58–61.

43   Chris Morris, "TV Host Barnes Pumps Out $23 Mil Suit against N.W.A.," *Billboard*, July 13, 1991, 9; "Violence Is Reflected in Actions as Well as Words," *USA Today*, June 21, 1991, 4D; Chris Morris, "N.W.A. Member Dr. Dre Pleads No Contest on Attack Charge," *Billboard*, September 1991, 11; Martha Sherrill, "Guess Who's Coming to Lunch? It's Easy-E, Mixin' with the GOP to Hear the Rap of the Commander in Chief," *Washington Post*, March 19, 1991; Mark Blackwell, "Niggaz4Dinner," *Spin* 7, no. 6 (September 1991): 55–57.

44   Pareles, "Outlaw Rock."

45   Jon Pareles, "Rap: Slick, Violent, Nasty and, Maybe, Hopeful," *New York Times*, June 17, 1990.

46   Gil Griffin, "Strong Words from Ice-T and N.W.A.," *Washington Post*, June 12, 1991.

47   Chris Morris, "Minnesota to Musicland: No N.W.A. Album to Minors," *Billboard*, August 10, 1991.

48   Paul Grein, "N.W.A. Album Charges onto Chart at No. 2," *Billboard*, June 15, 1991; "The Billboard 200," *Billboard*, July 6, 1991; Griffin, "Strong Words from Ice-T and N.W.A."

49   James T. Jones, "N.W.A.'s Career Gets a Jolt from Lyrics' Shock Value," *USA Today*, June 21, 1991; Alan Light, "Beating Up the Charts," *Rolling Stone*, August 8, 1991, 65.

50   Janine McAdams, "Low 'Priority': N.W.A.'s Chart-Topping Album; Violence, Misogyny Mar Un-Eazy-E 'Efil4zaggin,'" *Billboard*, July 6, 1991, 23.

51   J. Andrea Penix-Smith, "2 Live Crew, Eazy-E, NWA Set for Compton Rapfest," *Los Angeles Sentinel*, September 13, 1990, B10.

52   Jon Shecter, "Real Niggaz Don't Die," *The Source*, September 1991, 24.

53   Jon Pareles, "Should Ice Cube's Voice Be Chilled," *New York Times*, December 8, 1991.

54   Deborah Russell, "N.W.A. Displays a Winning Attitude; Stickered Album Is Nation's Top Seller," *Billboard*, June 22, 1991, 7.

55   Shecter, "Real Niggaz Don't Die."

56   Leland, "Droppin Science."

57  "Public Enemy No. 2 Rapped," *Toronto Star,* February 13, 1990, B1; "Record Chain Bans Rap Group's Album," *Globe and Mail* (Canada), February 13, 1990.

58  Lisa Barrett, "The Politics of Rap: Artists and Activists Sound Off and Speak Up," *Los Angeles Sentinel,* October 24, 1991.

59  Patrick Goldstein, "Rappers Don't Have Time for Newsweek's Attitude," *Los Angeles Times,* March 25, 1990.

60  Gregory Banks, "Violence in Rap: It's Time to Draw the Line," *Los Angeles Sentinel,* October 18, 1990, B9.

61  Marsh and Pollack, "Wanted for Attitude."

62  Steve Hochman, "Police Don't Give Rappers Bad Rap," *Los Angeles Times,* April 2, 1989.

63  Linda Deutsch, "21 LAPD Officers Involved in Beating of Black Motorist," *Press Telegram* (Long Beach), March 20, 1991, A1, in US Department of Justice, Federal Bureau of Investigation, FBI Records, the Vault, Rodney King, part 1 of 24, item 57, https://vault.fbi.gov/rodney-king; Kurt Streeter, "Months before He Died, Rodney King Told How the Beating by LAPD Officers Changed His Life," *Los Angeles Times,* March 3, 2016.

64  "Doctor Lists Injuries of Beaten Man," *Star-News,* March 9, 1991, A1, in FBI Records, the Vault, Rodney King, part 1 of 24, item 50.

65  Danny Pollock, "2 Local Victims React Differently to Police Brutality," *Star-News,* March 21, 1991, 1, in FBI Records, the Vault, Rodney King, part 1 of 24, item 222.

66  "Civilians' Video Cameras Undoing Rogue Officers," *Star-News,* March 8, 1991, A8, in FBI Records, the Vault, Rodney King, part 1 of 24, item 46.

67  "Video Footage of Arrest by Los Angeles Police Officers on March 3, 1991," in FBI Records, the Vault, Rodney King; Steve Padilla and Leslie Berger, "Cameraman's Test Puts Him in the Spotlight," *Los Angeles Times,* March 7, 1991; Kevin Uhrich, "It Turned My Stomach When I Saw It," *Star-News,* March 8, 1991, 1, in FBI Records, the Vault, Rodney King, part 1 of 24, item 47.

68  Hector Tobar and Richard Lee Colvin, "Witnesses Depict Relentless Beating," *Los Angeles Times,* March 7, 1991; Jennifer Lewis, "Tape Shocks Westside Police Commander," *The Outlook,* March 8, 1991, 5, in FBI Records, the Vault, Rodney King, part 1 of 24, item 36; Pamela Medve, "Video Stirs Emotions, Controversy," *San Gabriel Valley Tribune,* March 7, 1991, 1, in FBI Records, the Vault, Rodney King, part 1 of 24, item 37.

69    "Police Joked about Black's Beating Los Angeles Officer's Message Boasts of 'Big-Time Use of Force,'" *Toronto Star*, March 19, 1991. For a full transcript of transmissions between squad cars and the watch commander's office of the LAPD's Foothill Division related to the Rodney King beating, see Tracy Wood and Sheryl Stolberg, "Patrol Car Log in Beating Released," *Los Angeles Times*, March 19, 1991.

70    Janice Luder, "300 Protest Beating of Rodney King," *Star-News*, March 10, 1991, A1, in FBI Records, the Vault, Rodney King, part 1 of 24, item 55; "Hundreds of Protesters Demand That Gates Resign," *Los Angeles Times*, March 10, 1991.

71    Howard Gantman, "Bradley, Lawmakers Urge Probe of Brutality," *The Outlook*, March 7, 1991, in FBI Records, the Vault, Rodney King, part 1 of 24, item 23–24; Elaine Woo, "Rev. Jackson Joins Call for Gates' Ouster, Scolds Bradley," *Los Angeles Times*, March 17, 1991; Wood and Stolberg, "Patrol Car Log."

72    Ramona Ripston, "Chief Gates Must Step Aside," *Los Angeles Times*, March 7, 1991; Tim Kenworthy and Jill Walker, "Lawmakers Ask FBI to Probe Los Angeles Police for Brutality; Chief Gates Urged to Resign over Beating of Black," *Washington Post*, March 13, 1991; Yusuf Jah and Sister Shah-Keyah, *Uprising: Crips and Bloods Tell the Story of America's Youth in the Crossfire* (New York: Scribner, 1995), 122, 132.

73    Jerry Seper, "Black Caucus Wants Action on Alleged Brutality in LA," *Washington Times*, March 13, 1991; "Black Caucus Urges Broadened U.S. Inquiry into LAPD Beating Case," *Los Angeles Times*, March 13, 1991; John Yang and Jill Walker, "4 L.A. Officers Reported Indicted in Taped Beating; U.S. to Widen Probe of Alleged Police Brutality," *Washington Post*, March 15, 1991; "U.S. Widens Probe of Police Violence," *St. Petersburg Times* (Florida), March 15, 1991.

74    Charles Leerhsen and Lynda Wright, "L.A.'s Violent New Video," *Newsweek*, March 18, 1991.

75    Blackwell, "Niggaz4Dinner."

76    *NWA: The World's Most Dangerous Group.*

77    Gerrick Kennedy, "Ice Cube Reflects on the 25 Years since the Release of 'Death Certificate,'" *Los Angeles Times*, June 30, 2017.

78    Baraka, "Endangered Species."

79    Ice Cube, *Death Certificate*, album (Priority Records, 1991), CD; N.W.A., "Fuck tha Police"; John Leland, "Cube on Thin Ice," *Newsweek*, December 2, 1991, 69; Pareles, "Should Ice Cube's Voice Be Chilled."

80    Richard Harrington, "War of Songs Escalates," *Washington Post*, November 13, 1991.

81    Robert Christgau, "Review: Hard Again," *Village Voice*, November 15, 1991; Public Enemy, "Fight The Power," single (Motown, 1989), vinyl, 12".

82    Editorial, *Billboard*, November 23, 1991, 8.

83    Paul Grein, "'Certificate Accomplishes; Hammer Hits; Star Producers Shine Brightly on Hot 100," *Billboard*, November 16, 1991.

84    Marsh and Pollack, "Wanted for Attitude"; Baraka, "Endangered Species."

85    Dan Blackburn, *Of Presidents and Predators* (Page Publishing, 2018); Michelle Shocked and Bart Bull, "L.A. Riots: Cartoons vs. Reality," *Billboard*, 104, no. 25 (June 20, 1992): 6.

86    "Charting the Hours of Chaos," *Los Angeles Times*, April 29, 2002.

87    Rowan Scarborough, "Bush Mobilizes 4,500 Troops as Backup for Police," *Washington Times*, May 2, 1992; Robert Reinhold, "Riot in Los Angeles: The Overview," *New York Times*, May 3, 1992.

88    Max Robins, "Chopper Heaven in L.A. Hell," *Variety*, May 4, 1992, 111.

89    Dennis McDougal, "Few L.A. Outlets for Live Coverage of King Trial," *Los Angeles Times*, February 26, 1992.

90    Amy Wallace and David Ferrell, "Verdicts Greeted with Outrage and Disbelief: Reaction," *Los Angeles Times*, April 30, 1992.

91    Johnathan Croyle, "Central New York Reacts to the Rodney King Verdict in 1992," *Syracuse.com*, May 1, 2017.

92    David Mills, "Sister Souljah's Call to Arms," *Washington Post*, May 13, 1992, B1.

93    Russ Mitchell, "One Reporter's Two Nights in the Slammer," *Business Week*, May 18, 1992, 48, in Carton 37, Folder 1, Ronald T. Takaki Papers, Administration Papers, 1823–2009, Ethnic Studies Library, University of California, Berkeley.

94    "The Whole World Watches—and Reacts—to L.A. Riots," *Los Angeles Times*, May 5, 1992.

95    Tom Mathews, "The Siege of L.A.," Special Report, *Newsweek*, May 11, 1992, 30, in Carton 37, Folder 1, Ronald T. Takaki Papers Administration Papers, 1823–2009, Ethnic Studies Library, University of California, Berkeley.

96    Wallace and Ferrell, "Verdicts Greeted with Outrage and Disbelief."

97   Mathews, "Siege of L.A."

98   Mathews, "Siege of L.A."

99   Wallace and Ferrell, "Verdicts Greeted with Outrage and Disbelief."

100  David Whitman, "The Untold Story of the LA Riot," *U.S. News and World Report*, May 23, 1993; Mathews, "Siege of L.A."

101  Bryan Chan, "Photos: The 1992 Los Angeles Riots," *Los Angeles Times*, April 19, 2012.

102  Carolyn Bingham, "City of the Stars under Siege and Occupation," *Los Angeles Sentinel*, May 7, 1992, B3.

103  John Leland, "The Word on the Street Is Heard in the Beat," *Newsweek*, May 11, 1992, 52, in Carton 37, Folder 1, Ronald T. Takaki Papers Administration Papers, 1823–2009, Ethnic Studies Library, University of California, Berkeley.

104  Ice Cube, "F— 'Em (Insert)," *The Predator*, album (Priority Records, 1992), CD.

105  *NWA: The World's Most Dangerous Group.*

106  Sheila Rule, "Rappers Say the Riots Were No Surprise to Their Listeners," *New York Times*, May 26, 1992; Jimmie Briggs, "Pop Recordings," *Washington Post*, November 29, 1992; Kendrick Lamar, "N.W.A Told the Truth," *Billboard* 127, no. 24 (August 22, 2015).

107  Phil McCombs and Megan Rosenfeld, "Putting the Riots on the Record," *Washington Post*, May 5, 1992.

108  Stop The Violence Movement, "Self Destruction," single (Jive, 1989), vinyl, 12"; The West Coast Rap All-Stars, "We're All in the Same Gang," single (Warner Bros. Records, 1990), vinyl, 12".

109  Get The Fist Movement, "Get The Fist," single (1992; Mercury, 1992), vinyl, 12".

110  Ice-T, "Home Invasion," *Home Invasion*, album (1993; Rhyme $yndicate Records and Priority Records, 1993), CD.

111  Richard Harrington, "Ice-T and the Invasion of White Suburbia," *Washington Post*, March 24, 1993.

112  Kevin Zimmerman, "Live: Rap Music: Pop for the '90s?" *Variety* 341, no. 5 (November 12, 1990): 73–74.

113  Ice Cube, *The Predator*; Dr. Dre, *The Chronic*, album (Death Row/ Priority/Interscope, 1992), vinyl, LP, cassette, and CD.

114  Ice Cube, *The Predator.*

115  Ice Cube, *The Predator.*

116  Ice Cube, *The Predator.*

117  Ernest Hardy and August Brown, "The L.A. Riots: 20 Years Later; Rhythm of the Street," *Los Angeles Times,* May 2, 2012.

118  Kanye West, "The Immortals—The Greatest Artists of All Time: Dr. Dre," *Rolling Stone,* April 21, 2005.

119  "Talib Kweli and Hi-Tek Talk Dr. Dre, Detox, Gangsta Rap, Aftermath," *Hard Knock TV,* online music news program, Hardknock.TV, June 28, 2010, http://hardknock.tv/talib-kweli-and-hi-tek-talk-dr-dre-detox-gangsta -rap-aftermath/.

120  Hardy and Brown, "The L.A. Riots."

121  Havelock Nelson, "Rapping Up '93: After Chronic Growing Pains, Hardcore Gains Easy Acceptance, Hip-Hop Takes a Flying Leap into the Mainstream," *Billboard,* November 2, 1993; Eric Boehlert, "Rap's Grip on Suburbs Loosens as Teens Turn to Modern Rock," *Billboard,* June 3, 1995.

## Conclusion: LA County Blues

1  These cases include the deaths of Eric Garner, John Crawford, Michael Brown, Laquan McDonald, Tamir Rice, and Freddie Gray; in 2015, a mass shooting killed nine black parishioners inside the Emanuel African Methodist Episcopal Church in Charleston, South Carolina, a crime carried out by a twenty-three-year-old white supremacist; Jem Aswad, "Grammy Producer Ken Ehrlich Talks Kendrick Lamar's 'Provocative' Performance, Smacks Down 'All-White Tribute' Criticism," *Billboard,* February 15, 2016.

2  Micah Singleton, "Kendrick Lamar and the Grammys' Hip-Hop Problem—Twice as Good Still Isn't Enough," *The Verge,* February 17, 2016.

3  Michael Eric Dyson, *Between God and Gangsta Rap* (New York: Oxford University Press, 1996), 185; Ta-Nehisi Coates, *We Were Eight Years in Power: An American Tragedy* (New York: One World Publishing, 2017), 88; Chris Richards, "Kendrick Lamar Deserves the Pulitzer. Rap Is the Most Significant Music of Our Time," *Washington Post,* blog post, April 16, 2018.

4  Ernest Hardy and August Brown, "The L.A. Riots: 20 Years Later; Rhythm of the Street," *Los Angeles Times,* May 2, 2012.

5  EPMD, "Crossover / Brothers From Brentwood L.I," single (Rush / Def Jam, 1992), vinyl, 12".

6    Kevin Zimmerman, "Rap Music: Pop For the '90s?" *Variety* 341, no. 5 (November 12, 1990): 73–74.

7    David Samuels, "Yo! MTV Un-Wrapped," *Spin* 7, no. 6 (September 1, 1991), 44–45.

8    Zimmerman "Rap Music: Pop For the '90s?"

9    EPMD, "Crossover / Brothers From Brentwood L.I."

10    Mark Blackwell, "Niggaz4Dinner," *Spin*, September 1991, 55.

11    Dennis Hunt, "The Rap Reality: Truth and Money," *Los Angeles Times*, April 2, 1989, 80.

12    Mike Sager, "Cube," *Rolling Stone*, issue 588, October 4, 1990, 78.

13    Andy Gill, "Record Reviews: Taking a Rap on the Knuckles," *The Independent*, September 8, 1989.

14    *NWA: The World's Most Dangerous Group*, directed by Mark Ford (2008; VH1 Rock Docs, 2008), TV broadcast.

15    For research on the impact of noneconomic issues, specifically crime, in voting in elections during the 1980s and 1990s, see Jeff Cummins, "Issue Voting and Crime in Gubernatorial Elections," *Social Science Quarterly* 90, no. 3 (September 2009): 632–651.

16    Neil Best, "Ice Cube Recalls L.A. Raiders," *Newsday*, May 5, 2010.

17    Ice Cube, "AmeriKKKa's Most Wanted," *AmeriKKKa's Most Wanted*, album (Priority Records, 1990), vinyl, LP; N.W.A., "Fuck Tha Police," *Straight Outta Compton* (Ruthless/Priority, 1988), vinyl, LP.

18    Chris Richards, "Kendrick Lamar Deserves the Pulitzer; Rap Is the Most Significant Music of Our Time," *Washington Post*, April 16, 2018.

19    Lawrence W. Levine, *Black Culture and Black Consciousness: Afro-American Folk Thought from Slavery to Freedom* (Oxford, UK: Oxford University Press, 1978), 222, 238; Jack Dolan, "Police in Six Southern California Counties Have Shot More Than 2,000 Suspects since 2004. Only One Officer Was Prosecuted—He Was Acquitted," *Los Angeles Times*, February 19, 2016.

20    Dennis Hunt, "The Rap Reality: Truth and Money: Compton's N.W.A. Catches Fire with Stark Portraits of Ghetto Life," *Los Angeles Times*, April 2, 1989.

21    Ras Baraka, "Endangered Species," *The Source*, September 1991, 34.

22    Hardy and Brown, "L.A. Riots: 20 Years Later."

# ACKNOWLEDGMENTS

Over the years, writing has felt like a lonely journey. I experienced the thrill of discovery alone. I generated my own momentum. I stared at the blinking cursor in solitude. I set my own standards, suturing my self-esteem when I failed to meet them. When it seemed that maybe I'd exceeded them, I celebrated by myself with bad TV and a good beer.

The work of writing is, in many ways, a solitary thing. But, as I've been lucky to discover, composing a book is something else entirely. It really does take a village to nurture scholarship in its most fragile state into something mature enough for publication. I am so very fortunate, then, to have had the generous and patient support of friends, loved ones, colleagues, students, pros in the publishing world, and experts tied to the story I sought to tell. Collectively, these people are responsible for everything wonderful about this book. I, alone, am to blame for everything else.

The research for this book depended upon the expertise of librarians and staff at dozens of institutions. I must specifically thank those I bugged relentlessly at the Margaret Herrick

Library of the Academy of Motion Picture Arts and Sciences, the Charles E. Young Research Library and the Center for Oral History Research at UCLA, the Ethnic Studies Library and the Bancroft at UC Berkeley, the Los Angeles Public Library, the Inglewood Public Library, the California State Library, and, most gracious of all, the Southern California Library for Social Studies and Research, a Vermont-Slauson gem. Generous fellowships provided by the Arthur Ferreira Pinto Foundation and UC Berkeley's Graduate Division allowed me to travel for research and pay rent as a doctoral student. Financial support from San Francisco State University, my home institution, provided me with the resources and the precious leave time to continue research, rewrite the dissertation, and workshop the manuscript at conferences.

In the late stages of research, I sourced images to include in the book, making every effort to identify rights holders and secure permission for the use of copyrighted material. Thus, I'm grateful for the good people at the Studio for Southern California History, UCLA's *Los Angeles Times* Photographs Collection, *The Crisis*, the *Los Angeles Sentinel*, *Rafu Shimpo*, and *Black Radio Exclusive*. They all kindly answered my requests for permission to use images or pointed me to those who could grant that permission. My gratitude also goes to the Historical Society of Southern California and its Ahmanson Foundation Grant for Book Publication, which funded the sometimes expensive process of gathering rights and clearances. I give special thanks to Greg "Egyptian Lover" Broussard for sharing a piece of his Uncle Jamm's Army past, and to Susan Yano, who lent me a rare snapshot of her late husband's reign at the Roadium swap meet.

This book began as a dissertation that I almost didn't write. As a graduate student at UC Berkeley, I had a bad case of Imposter Syndrome, which made the idea of writing about 1980s popular culture—and rap, specifically—feel absurd. I was drawn to the research, but I worried that the people I revered, who had taken a chance on me, would be deeply disappointed (and concerned about my job prospects) if I chose to veer so far off the beaten path of traditional historical scholarship. But my advisors, Leon F. Litwack and Waldo E. Martin, Jr., along with Scott Saul and Kerwin Klein, only encouraged me, not once doubting that the work mattered. I am forever grateful to Leon Litwack for what he has impressed upon me about good writing. No one, except perhaps my bibliophile husband, is more hardcore about the merits of clear prose, and no one has better prepared me for how frustrating it can be to produce writing that isn't, well, frustrating. I relished being Leon's last doctoral student, and I still relish his friendship. Waldo Martin is the reason I finished the dissertation at all. I became a mother halfway through my graduate program—something that wasn't then and still isn't common for women pursuing PhDs. No one owed me any sympathy for all the new and unexpected pressures I felt as a new mom on a filing deadline, yet Waldo offered it again and again. I'm as grateful for his kindness as I am for our many, many impassioned discussions about Mary J. Blige.

At Berkeley, I was also lucky to have the support of Scott Saul in the English Department. Scott wrote the book on Richard Pryor that I wish I'd written, so I consider myself lucky to have had his support and his feedback. I'm not sure Kerwin Klein knows how much influence he had on my decision to write about rap. When I was an undergrad at Berkeley in the 1990s, I took his California History class and he assigned an article about Ice Cube and the LA riots. It was a piece by Jeff Chang, then a graduate student but also someone I knew for his ties to the Bay Area indie record label Solesides (later Quannum), where I worked in promotions. I was stunned that at UC Berkeley a history professor would be so bold as to discuss recent pop culture in his classroom, and I was floored by the fact that we were required to read something about rap, written by someone in the hip-hop scene I was a part of. If there's a seed from which this book grew, it's Kerwin's teaching. As a graduate student, Kerwin remained a beacon for me; I am particularly privileged, given how elusive he was known to be, that he spent as much time as he did with me discussing Los Angeles, music, writing, and teaching.

The manuscript I presented to Harvard University Press was the product of truly invaluable feedback from advisors, fellow graduate students, colleagues, friends, students, and family. As proud as I was of the dissertation when I filed it, I quickly resolved to take it down to the studs and rebuild the whole thing. It would have been a hopeless undertaking were it not for the generous suggestions, edits, and critiques offered by those I've already mentioned, and also by A. B. Wilkinson, Alejandro Garcia, Joe Duong, Kerima Lewis, Joe Orbock, Rachel Bernard, Sarah Stoller, Sarah Gold-McBride, Jeannette Eileen Jones, Kalenda Eaton, Michael Johnson, Emily Lutenski, Meina Yates-Richard, Jeanelle Hope, and Miguel Juárez. I'm also thankful to two anonymous readers who, though tough critics, ultimately convinced me that I had a "page-turner" on my hands.

Dear friends and others who know more than I do about the topics in these pages graciously contributed ideas, and even connections. Pam "The Funkstress" Warren, Josh Bea, Erik Kjensrud, Daniel Green, Justin Bradshaw, Patrick Diaz, Jason Castillo, Marc Burrell, Andrew Nosnitsky, Brian Warwick,

Mike Davis, Billy Jam, Greg "Eqyptian Lover" Broussard, and "Greg Mack" MacMillan are among those who added dimensions to the book. Two fellow historians and brilliant friends, Amy DeFalco Lippert and Daniel Immerwahr, are owed thanks for providing moral support through revisions and then shepherding me through the sometimes daunting publishing process.

I pitched this book to Andrew Kinney at Harvard University Press on a whim. My expectation was that the meeting would go about as well as the one in which Jerry Heller tried to convince Capitol Records chairman Joe Smith to sign NWA. That is to say, I didn't anticipate it would result in any partnership and I worried he might think I had a screw loose. When Andrew revealed himself to be a dyed-in-the-wool hip-hop fan who knew DJ Quik as well as he knew Kool Moe Dee, I thought I might be able to convince him that Harvard should publish this book. I didn't have to. Andrew made it his own mission. As my editor, his advocacy has been beyond vital, and his confidence in the project has kept me sane.

I've benefited from so much outstanding talent, professionalism, generosity, and patience at Harvard University Press. The fine people there truly are the village that it took to make this book special. In addition to Andrew's support, I'm grateful for the work of Olivia Woods, Stephanie Vyce, Anne Mcguire, Tim Jones, and Melody Negron. I'm especially indebted to Julia Kirby, who edited the final manuscript. Indeed, I nearly dedicated the book to Julia rather than to my children. My life is as charmed as it is because of my kids, and this book is as good as it is because of Julia's edits.

Marlene and Steve Angeja, my mother and father, have cheered me on, sacrificed their time, read drafts, babysat, pushed me, and loved me. They, along with my brother and my stepmother, made it possible for me to balance my professional goals with motherhood. But more than that, my mom and dad, in their own ways, modeled courage and determination. I've needed lots of both all along the way, so I'm thankful for who they are.

No one has been closer to this journey—with all its stress and joy—than Ross Viator. I'm lucky to have his friendship, to share his passion for music, and to be able to obsess with him over words. I am also privileged to have someone so smart and sweet in my life to help me accept my mistakes and celebrate my victories. I'm not sure a book about rap can be considered a love letter. But if it can, this one is to him.

# INDEX

Page references in *italics* indicate a figure.

Basie, Count, 5
"Batterram" (song): debut, 18; influence, 61; lyrics, 19, 23, 24, 56, 59–60, 134; popularity, 56, 58, 59, 93, 213; production, 19, 55–56, 58, 133–134, 218; promotion, 81
battering ram vehicle. *See* V-100 armored vehicle
Beastie Boys (music group), 104, 108, 126, 131
Beavers, George, 8
Biden, Joe, 236
Big Boi (Antwan Patton), 203
*Billboard Magazine*, 67, 112, 113, 166, 167, 171, 175, 297n17
Birks, Dania "Baby-D," 174
Blackburn, Dan, 242, 243
Black Entertainment Television, 187
Black Flag (music group), 67, 68, 74
"Black Korea" (song), 240, 241
#BlackLivesMatter movement, 256
Black Panther Party, 28, 29, 50, 81, 165
*Black Radio Exclusive* (magazine), 169
Black Sabbath (music group), 68
Black Thought (Tariq Trotter), 215
black youths: attitude to politics, 226; joblessness, 13; marginalization, 61; mentality, 1; musical tastes, 18; older generation's views of, 14–15; police abuse, 21, 47–48
Blondie (Debbie Harry), 74, 185
Bloods street gang, 19–20, 21, 39, 89
Blow, Kurtis, 97–98, 128, 185, 290n38
Blue, Hazel, 33, 34
Blue Records. *See* Dootone Records
blues music, 16, 264–265

Bobcat (Bobby Ervin), *78*
Bolton, Glen. *See* Daddy-O
Boogie Down Productions (music group), 129, 164, 214
Bowie, David, 187
*Boyz N the Hood* (film), 240, 242, 247
"The Boyz-N-The Hood" (song): commercial success, 135–136, 175–176; impact on listeners, 137; KDAY radio debut, 135; label, *124*; lyrics, 125–126; popularity, 153, 162, 218; production, 125, 126, 133, 134, 136, 140–141; promotion, 135, 137, 140; sources, 126; target audience, 135
Bradley, Tom: concern about choke hold deaths, 50; criticism of, 41, 42; historic election of, 13; during 1992 Los Angeles riots, 243; police spying on, 43; public statement on law enforcement, 41; response to Rodney King beating, 236; support of Daryl Gates, 21; on urban terrorism, 22
Brathwaite, Fred. *See* Fab 5 Freddy
breakdancing, 72, 73, 94
*Breakin' 'n' Enterin'* (film), 72–73, 74–75, 114
Broadus, Calvin, Jr. *See* Snoop Dogg
Broussard, Greg. *See* Egyptian Lover
Brown, James, 132, 185
Brown, Jerry, 43
Brown, Rose, 245
Buckley, Steve, 77
Burns, Juana "MC J.B.," 174
Bush, George H. W., 146, 227

*Night Tracks* (television program),
191, 192

NWA (music group): audience, 178;
boycott of music and events of,
219–220, 226; commercial
success, 204, 229–230, 232,
260–261; controversy over
name, 200; creation, 153;
criticism, 233–234; cultural
influence, 214–215, 230, 232;
debut album, 153–154, 155;
Detroit concert, 220; dis-
solution, 228; *Efil4zaggin*,
229–230, 232; FBI attention
to, 208, 224–225, 226–227;
first music video, 157; free
speech debate, 205, 231;
"Gangsta Gangsta" single,
257; independent status,
155–156; interviews, 209–210;
marketing strategy, 162, 197,
201, 206–207; members, 153;
misogyny, 229, 230; music
style, 156, 178, 212, 262–264;
national tour, 222; *100 Miles
and Runnin'*, 227; popularity,
205, 220–221, 227, 228, 231,
232; promotion, 165, 179, 229;
publicity, 155, 162–163, 204,
205–206, 227, 228; reputation,
155, 178, 212; showcase in
Washington, DC, 222–223;
street credibility, 203, 210;
Toledo appearance, 221; on
*Village Voice* cover, *225*; on
*Yo! MTV Raps* show, 201,
202–204. *See also* "Fuck tha
Police" (song); *Straight Outta
Compton* (album); "Straight
Outta Compton" (video)

O'Callaghan, Lloyd, 33, 35
O'Connor, Len, 9
Operation Hammer: criticism, 147;
gang sweeps, 157–158; launch,
144–145; media coverage, 152;
public support, 146; scale,
145–146
Operation Safe Streets, 148
"Organizing Against Police
Brutality" event, 29
Osbourne, Ozzy, 68, 69
Otis, Johnny, 1, 14
Owen, Frank, 66

Palace (nightclub), 88
Pardee, Rudy, 140
Pareles, Jon, 190, 228
"Parents Just Don't Understand"
(song), 168
Parents Music Resource Center, 68,
208, 230
Parker, William, 9, 27, 31, 44
Parr, Russ, 58
Patterson, Jack, 18, 105, 170
Patterson, Lorenzo. *See* MC Ren
Paul, Cameron, 174
Penguins (music group), 12
Penn, Sean, 148
Philibosian, Robert, 20
Phillips, Johnny, 137
Phillips, Linda, 244
Pittman, Bob, 186
police brutality, 222, 223, 224, 227,
234–235
*Predator, The* (album), 250–252
Prince (Prince Rogers Nelson), 14,
80, 113, 114, 126, 184, 187
Priority Records: business model,
173, 179; creation, 171, 172;
featured in music magazines,